Guide to
The Jersey Shore
From Sandy Hook to Cape May

Second Edition

by Robert Santelli

A Voyager Book

The Globe Pequot Press

Chester, Connecticut

For my mother and father,
Dorothy and Robert Santelli

Library of Congress Cataloging-in-Publication Data

Santelli, Robert.
    Guide to the Jersey shore: from Sandy Hook to Cape May / by Robert Santelli. — 2nd ed.
    Rev. ed. of: The Jersey Shore: a travel and pleasure guide.
        p.   cm.
    "A Voyager book."
    Includes index.
    ISBN 0-87106-302-6
    1. Atlantic Coast (N.J.)—Description and travel—Guide-books.
    2. New Jersey—Description and travel—1981—Guide-books.
    I. Title.
F132.3.S26 1990
917.4904'43—dc20
                                                    90-49794
                                                        CIP

Manufactured in the United States of America
Second Edition/First Printing

Acknowledgments

For all their help and encouragement, I am indebted to the following: Betty Lou Applegate, Jack Aprill, Savo Balic, Pat Clarke, Wayne Hartman, Ranger Tom Hoffman, Pat Hyde, Angel and Jack Jeandron, Connie Kosten, August and Dot Draft, Jackie Kraft, Blair Learn, Sam Melton, Pauline Miller, Gertrude Neidlinger, Mary Roche, Jack Santelli, Chief Ranger Pete Segge, Karen Siciliano, Charles Tomasello, Ranger Randy Turner, Joanne Van Roden, John Wynbeek, Dora Visco and B. Michael Zuckerman, and the Cape May County Historical Association, the Mid-Atlantic Center for the Arts, the Monmouth County Division of Tourism, the Monmouth County Historical Association, the Ocean County Historical Association, the Pinelands Cultural Society, the Renault Winery and the Southern Ocean County Chamber of Commerce.

A special thanks goes to Laura Strom, Norma Ledbetter, Bruce Markot, Sally McMillan, Jennifer Mullennix, Judy Davis, Barbara Campbell and the rest of the Globe Pequot and East Woods Press crews; to Pam Kraft and Denise Fike, both of whom contributed artwork and ideas for the cover of this book; and to Jim and Janis White for their warm hospitality.

Finally, I own an extra-special thanks to my agent and friend, Sandy Choron, for guiding me all the way; to my wife, Cindy, my two daughters, Jaron and Jenna, and my son Jake, for being most patient and loving down the stretch; and to my mother and father, for relocating the family to the Jersey Shore way back when.

About the Author

Born and raised on the Jersey Shore, travel and sports writer Robert Santelli contributes frequent articles to *New Jersey Monthly*, *Bicycling* magazine, *Surfer* magazine, and *Caribbean Travel and Life*. A music critic and travel correspondent for the *Asbury Park Press*, he is also the author of *Short Bike Rides in New Jersey*, published by the Globe Pequot Press.

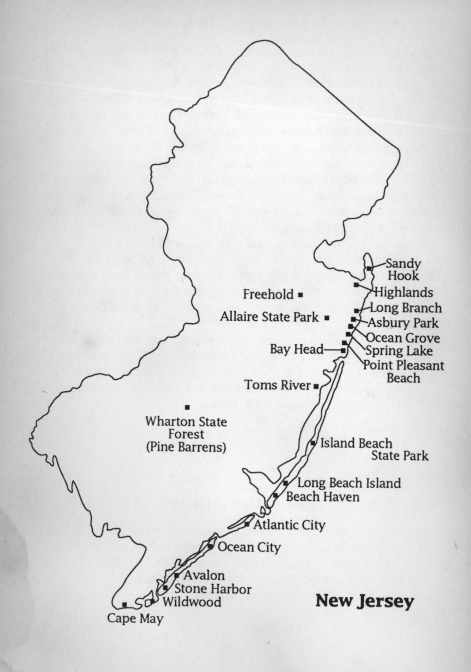

Sandy
Hook
Highlands
Long Branch
Asbury Park
Ocean Grove
Spring Lake
Point Pleasant
Beach

Freehold ■

Allaire State Park ■

Bay Head ■

Toms River ■

■ Wharton State
Forest
(Pine Barrens)

Island Beach
State Park

Long Beach Island
Beach Haven

Atlantic City

Ocean City

Avalon
Stone Harbor
Wildwood

Cape May

New Jersey

Contents

Introduction

The ritual begins in earnest July Fourth weekend. Cars crammed with kids, coolers and suitcases; surfboards strapped on the roofs; boats on trailers pulled behind: These crowd New Jersey highways like the Garden State Parkway and the Atlantic City Expressway. Traffic thickens at the tollbooths and exits; impatience tears at the soul. The sounds of Bruce Springsteen and Jon Bon Jovi blare from car stereos and provide the perfect soundtrack for the brewing excitement. It's summertime, and that means it's time to head to the Jersey Shore.

The annual summer migration to the Jersey Shore goes back further than the completion of the Parkway or Expressway, further even than the invention of the automobile. The original Shore vacationers, the Lenni Lenape Indians, began summering at the Shore centuries ago. Each summer many left their inland villages in June to escape the summer heat. At the Shore they fished, hunted and collected oysters, clams, berries and beach plums. Then in September they returned to their villages and made ready for the approach of winter.

Dutch and English farmers and whalers began settling at the Shore in the mid-seventeenth century. As word spread of the area's glorious summer climate, wealthy colonists from Philadelphia began visiting the Jersey Shore for the soothing qualities of the salt air and cooler temperatures. Eventually, guesthouses and inns were built to accommodate such visitors and their families. Thus, the Jersey Shore became the young nation's most popular summer resort, and Cape May and Long Branch, its very first resort towns.

Today, millions of people visit the Jersey Shore each summer for a variety of reasons. Most, of course, come for its sun, sand and surf. But others come for its restaurants, for its fishing and boating, for its nightlife and for its history. Tourists, for instance, from all 50 states and a number of foreign countries visit Victorian Cape May each year.

Some have more specialized interests, like gambling. Atlantic City alone annually attracts upwards of 25 million visitors to its luxurious casinos and its famous boardwalk. After just a few short years, Atlantic City rivals Las Vegas as the gambling and entertainment capital of America, and maybe even the world.

Some visitors spend their entire vacations at the Shore, residing in tiny bungalows or beach cottages that have been in the family for years. Others take day or weekend trips to Sandy Hook, Seaside Heights or Sea Isle City. Mostly they come by car. Some take trains or buses. But come they do. Thanks to the Jersey Shore, tourism is now one of New Jersey's largest industries.

The Jersey Shore coastline is 127 miles long. It extends from the northernmost tip of Sandy Hook, which continues to grow each year due to new sand deposits carried by swift ocean currents, to the southern-most tip of Cape May Point, a tiny beach town that sits in the shadow of the Cape May Point Lighthouse. In between these two boundaries is a rich, exciting diversity of landscape and activities that goes far beyond the standard allure of the Jersey Shore.

It is indeed true and certainly no secret that New Jersey's beaches are among the finest on the Eastern Seaboard. As already mentioned, they are the Shore's prime attraction, as they well should be. But beyond the beaches and sand dunes, the boardwalks and bungalows, there is more, so much more, to see, to do and to experience that it's no exaggeration to say the Shore has something for everyone.

Here's proof. Are you a history buff? The Shore is steeped in revolu-tionary war drama, Victorian memories, pirate legends and lore, and tales of maritime adventure on the open sea. Like to shop for antiques? Try the Route 9 corridor just north of Cape May, sometimes referred to as "Antique Alley." Enjoy museums? The Cape May County Museum can keep you fascinated for hours. So can the Twin Lights Museum. It recalls the bygone days of the U.S. Life Saving Service and the wireless telegra-phy experiments of Guglielmo Marconi. You'll see lions, tigers and bears at the Cape May County Zoo, and you'll marvel at the thousands of mi-grating birds resting at the Brigantine section of the Edwin B. Forsythe National Wildlife Refuge. And you won't see a more unusual collection of seashells than what you'll find at Ocean City's Seashell Museum.

Interested in lighthouses? The Jersey Shore possesses some of the oldest in America as well as some of the most famous. Visit the Sandy Hook Lighthouse, or Old Barney or Twin Lights. Feel like camping or ca-noeing in a true wilderness area? Spend some time in the Pine Barrens, one of the great remaining forest areas on the Atlantic Coast. What about car racing? Set aside Saturday nights and venture to Raceway Park or Wall Stadium. Perhaps horse racing is more your style. Then it's off to Monmouth Park, Freehold Raceway or Atlantic City Raceway. Is rock 'n' roll in your soul? Asbury Park has one of America's great music halls, the Stone Pony, proving ground for Bruce Springsteen and Bon Jovi, Southside Johnny and the Jukes, and many others.

I could go on, but you get the picture. With such diversity comes choice, and often too many choices result in indecision. Everything looks and sounds good. You have two days or two weeks to spend at the Jersey Shore. Where should you go? What should you see? What should you do?

Questions like these prompted the writing of *Guide to the Jersey* Shore. The book is not a definitive guide to the Jersey Shore. It wasn't intended to be. Rather, its primary function is to serve as a companion to one's discovery of the Jersey Shore: of its beaches and boardwalks and beach towns, yes, but also of its many other wonderful traits and attractions.

During the course of researching material to include in this book, I traveled up and down the coast and visited virtually every town from Sandy Hook to Cape May Point. Having grown up on the Jersey Shore and worked there as a writer and teacher, I was aware of all its glowing attractions and a good many of the more unheralded ones, too. Yet, I still found much that I never knew existed.

Driving or bicycling or walking through towns such as Sea Bright, Bay Head, Leed's Point, Atlantic City and Stone Harbor; boating on Barnegat Bay and the Manasquan River; hiking along trails in Allaire State Park and through the marshland at the Wetlands Institute; and surfing at Sandy Hook and Seaside Heights made me realize that the Shore was truly diverse in its form, its features and its culture. But despite this, I also uncovered a subtle sense of unity, which, I hope, comes through in the book.

The chapters are arranged geographically, from north to south. Although each chapter deals with a specific section of the Shore—the North Jersey Shore, the Barnegat Peninsula, Long Beach Island, and so on— and though each possesses its own personality and highlights, it is the Atlantic Ocean and its grand influence that bond these regions. Nearly all activities and attractions, historic sites and natural areas are somehow, some way linked with others by way of their relationship with the ocean. The only possible exception is the chapter entitled "The Inland Shore." But even there you'll find ties to the sea in one form or another.

All nine chapters contain a potpourri of information and personal observations designed first to introduce, and then to help select, places to see and things to do. Two chapters, Atlantic City and Cape May, deal almost exclusively with those two immensely popular resort towns. There was so much to write about them that they insisted on their own chapters.

At the conclusion of each chapter, you will find a short list of recommended restaurants. I ate at many of the ones mentioned and many not mentioned, too. But I did not eat at all of them. To eat at and judge *every* restaurant on the Jersey Shore would have been an impossible task. There are so many—literally hundreds—that the time it would have taken to sample meals at every one of them would have curtailed research in other more important areas.

Yet dining is an essential and enjoyable part of any vacation or visit to the Jersey Shore. Thus, to provide some sort of guidance, I researched what restaurant critics had to say about Shore restaurants, considered readers' restaurant polls in reputable magazines such as *New Jersey Monthly,* carefully listened to word of mouth and, finally, used my own taste buds and sense of epicurean quality wherever I could to judge which restaurants should be recommended and which should not. What resulted are nine separate restaurant lists that a visitor can choose from and be reasonably assured of a fine meal anywhere on the Shore.

I also included a category concerning the price of meals, albeit, please bear in mind menus and prices can and do easily change. The price code is based on dinner prices only. Inexpensive means an average meal (minus drinks, remember) costs about $10 or under. Moderate means $10 to $15. Expensive means over $15.

As for lodgings, there are almost as many hotels, motels, inns and guesthouses at the Jersey Shore as there are restaurants. A large percentage of them, however, contain standard accommodations, namely, a room simply furnished and decorated, complete with a color television and Bible. Many have pools and/or beach privileges. Too many have overly familiar nautical names and themes: Sea Drift, Seascape, Driftwood, Sunset View, Ocean View, Bay View, Captain Jack's, Ebb Tide and High Tide.

Did you know that . . .

There is a town called Jersey Shore? Strangely enough, it is located in Pennsylvania, not New Jersey.

It would have been pointless to attempt individualized descriptions of such hotels and motels, since so many seem to have come from the same mold. Also, without actually having stayed overnight in each and every one, it would have been unfair to try to rate them. So I didn't.

There are, though, some truly special lodgings at the Jersey Shore. The grand hotels of Atlantic City, for example, and the charming bed and breakfasts of Cape May deserve special attention and get it. For those not wishing to indulge in luxury while in the Atlantic City area or experience Cape May's Victorian bed and breakfast splendor, but still requiring a place to stay for the night or week, I have provided the addresses and telephone numbers of tourist centers, chambers of commerce and accommodations agencies, which will assist you in finding the lodging that best suits your taste and budget.

Finally, I was reluctant to include admission fees to places like museums, beaches and parks simply because such information is apt to change and could date the book prematurely. In the case of meals, there is room to play with; an average meal costs between . . . But with admission fees, one is dealing with precise figures. Therefore, I merely mentioned that an admission fee is required to gain entrance and left it at that.

Despite such limitations what *is* included in the book should be more than enough for you to begin your discovery of the Jersey Shore. So set aside preconceived notions. Gas up the car. Pack your bathing trunks, hiking shoes, fishing pole, camera and suntan lotion. There's more at the Shore than you think.

1

 The Bayshore and Sandy Hook

Years ago, the communities nestled along the southern edge of Raritan and Sandy Hook bays were an integral part of the Jersey Shore. Before completion of the Garden State Parkway in 1957, visitors from northern New Jersey and New York drove down Route 35 and then onto Route 36 to spend a day, a weekend or a week on the Bayshore. Before that, steamships brought passengers to Keansburg and the Highlands area from lower Manhattan.

Anglers came to Keyport, Port Monmouth and Leonardo for the excellent fishing in the waters just off these bay towns. Families came to Keansburg to swim off its bay beaches during the day and walk its boardwalk, with its amusement rides and penny arcades, at night. Young couples spent romantic evenings in the guesthouses and inns that dotted Atlantic Highlands and the Highlands.

The opening of the Parkway registered a heavy blow to the Bayshore tourist trade, however. The new highway provided easy access to resort communities in southern Monmouth and Ocean counties. Suddenly, even Atlantic City no longer seemed all that far away. Many vacationers began bypassing the Bayshore for the beaches and boardwalks in Shore towns such as Manasquan, Point Pleasant Beach and Seaside Heights.

But even more crippling to Bayshore tourism was the pollution that flowed out of the refineries and factories on the northern and western shores of Raritan Bay. Such unchecked discharge into the bay ultimately made it one of New Jersey's dirtiest waterways.

Sandy Hook Bay, which lies farther east, was also victimized by pollution. By the mid-seventies, the fish and shellfish once caught and eaten in abundance by anglers were now condemned. Swimming in the bays became a health hazard. Without clean water, the Bayshore was all but forgotten by many Jersey Shore visitors.

Fortunately, the Bayshore is on the verge of a major comeback. Many Shore-based environmental groups report that baywaters are cleaner than they were ten years ago, thanks to tough antipollution laws recently passed by the New Jersey state legislature. Environmentalists stress, however, that even stricter antipollution laws—and enforcement of them—are necessary if the bays are to regain their full health.

In 1985, the state unveiled its Bayshore Development Plan to help local Bayshore communities improve their economies and their ability to attract vacationers once again. Waterfront development projects are in the works in some Bayshore towns, and many visitors are rediscovering the area's museums and historical sites as well as its first-rate seafood restaurants.

Did you know that . . .

Legendary impresario P. T. Barnum once owned a house in Keyport. Dancing great Fred Astaire made his theatrical debut in the town's Old Palace Theater in 1910. He was 11 years old.

Boating was one activity that was not seriously affected by the Bayshore's decline in the seventies and eighties. It is still much enjoyed on Raritan and Sandy Hook bays, as evidenced by the area's many marinas and boatyards. These bodies of water provide both shelter from and access to the Atlantic Ocean to the east.

Some people still come to the Bayshore out of habit. Tradition seems to count for something here. It's a place where dance pavilions were once filled with GIs home on leave and girls eager for a man in uniform. It's a place where perhaps our parents or grandparents came for that much-deserved week-long vacation. It's a place that had its day in the sun, so to speak, and is now only filled with faded memories.

But if all this is true, why, one might wonder, is Route 36, that ribbon of highway that runs parallel with the Bayshore, bumper to bumper with cars on Saturday mornings in July and August? And why is it even worse, or so it always seems, on Sunday afternoons and evenings when thousands of cars inch their way west to the Parkway? The answer is simple: Sandy Hook.

Part of the Gateway National Recreation Area (which also includes the

Jamaica Bay Wildlife Refuge in Brooklyn and Queens, Breezy Point in Queens and Great Kills Park and Miller Field in Staten Island), Sandy Hook, in recent years, has become one of the most popular recreation spots in the New York-New Jersey Metropolitan area. Approximately 20,000 people a day converge on this sandspit at the top of the Jersey Shore each summer day. It's not uncommon for the Sandy Hook park rangers to close the gates to vehicular traffic as early as 10 o'clock in the morning on hot summer weekends and holidays to avoid extensive overcrowding and abuse of the facilities there.

Sandy Hook's proximity to the metropolitan area and the vast number of things to see and do there make it the pride of the North Jersey Shore. Few areas north of Atlantic City offer so much to visitors, not only during the summer, but throughout the year. No longer is Sandy Hook simply a place to go when the sun is shining and the temperature 80 degrees. Many of the activities detailed below are year-round activities. And those who love walking on a windswept beach before or after summer will find Sandy Hook irresistible.

One thing a visitor to the Bayshore and Sandy Hook should keep in mind, however: this area is almost exclusively a day-visit area. You'll find few quality hotels or motels in the Bayshore vicinity and practically no inns, bed and breakfasts or guesthouses that meet minimum standards. There are no places to pitch a tent and camp, either. Families that travel long distances to enjoy Sandy Hook or the Highlands should look for accommodations in nearby Sea Bright. Generally speaking, the farther you go south of Sandy Hook, the better your chances are of finding suitable accommodations.

Keyport

Keyport lies at the crossroads of Routes 35 and 36 on the southwestern shore of Raritan Bay. Because of its proximity to New York—look across the bay on a clear day and you can see both Brooklyn and lower Manhattan—a thriving boat-building industry made the town the largest in Monmouth County in the mid-1800s. Steamboats were built and repaired in Keyport boatyards. One of them, the *River Queen,* was used during the Civil War by President Lincoln and Union generals for war conferences on the Potomac River. Keyport boat builders also built Sea Bright skiffs, wooden boats that were later used with great success for rum-running during Prohibition.

The **Steamboat Dock Museum,** located on the corner of American Legion Drive and Broad Street, has photos and memorabilia that depict Keyport's golden era of shipbuilding. The one-story structure that houses the museum was once a steamboat repair shop. (Run by the Key-

What to Do with Fish after You Catch Them

1. If you plan to take home what you catch, make sure you have a cooler full of ice on hand. Do not use garbage cans; they don't have drains to allow melted ice and water to escape. If the fish you catch lies in such water, it will quickly lose its flavor and perhaps even spoil.

2. Clean your catch as soon as possible. Cleaning a fish takes practice. And practice makes perfect. The key to cleaning a fish? A very sharp, thin-bladed fillet knife. Fishermen experienced in cleaning fish say a semiflexible blade is best. You'll also need a scaler (especially if you plan to keep the skin), a board on which to clean and scrape the fish, and plastic bags.

3. Thoroughly clean the fish of slime, innards and scales. Wash the fish clean and make sure no blood is left in the cavity. Rid fish such as tuna and bluefish of brown meat just beneath the skin; this is where the oil is found that gives improperly cleaned fish a "fishy" taste.

4. Pack your cleaned fish in plastic bags. Make sure there is plenty of ice in the cooler. Don't overstock fish in your cooler at the expense of ice.

5. Upon arriving home, remove the fish from cooler and place in freezer if you do not intend to eat immediately.

port Historical Society, the Steamboat Dock Museum is open Sundays June through September. Admission is free.)

Boat building continues today in Keyport in yards owned by Hans Pedersen & Sons, Olav Olsen, and Master Shipwrights. If you're not interested in buying a boat, you can rent one at Bayside Bait & Tackle, across from the Steamboat Dock Museum. Fourteen-foot aluminum boats ideal for crabbing or fishing are available for rent by the half day or day. If you have your own boat, you can launch it at Bayside Bait & Tackle for a small fee. Landlubbers can fish or crab off the Keyport Fishing Pier on American Legion Drive.

Keansburg

Keansburg's primary attraction is its **Amusement Park** on Beachway Road. Though often referred to as Keansburg's boardwalk area, there are no wooden planks to stroll on. Instead, a black asphalt walkway allows the visitor to wander through a maze of old-fashioned concession stands and amusement rides.

Compared to Jersey Shore resorts like Wildwood and Ocean City, Keansburg is in desperate need of a facelift. But therein lies its appeal to some. You'll find kiddie rides that belong in some museum, a water slide, wheels of fortune, a sausage and peppers stand here, a pizza parlor there and, believe it or not, an eatery on Beachway Road called **Terminal Lunch.** With the right frame of mind, Keansburg can be fun. Not recommended, however, for those with high-brow intentions or the need for first-class facilities.

Port Monmouth

To gain a full understanding of the history of the Bayshore, visit the **Spy House Museum.** (Call 908–787–1807 for museum hours.) Spy House is overflowing with artifacts and exhibits, dating as far back as the seventeenth century. There is, in fact, so much on display that it can be difficult to view everything and put all that you've seen into a historical perspective. But there is no better museum anywhere on the Jersey Shore when it comes to telling the story of the earliest Bayshore families, depicting the area's role in the American Revolution and learning about the work habits and culture of Bayshore watermen.

The Whitlock-Seabrook House, which is part of the Spy House Museum complex, was built in 1663. It was the first house constructed on the Jersey Shore and is an excellent example of early American architecture and craftsmanship. The Whitlock-Seabrook House became known as the "Spy House" during the revolutionary war. George Washington's chief spy, Col. John Stilwell, sent messages concerning British ship movement in the bay to patriots in the house, which, during the war, was an inn. Fellow patriots waiting in whale boats hidden in nearby shoals were then dispatched to sink or damage the British ships.

Inside the museum, audiotape tours are available, as are numerous pamphlets and handouts pertaining to the history of the house and its environs. Admission is free.

Belford

Belford is home to one of four commercial fishing fleets on the Jersey Shore. (The other three are in Point Pleasant Beach, Barnegat Light and Cape May.)

The **Belford Seafood Co-op,** located at the junction of Main Street and Port Monmouth Road, is where the catch of the day ends up. The Co-op distributes fish to area restaurants and to others in northern New

Jersey and New York City. One can purchase fish here somewhat cheaper and fresher than at fish markets beyond those at the Jersey Shore. None of the fish, however, are cleaned or cut into fillets if you buy them right off the dock. Best bet: ling and whiting, and, when available, lobster. The Co-op is open seven days a week. Call (908) 787–6500 for more information.

Leonardo

Leonardo, located on the southern shore of Sandy Hook Bay, is another important Bayshore town for boaters, since the Leonardo State Marina is located here. A popular launch area for those without permits or privileges at private basins and marinas, Leonardo, as one might expect, is quite busy during the summer.

For those wishing to launch a boat, stop first at the marina's main office on Concord Avenue and purchase a launch ticket, good for one boat for one day. Annual permits, valid from April 1 to October 31, are available at the office, too, and well worth it if you plan to launch from Leonardo on a regular basis. The marina is open year-round and 24 hours a day during the summer. Boaters wishing berths in the marina, take note. According to marina officials, there's an eight-year waiting list in all three boat-size categories: 30, 40 and 50 foot.

Lighthouse buffs will want to visit **Conover Beacon,** one of three lighthouses in the Bayshore/Sandy Hook area. (The other two are Twin Lights in Highlands and the Sandy Hook Lighthouse at Fort Hancock on Sandy Hook.) Built in 1856, Conover Beacon was one of a pair of light-towers that helped guide boat captains into the Chapel Hill Channel in Sandy Hook Bay. The second light-tower in the pair is located a few miles from the coast, in Middletown. Known as the Chapel Hill Beacon, it, too, was built in 1856. However, since it now rests on private property, it is no longer possible to visit. You can, though, find photos of the light-tower as well as a keeper's log at the Twin Lights Museum.

Conover Beacon is located on Sandy Hook Bay at the end of Leonardo Road. Its red and white tower is quite simple in design. But in days gone by, its importance was great as navigation in Sandy Hook Bay would have proved hazardous without it and the Chapel Hill Beacon beaming brightly through darkness and fog.

Also located in Leonardo is the bay section of **Earle Naval Station.** (The main section is inland in Colts Neck Township.) Earle supplies logistics, weapons and matériel support to navy warships. Understandably, it is off-limits to tourists. The nearly three-mile-long loading pier that juts out into Sandy Hook Bay is, however, easily visible from the Leonardo State Marina. With six deep-water berths, it's not unusual to see warships moored there. Three ammunition cargo ships call Earle their homeport: the USS *Suribachi,* the USS *Nitro* and the USS *Butte.*

Atlantic Highlands

People often confuse Atlantic Highlands as being part of Highlands or vice versa. Despite the similarity in names and the proximity to each other—they are Bayshore neighbors—Atlantic Highlands and Highlands are separate communities.

Whereas Highlands concerns itself with the Jersey Shore tourist trade in the form of top-notch seafood restaurants, the Twin Lights Museum and plenty of party fishing boats to choose from for a day on the ocean with rod and reel, Atlantic Highlands is primarily a residential community and does not see itself as a tourist town. Even so, the town does have a very fine municipal marina and its own fleet of party boats. It also possesses a few things to do that should not be overlooked by those visiting the area or passing through on their way to Sandy Hook.

Things to Do

Go Fishing on Sandy Hook Bay or the Atlantic Ocean. Small skiffs, rowboats and small motorboats are for rent at places like **Chuck's Boats** (908–291–2275) on Simon Lake Drive, the road that runs parallel with the harbor. A nearby tackle shop sells bait. If ocean fishing is more your fancy, plan to fish on one of the many party boats that make daily trips to fishing holes offshore. All the boats have signs posted on their respective docks, which give essential information such as departure times, price of the trip and what kinds of fish are running.

Take a Ride on Scenic Drive. Scenic Drive is actually Ocean Boulevard. It extends from First Avenue in downtown Atlantic Highlands, just a couple of streets south of the Atlantic Highlands Municipal Marina, to Mt. Mitchill Scenic Overlook. The drive is short (three to four miles), but the views are excellent. Sandy Hook, Sandy Hook Bay, lower Manhattan, parts of Brooklyn including Coney Island, and even southern Long Island can be seen. On an especially clear day, New York's Twin Towers and the Empire State Building are within sight. Be sure to stop at the vista in front of the **Hofbrauhaus Restaurant;** it has the best view on Scenic Drive.

Visit Henry Hudson's Spring. The Italian explorer Giovanni da Verrazano was the first European to explore the Sandy Hook area and Raritan Bay, in 1524. Henry Hudson, exploring the area in 1609, sent some of his men searching for fresh water in what is today Atlantic Highlands. What they found was a spring that the Lenni Lenape Indians used for their freshwater needs.

While on Ocean Boulevard (Scenic Drive), turn left onto Lawrie Road, then left onto Hilton Road to Bay Side Drive. This will lead you to what is known as Henry Hudson's Spring or Henry Hudson's Spout. Water still trickles from the spouts in the rocks, and a marker located behind the stone wall explains the historical importance of the site.

Visit Mt. Mitchill Scenic Overlook. Part of the Monmouth County Parks System, Mt. Mitchill, which rises 266 feet above sea level, is the highest point not only on the Jersey Shore, but on the entire Atlantic Seaboard. It offers a majestic view of Sandy Hook and Raritan bays and the lower part of the New York skyline. Scenic Drive ends at Mt. Mitchill.

Mt. Mitchill has pay binoculars available for even better views and a small picnic area for public use, complete with barbecue pits. A plaque located at the four flagpoles is dedicated to the Americans held hostage in Iran in 1980.

Highlands

Highlands is the seafood capital of the North Jersey Shore. It has more fine seafood restaurants and small chowder-style shanties than anywhere else in the area, and nearly all of them have nautical settings of some sort. Some even have docks on the premises, so those arriving by boat can moor there.

Most of the major restaurants in Highlands are well known. Few serious seafood lovers have not heard about or eaten at **Bahr's, Longjohn's,** the **Clam Hut** or **Doris and Ed's,** where the fish is fresh and the clam chowder is seasoned to perfection.

Highlands, however, has more to offer visitors than delicious seafood. Take a ride along the waterfront, and you'll discover more party fishing boats than any visiting deep-sea fisherman will ever need. Before you select one, however, be sure to ask around as to where different boats are currently doing much of their fishing, and check this information against the fish stories you'll undoubtedly hear dockside.

Did you know that . . .

James Fenimore Cooper's novel *The Water Witch,* although written in Paris, is set in Highlands. Cooper was a frequent visitor to the town in the 1820s.

Most boats fishing out of Highlands or Atlantic Highlands in the summer will be going for bluefish, fluke, weakfish or porgy. During the winter, ling, cod and whiting make up the main catch. For half-day trips and overnight trips, party boats will venture as for as 40 miles offshore in search of fish.

Highlands is also full of history. As early as 1663, the area was being considered for settlement by Dutch and British colonists. In 1678 Richard Hartshorne, for whom the woods in nearby Middletown are named, acquired use rights for Sandy Hook from the Indians for 13 shillings. He then purchased the Highlands area from the original English settlers there.

During the revolutionary war, the Sandy Hook/Highlands vicinity was controlled by British soldiers and colonists loyal to the Crown. When they captured a Monmouth County Continental Militia commander, Capt. Joshua Huddy, they imprisoned him and eventually took him to Highlands, where he was hanged for a murder he did not commit. Visitors can view a marker set at the hanging spot in Huddy's honor. It's located in the park on Waterwitch Avenue that bears the name of the patriot.

In the mid-1800s, Twin Lights was built atop Highlands. One of the most powerful lighthouses in the world at the time, its lights could be seen as far as 70 miles at sea, said sailors. It was also here that Guglielmo Marconi demonstrated the first commercial use of wireless telegraphy, in 1899. Today Twin Lights is a museum and state historical site and should be considered a "must visit" for anyone coming to Highlands. (See below for detailed information on the Twin Lights Museum.)

Tourism was a thriving business in Highlands as far back as a century ago. In the early 1900s, hotels and inns were found on almost every street, restaurants were overflowing with patrons and Highlands' bay and river beaches were crowded with swimmers and beachwalkers. Highlands was the perfect day-trip or weekend outing for New Yorkers. There was a pier in Atlantic Highlands where steamships from Manhattan docked and unloaded passengers. A seashore railroad line passed through Highlands and took visitors to other Jersey Shore resorts like Long Branch and Red Bank. It was Highlands' golden era, to be sure, and the town profited immensely from it.

Did you know that . . .

Gertrude Ederle, the first woman to swim the English channel, spent her summers in Highlands and learned to swim there. She swam the channel in 1926. A Highlands park is named in her honor.

When the steamships stopped coming in the early 1930s, much of the town's tourist trade began to dry up. One by one, the hotels and guesthouses went out of business. Fortunately, Highlands held on to its reputation as a good place to fish and an even better place to eat seafood. But today, if you visit Highlands and plan to stay overnight, you'll have little luck locating decent lodging. **Conner's Hotel,** a pleasant family-run operation (326 Shore Drive, 908–872–1500) is the only recommended accommodation in Highlands.

Highlands' maritime heritage and history still drift through its side streets. Walking or driving by the town's waterfront, you can easily imagine a popular, turn-of-the-century resort filled with shops and visitors, with boats in the harbor and steamships in the bay.

Things to Do

Visit the Twin Lights Historical Site. A visit to Twin Lights is an ideal way to spend an afternoon followed by dinner at any of the fine seafood restaurants just down the hill. The museum and related exhibits at Twin Lights provide the visitor with not only the story of one of America's most fascinating lighthouse structures but also the best collection perhaps anywhere of photographs and equipment used by the U.S. Life Saving Service, forerunner of the U.S. Coast Guard. In addition, there's an excellent exhibit that deals with Guglielmo Marconi's famous demonstration of wireless telegraphy and superb examples of the unusual hunting and fishing boats built at the Jersey Shore many years ago.

Plan to visit Twin Lights on a clear day. Sitting on the bluffs overlooking the Shrewsbury River 200 feet above sea level, Twin Lights, like nearby Mt. Mitchill, offers a wonderful panoramic view of lower New York, Sandy Hook and surrounding waters. Museum visitors wishing to spend the better part of a day at Twin Lights might want to picnic on the grounds. Facilities for picnicking include tables and barbecue grills.

If you're coming from the Garden State Parkway and Route 36, you can reach Twin Lights by turning right just before the Highlands Bridge, which connects Highlands with Sandy Hook. This will lead you to Portland Road. Bear right onto Highlands Avenue and follow the signs to the entrance of Twin Lights.

The biggest attraction at Twin Lights is, of course, the double lighthouse. It is, as you'll quickly discover, not your typical lighthouse. Looking at it from the bottom of Highlands or from Sandy Hook, one might think the two tall towers to be those of an old fortress. The structure consists of the two lighthouse towers connected by a long, narrow building, which once contained quarters for the keepers of Twin Lights and their families. Today, the building is the home of the Twin Lights museum and auditorium.

Look closely at the lighthouse towers, and you'll see that despite the term *twin lights,* they're not *really* twins. No one knows for certain why architect Joseph Lederle chose to give the North Tower an octagonal shape and the South Tower a square one, but he did. One should also know that the present Twin Lights were constructed in 1861–1862 and are not the original towers that stood atop Highlands. Those were built in 1828 and consisted of two unconnected towers.

Visitors to Twin Lights are permitted to climb the North Tower, which, although the lighthouse was officially decommissioned in 1949, still blinks from dusk to dawn. The steps are steep and narrow—there are 64 of them—but the climb is worth your effort. As one might expect, the view from the top is superb. Special permission is needed to enter the South Tower.

After climbing the North Tower and enjoying the vista, plan to spend some time in the Twin Lights Museum. It is one of the best museums on the Jersey Shore and contains a number of interesting artifacts, photographs, documents and exhibits that chronicle the history of Twin Lights. There's also a working replica of Guglielmo Marconi's original wireless telegraph equipment.

In 1899, due to Twin Lights' high elevation and proximity to New York, Marconi built the first wireless telegraph antenna in the United States on the grounds. His wireless telegraphy equipment enabled the citizens of Highlands to receive information about the return of Commodore Dewey's fleet after its victory at Manila Bay during the Spanish-American War. The same equipment also enabled the *New York Herald* to be the first newspaper to report news of the 1899 America's Cup Race off the North Jersey Shore.

Other interesting exhibits in the museum include the one that deals with the history of the U.S. Life Saving Service. (See below for more information on the U.S. Life Saving Service.) Be certain to check out the Francis Life Car, an iron container that was used to bring people ashore from sinking, wrecked ships. There's also an interesting collection of locally built skiffs that were used for hunting and fishing in bays and rivers along the coast. On display are examples of the Sea Bright Skiff, the Shrewsbury Crab Skiff and the Barnegat Sneakbox.

But the most fascinating exhibit is the one that deals with the boat, *The Fox.* In 1896, *The Fox* was the first known boat to cross the Atlantic Ocean without the use of sail or steam. Two Highlands fishermen, Frank Samuelson and George Harbo, accepted the challenge of rowing across the Atlantic initiated by the New York magazine, *Police Gazette.* They completed their journey in 62 days and earned $10,000 in prize money put up by the New York magazine's publisher, Richard Fox (hence the name of the boat).

The men rowed from New York harbor to LeHavre, France. A replica of *The Fox* is in the museum, as well as a series of paintings dealing with their voyage by maritime artist Henry Luhrs and copies of photographs and equipment used by the men.

Just outside the museum you'll see a boathouse. It was the first lifeboat station built on Sandy Hook, opposite Spermaceti Cove. Constructed in 1849, one year after the U.S. Life Saving Service was founded and began rescuing shipwreck victims off the New Jersey Coast, it is the only one remaining of the original eight Life Saving Service boathouses.

Beyond the boathouse is the Twin Lights Generating Station, which now contains an original Fresnel lighthouse lens from the South Tower as well as an audio program that explains the intricate development of the lens.

Just across from the generating station is the Twin Lights Auditorium, where visitors can see films and slide shows depicting the history of Twin Lights and neighboring Sandy Hook. The films and slide shows are usually shown on weekends and holidays when attendance at Twin Lights is heaviest, or upon request. Park staff announce which film or slide show will be shown as well as the starting time over the park's public address system.

After visiting the generating station, walk around to the front of the Twin Lights building, the side facing the ocean, where there is another audio program at the brick overlook. It gives a brief but valuable historical sketch of the Highlands area and should not be missed. Those not wishing or unable to climb the North Tower will want to enjoy the view here.

Just behind the overlook is a cannon. Dubbed the Twin Lights Mystery Cannon after its discovery during a renovation of the original Twin Lights in 1841, its purpose at Twin Lights is still not known.

Finally, on the north side of the Twin Lights structure you'll find one last audio program, this one explaining the story of Marconi and his work at Twin Lights, told by his daughter, Gioia Marconi Braga. This is located just above the picnic area, on the spot where Marconi's antenna stood.

Twin Lights is open daily. Site grounds are open until sunset. The park is closed on Thanksgiving, Christmas, and New Year's Day. There is no admission charge. For more information, call (908) 872–1814 or (908) 872–1886.

Searching for Captain Kidd's Treasure. If you spot a solitary figure scanning the sand with a metal detector at the edge of a Highlands street, there's a chance he's searching for a few old doubloons, though he may not admit it. Legend has it that the notorious pirate, Captain Kidd, buried treasure somewhere on the bay side of Sandy Hook. Few

The U.S. Life Saving Service

What would become known as the U.S. Life Saving Service began in 1848 after a New Jersey Congressman, Dr. William A. Newell, convinced the federal government to appropriate $10,000 to construct and equip lifesaving stations along the Jersey Shore.

New Jersey was the logical birthplace for the U.S. Life Saving Service. During the eighteenth and nineteenth centuries, before the advantages afforded ship captains with the use of modern navigational equipment, there were a large number of shipwrecks off the Jersey coast. Many people lost their lives and millions of dollars worth of cargo went to the bottom of the sea.

Although shipwrecks occurred with unsettling regularity from Cape Cod to Cape Hatteras, New Jersey recorded some of the worst disasters and proportionately more of them. The reason was twofold. First, New York possessed one of the country's busiest harbors with a large amount of ship traffic even back then, and much of it passed along the Jersey coast. Second, the Jersey coast was notorious for its dangerous, shifting sandbars and shoals. When the wind blew from the northeast, as it frequently does during storms, sailing ships were blown toward shore or forced to seek refuge close to it. Often they hit a sandbar and, because of gales and particularly rough seas, were wrecked.

The money Congress spent on creating the Life Saving Service went to purchase lifesaving equipment and the construction of life-saving stations. Originally, the stations were simple and rather crude; they contained provisions and lifesaving equipment. When a wreck was spotted, surfmen would launch boats from the beach and rescue shipwreck victims.

If the ocean was too rough, the surfmen would fire a shot line to the ship, rig other lines and pull people to safety using the Francis Life Car. Over the years, hundreds of people escaped death by riding to safety in one of these containers. You can see two original Francis Life Cars at the Twin Lights Museum.

Originally, eight stations were built for the Life Saving Service on the Jersey coast. They were located from Sandy Hook to the southern edge of Long Beach Island. As the Life Saving Service matured, stations were constructed approximately 3½ miles apart on the coast, with foot or horse patrols covering the beach area in between. New Jersey eventually had 41 lifesaving stations in all.

The U.S. Life Saving Service was gradually extended to cover not only New Jersey's coastline, but the remainder of the Atlantic Coast, the Gulf and Pacific Coasts and even the shorelines of the Great Lakes. After a reorganization of the Life Saving Service was completed in 1875, better records of rescues and rescue attempts were kept. From 1872 to 1915, when the Life Saving Service merged with the U.S. Revenue Cutter Service to form the U.S. Coast Guard, over 175,000 people had been safely rescued from the angry sea.

people actually searched for the buried treasure until 1948, when an old fisherman found some gold coins in the sand off Cedar Street. When news spread of his discovery, it was widely assumed the coins were part of the lost treasure of Captain Kidd. People flocked to the bay beaches of Highlands and sifted the sand there with hopes of striking it rich. Other coins were found, but the treasure wasn't. Although the gold coins were never truly linked with Kidd's treasure, the legend lives on.

Go Fishing for Jersey Jumbos. Jersey Jumbos are bluefish. They're not only exciting fish to catch, but they're good eating fish too. The Jersey Shore is noted for its excellent bluefishing. Bluefish are inshore fish and travel in schools. You can spot a school by looking for flocks of seagulls overhead; they eat what bluefish in a feeding frenzy don't. The bluefish is a fighter, so don't count on a particularly easy catch. But that's what makes bluefishing fun—and challenging. Be careful handling bluefish. They have sharp teeth and can do damage to an unsuspecting fisherman whose fingers are in the wrong place. Most of the Highlands' party boats advertise bluefishing. Two of the best bluefishing grounds on the north Jersey Shore are Shrewsbury Rocks and Ambrose Light Tower. The best time to go for bluefish is July through September.

Sandy Hook

Back before Giovanni da Verrazano and Henry Hudson explored the waters around Sandy Hook, the Lenni Lenape Indians regularly visited the thin, ever-changing strip of barrier beach to gather its natural resources. The Indians came to fish, to gather shells and beach plums and to cut down dead cedar trees to make canoes.

Even though Richard Hartshorne acquired use rights for Sandy Hook in 1678, it wasn't until 1762 that merchants from New York City purchased the northern tip of Sandy Hook to erect a lighthouse in order to make navigation into and out of New York harbor easier for visiting ships. The Sandy Hook lighthouse began operation two years later. Today, its the oldest operating lighthouse in America.

Did you know that . . .

When the Sandy Hook Lighthouse was completed in 1764, it stood 500 feet from the tip of Sandy Hook. Today the lighthouse stands 1¼ miles from the tip. A giant sand build up at the north end of the peninsula, due to ocean currents and waves, has enabled Sandy Hook to grow substantially over the years.

Sandy Hook's strategic location was realized as early as the late 1600s, when plans were drawn to erect a fort there. Gun emplacements could easily guard entrance to the harbor because the channel leading to it passed right by the tip of Sandy Hook. The fort, however, was never built.

The British knew how valuable Sandy Hook was, and during the War for Independence, British regulars and Loyalists, or Tories, controlled it, despite attempts by the Americans to take the sandspit. It proved particularly valuable to British Gen. Henry Clinton, who, after the Battle of Monmouth in 1778, fled to Sandy Hook from where he and his troops then escaped to New York.

Shortly before the Civil War, construction of a large fort was begun at Sandy Hook. It was to be used as the first line of defense of the New York and New Jersey harbor area, supplementing the other coastal forts closer to the New York City port. Never officially named, because it was never completed, the partially erected fort was simply known as "Fort at Sandy Hook."

The only permanent fort built at Sandy Hook was **Fort Hancock.** The U.S. Army Proving Ground used land there to test guns, ammunition and armor plate from 1874 to 1919. During World Wars I and II, Fort Hancock was an important coastal defense fort and heavily fortified with the most powerful guns of those eras.

Early in World War II, it was especially feared that Germany might try to attack New York and bomb its harbor; therefore, the gun emplacements at Fort Hancock were extremely important in the defense of the city. Many of the gun batteries and bunkers can be seen today, decaying amid beach grass and sand dunes. Some are extremely dangerous to walk on and explore. Obey the warning signs.

After World War II, Fort Hancock's big guns were dismantled, made obsolete in coastal defense, due largely to the superiority of air defense. In the guns' place came first antiaircraft guns, then Nike Ajax missiles and, still later, larger Nike Hercules missiles. The Nike missiles at Sandy Hook were part of the last defense system seen there. In 1962, the southern two miles of Sandy Hook were leased by the State of New Jersey from the U.S. Army for use as Sandy Hook State Park. In 1972, Gateway National Recreation Area was created, which included Sandy Hook. And in 1975, Fort Hancock was officially turned over to the National Park Service.

Despite the historical significance of Fort Hancock, most people who come to Sandy Hook for the day come to go swimming. If you plan to visit Sandy Hook in the summer, expect large crowds. Try to avoid visiting the park on summer weekends or holidays, since there is no guarantee you'll get in unless you arrive early. For those not interested in swimming, the best time to visit Sandy Hook is in spring or fall. The weather is usually pleasant, and there are no crowds, except, perhaps, on weekends.

There is also no reason why one should not consider a visit to Sandy Hook in late fall or even winter. Fishermen use the facilities at Sandy Hook year-round. What you'll find in the off-season are uncrowded hiking trails, excellent beachcombing and the opportunity to visit Fort Hancock and its sites at your own pace. Be advised, however, that in January and February Sandy Hook can be bitter cold. Icy winds often blow across the barrier beach, making hiking or exploring Fort Hancock enjoyable only if you're properly dressed.

If you arrive by car during the summer season (Memorial Day weekend through Labor Day), there is a recreation user fee. Bicyclists are free; so are those who walk in. Actually, bicycling around Sandy Hook is an excellent way to see and enjoy the sites. The roads are flat and well paved, which makes for easy cycling. Those who cycle also have easy access to many of the sites without having to worry about parking, a major problem at Sandy Hook in the summer.

In order to familiarize yourself with Sandy Hook and learn about the wide range of programs and activities available to visitors (see below), your first stop should be the Spermaceti Cove Visitor Center. It's located on the right side of the park's main thoroughfare, just beyond Parking Area D and directly across from Spermaceti Cove on the bay side. The building, once a U.S. Life Saving Service Station, was built in 1894. Plan to spend enough time here to catch the 10-minute slide show, which provides a good introduction to Sandy Hook, and to visit the displays that deal with the ecology and history of the area. Antique beach apparatus, once used by the Sandy Hook surfmen (as men of the U.S. Life Saving Service were called) are also on display.

On your way out, pick up the free brochures and pamphlets available to visitors. They range from self-guided walking tours to information pertaining to seashells found on Sandy Hook beaches. The ranger on duty there will also be able to answer any questions you might have.

Leave the Visitor Center and continue into the park. A half mile or so up the road is what's known as Parking Area F, a fishing beach. Even if you're not an angler, proceed up the road. Just before the parking lot adjacent to the beach, notice the old ammo bunkers once used to store artillery shells for battery guns. Across from the ammo bunkers are what *look* like machine-gun bunkers. Actually, they were sentry checkpoints.

Although there are no markers indicating such, this South Beach Area was where, some say, World War II was really won. It was here that a top secret radar testing site existed in the 1930s. Experiments carried out here helped scientists from nearby Fort Monmouth (see chapter 3) complete the all-important development of radar. This, of course, enabled Allied forces to pick up, on a screen, bleeps indicating the approach of enemy aircraft. Radar might not have *really* won the war for America and her allies, but there can be no doubt it played a significant role.

Returning to the main road, continue heading north into the park. Eventually you'll come to a fork in the road. One route will take you directly to the Fort Hancock National Historic District; the other will take you there, too, but by way of Gunnison Beach, Battery Gunnison and North Beach. Take the latter route.

Battery Gunnison is the remains of two 6-inch gun emplacements built in 1904. One can climb atop the battery, walk through the maze of rooms and tunnels and view the guns up close. Gunnison Beach separates the battery from the ocean. North Beach is the northernmost beach on Sandy Hook that is protected by lifeguards and open to swimmers. If you plan to swim or spend the day on the beach, take the time to ride up to North Beach. It is the nicest of all Sandy Hook beaches and has the best views of ships approaching New York harbor.

West of North Beach is Fort Hancock. Continue on the main road—you'll see Sandy Hook's famous lighthouse standing tall against a backdrop of blue sky—and follow it to the fort. (For a complete tour of Fort Hancock, see below.)

Once you've visited the sites at Fort Hancock and spent some time in the museum there, you'll be on the bay side of Sandy Hook. If it's a clear day, you'll be able to see across Sandy Hook Bay to Atlantic Highlands and Highlands, including Twin Lights. Heading south on the main road, you'll pass by Horseshoe Cove and the Halyburton Monument, where the remains of British sailors dating back to the revolutionary war were found years ago.

Further down the main road, to your right, is the **Sandy Hook Holly Forest.** This is a wildlife sanctuary. This means it's illegal to pick plants or harm the wildlife in any way. In the forest you might catch a glimpse of one of many types of birds that frequent Sandy Hook. Sandy Hook is on what's called the Atlantic Flyway, and a number of migrating birds seek shelter and food here. The oldest holly tree in the forest is estimated to be over 150 years old. Yet, because of the salt air, the trees are stunted and never reach the height of a normal holly tree. (The Holly Forest is accessible only by guided tour.)

After the Holly Forest are three bayside islands that lie close to shore. Skeleton Hill Island and South Island at Spermaceti Cove and Plum Island farther south are all accessible if you don't mind wading out to them. You're apt to find some interesting marine life on them. A mile or two farther down the road, and you'll come to the exit and entrance of the park.

Things to Do

Go on a Self-guided Tour of Fort Hancock. You can pick up the free pamphlet, *Fort Hancock History Tour,* at the Spermaceti Cove Visitor Center or at the Sandy Hook Museum in Fort Hancock. Bicycling through the fort is better than driving, except, of course, during the winter. Walking is probably the best way to explore Fort Hancock, however. On the tour you'll pass a number of derelict buildings and undoubtedly will wonder why they haven't been demolished or restored. The National Park Service, it seems, is in a frustrating bind. Presently, there's little money available to restore such buildings.

Some of Fort Hancock's buildings are in good shape; these have been renovated little by little since the Park Service gained control of the fort in the mid-1970s. There are a number of fine houses on Officer's Row, for example, the scenic boulevard that runs parallel with Sandy Hook Bay. The buildings that house the ranger headquarters and the Sandy Hook Museum have also been restored. But much more money needs to be poured into Fort Hancock if its historical value is to be fully appreciated and preserved.

After touring Fort Hancock, make sure you see Battery Potter—America's first and only "steam-powered, disappearing gun battery." From spring through fall rangers lead tours into the battery's tunnels. Nearby is the Rodman Gun—this huge Civil War-era gun was one of the largest muzzle-loading cannon ever made. The Fort Hancock gun is one of only two that still exist today. Nearby is the Sandy Hook Museum. Located across from the parade field, this one-room museum contains small exhibits, photos, memorabilia, maps and illustrations depicting the history of Fort Hancock. History House—currently the home of the Sandy Hook Veterans Historical Society—used to be the residence of a lieutenant and his family stationed at the fort around the turn of the century. Open only on weekends. The Sandy Hook Lighthouse—located on the grounds of Fort Hancock—is still in operation under the jurisdiction of the U.S. Coast Guard. (The Sandy Hook Coast Guard Station and adjoining complex is on the bay side, northwest of Fort Hancock. It is off-limits to visitors.) Because it is not open to visitors, the Sandy Hook Lighthouse hasn't captured the hearts of the public as has "Old Barney," the Barnegat Lighthouse on Long Beach Island (see chapter 5). Yet the octagon-shaped Sandy Hook Lighthouse played an important role in the American Revolution. Despite repeated attempts by American patriots to destroy it, the lighthouse enabled British ships to gain entrance to New York harbor.

Walk Old Dune Trail. Old Dune Trail begins at the Spermaceti Cove Visitor Center. You can get a free copy of a pamphlet there that explains what plants you'll find along the one-mile loop. Stay on the path; over two-thirds of Sandy Hook is vegetated by poison ivy. Also, bring along insect repellent. Mosquitoes and nasty green head flies abound in the summer. There are numerous other trails and walks on Sandy Hook. Ask a ranger for details.

Watch a Lifesaving Drill. During July and August, park rangers dress up as surfmen of the U.S. Life Saving Service and reenact a lifesaving drill on the beach near Spermaceti Cove Visitor Center. They fire an authentic reproduction Lyle Gun, an important piece of equipment in bringing to shore shipwrecked victims, and explain the various functions and lifestyle of a typical turn-of-the-century surfman. Call (908) 872–0115 for more information.

Go Bird-watching. Birds constitute the largest percentage of wildlife on Sandy Hook. Using a pair of binoculars, you might spot warblers, sandpipers, marsh hawks, a great blue heron, an osprey, a great horned owl, woodpeckers, black ducks and clapper rails.

Go Swimming. The most popular activity on Sandy Hook during the summer is swimming. Areas B, C, D, and E, Gunnison Beach and North Beach have lifeguards. There's even a nude beach south of Battery Gunnison. Although the sand isn't the best quality—grayish white in color and coarse—and the water isn't the cleanest found on the Jersey Shore, Sandy Hook's beaches are crowded during July and August.

Go Surfing. Surfer's Cove, situated where the seawall ends near Parking Lot C, is the best spot on Sandy Hook to catch summer and autumn waves. On days when the waves are small, ride a longboard. When the swell picks up, thruster model surfboards perform best.

Go Sailboarding. Most of the sailboarding at Sandy Hook is done on the bay side of the peninsula, across from Area C. Beginners especially like the flat, glassy conditions that usually prevail and the shallow water. The privately run concession stand adjacent to the Parking Lot at Area C rents sailboards and gives lessons as well.

Go Jogging. Early morning or early evening joggers will find the roads and scenery on Sandy Hook to their liking. Don't run when traffic is heavy. You can get information on specified distances from rangers.

Hunt for Seashells. Before you do, pick up literature on shells found at Sandy Hook at the Visitor Center. The pamphlets will help explain what you'll find walking on the beach. Common shells include Atlantic slipper shells, periwinkles, whelks, Eastern oyster shells, razor clams, Atlantic ribbed mussels and Atlantic bay scallop shells.

Enjoy a Puppet Show with the Kids. During the summer, free puppet shows for children, starring Sissy Seagull, Clem Clam and others are presented on the beach in front of the Spermaceti Cove Visitor Center. Call the center for details.

"Go Bunkers" on a Bunker Tour. Tours of gun batteries and bunkers within the Fort Hancock historical district are popular with history and military buffs. Tours are offered on selected Sundays during the spring and fall. Reservations are a must, as are flashlights. Call (908) 872–0115.

Star Gaze. Spend an evening peering through a telescope and view the heavens. A park ranger leads discussions on astronomy in the summer and fall. There's also a slide show that's presented to familiarize would-be astronomers with the basics of star gazing. It's recommended, but not necessary, that you bring your own telescope. For more information, call (908) 872–0115.

Go Fishing. There are special fishing areas for surf fishermen at Sandy Hook. Anglers can try their luck on the bay side, too. Night permits are available at the Ranger station. Rangers even provide surf-casting instructions and workshops during the summer. Fish anytime, but autumn is best.

Go on a Canoe Cruise. On Sundays in July and August, one can spend several hours paddling around Spermaceti Cove. Bring something to eat, for the group stops on Skeleton Hill Island for lunch and explores the island afterwards. Reservations are required. Bring your own canoe or use one of the park's five canoes. This is an excellent activity for couples, families and canoe clubs. For more information call (908) 872–0115.

Where to Eat on the Bayshore

Bahr's, 2 Bay Avenue, Highlands, (908) 872–1245
Price Code: Moderate   Menu: Seafood
Bahr's is one of the Bayshore's most popular seafood restaurants. Dockside dining on the Shrewsbury River. Nautical decor inside includes Highlands memorabilia and old photos of ships.

Careless Navigator, 1 South Bay Avenue, Highlands, (908) 872–1616
Price Code: Inexpensive   Menu: Mostly seafood
Good lunch menu that includes tasty seafood sandwiches. Located under Highlands Bridge. Some tables have water view of Shrewsbury River.

Clam Hut, Foot of Atlantic Street, Highlands, (908) 872–0999
Price Code: Moderate   Menu: Seafood
Menu at the Clam Hut is similar to Bahr's; good lobster and other seafood specials, nautical ambiance.

Doris and Ed's, 36 Shore Drive, Highlands, (908) 872–1565
Price Code: Expensive   Menu: Gourmet seafood
The number-one seafood restaurant north of Atlantic City. Meticulously prepared, truly delicious appetizers and main courses, out-of-this-world desserts. Ask for a table with a water view. Reservations a must.

Ten Tips for Dining at the Jersey Shore

1. Read restaurant reviews. Magazines, such as *New Jersey Monthly* and *Atlantic City,* and Shore newspapers like the *Asbury Park Press* and *Atlantic City Press* regularly print restaurant reviews. Read and then file the ones that sound especially enticing.

2. Find out beforehand if the restaurant you choose to dine at has a liquor license. If you enjoy a drink with your meal, bring your own bottle of spirits.

3. Stay away from popular restaurants on weekends and especially on holidays.

4. Keep an eye out for days in which a particular restaurant offers "Lobster Specials" or "All the Shrimp You Can Eat"—and then select another evening to dine there if it's peace and quiet and good service you prefer.

5. Whenever possible, make advance reservations in order to avoid long lines. Wherever possible, ask for a table with a view of the water.

6. Choose a restaurant that's open year-round over one that's seasonal. You're more apt to get better service, bigger portions and higher food standards.

7. If it's seafood you enjoy, try to select a restaurant that has an adjoining fish market. This way you know what you order is fresh. Often you even get the chance to pick out your own fish or lobster.

8. If ordering seafood anywhere else on the Shore, don't be afraid to ask if the catch is fresh. Yes, there are Shore restaurants that use frozen fish.

9. Avoid eating dinner on the boardwalk. No matter how tempting the scent of sausage and peppers, foot-long heroes and fried clam sandwiches are, save the boardwalk eating experience for a snack or beach lunch.

10. Be wary of fish dinners that are smothered in sauce. It's not uncommon to get more sauce than fish.

Hofbrauhaus, 301 Ocean Boulevard, Atlantic Highlands, (908) 291–0224

Price Code: Moderate   Menu: German

For those tired of seafood. Sauerbraten, wiener schnitzel and other German specialties. Great view of Sandy Hook Bay from across the street.

Long John's Ltd., 18 Beach Boulevard, Highlands, (908) 872–1771
Price Code: Moderate   Menu: Seafood
Dockside dining, daily seafood specials. Competes with the Clam Hut and Bahr's for the same seafood crowd.

Memphis Pig Out, 67 1st Avenue, Highlands, (908) 291–5533
Price Code: Moderate   Menu: Ribs and chicken
The place on the North Jersey Shore for hickory-smoked ribs, pork shoulder and chicken. Dinner only.

Moby's Restaurant, 2 South Bay Avenue, Highlands, (908) 291–4430
Price Code: Inexpensive   Menu: Seafood
Paper plate dining, outdoor tables. The clam chowder is tops; so is the view.

2

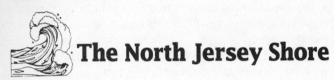

The North Jersey Shore

Just south of Sandy Hook, and extending all the way down to the Manasquan Inlet, is what's usually referred to as the North Jersey Shore. It begins with Sea Bright, a town that's forever in danger of being swept away by the sea, and ends at Manasquan, a town that also acts as the southernmost coastal boundary of Monmouth County. In between is a string of towns—Belmar, Asbury Park, Deal, Spring Lake, Long Branch and others—that comprise the most densely populated section of the Jersey Shore, due to its large year-round residency.

As more and more workers opt for the commuting life, the seasonal stigma of the North Jersey Shore continues to disappear. Each day—in summer and in winter—the train that runs along the coast and ends up in New York City is filled with white-shirted commuters reading the *New York Times* and *Wall Street Journal*. Those whose place of work is northern New Jersey drive along the Garden State Parkway. Finally, more and more commuters to Philadelphia and western New Jersey cities such as Trenton and Princeton are living in the southern half of the North Jersey Shore and traveling across the state via Route 195.

The accessibility of the North Jersey Shore to Philadelphia and New York/northern New Jersey has permanently altered the makeup of the area. Unlike beach towns farther south along the Jersey coast, there are no more "summer-only" beach towns on the North Jersey Shore. This, of course, does not mean that the North Jersey Shore doesn't attract hordes of tourists anymore or doesn't cater to tourism. On the contrary.

In terms of sheer numbers, more visitors are vacationing in this part of the Jersey Shore than ever before. But a ride down to Spring Lake or Brielle in the middle of the winter will find thriving communities functioning just like anywhere else in the state.

The towns of the North Jersey Shore may be linked geographically and be similar in the transformation from seasonal to year-round living, but they constitute an area that is, nevertheless, one with many different personalities. This makes it all the more interesting for the visitor to explore. The North Jersey Shore is actually a study of contrasts. Asbury Park, despite being a mere four miles from Spring Lake, is a far cry from its neighbor in many ways. The same can be said about Deal and Long Branch, Bradley Beach and Sea Girt, Belmar and Brielle. And no town on the North Jersey Shore is like what one will find in Ocean Grove. One can spend days, even weeks, exploring the North Jersey Shore and never fully digest its grand diversity.

A hundred years ago when popular seashore resorts like Long Branch attracted wealthy New Yorkers and United States presidents, and huge mansions and luxurious summer cottages sat overlooking the Atlantic Ocean, the area was known as New Jersey's Gold Coast. It was the summer playground of the rich and famous. Millionaires like Solomon Guggenheim built grand summer palaces here; Diamond Jim Brady and the actress Lily Langtry were frequent visitors to Long Branch. Presidents Grant, Garfield, Arthur, Harrison, McKinley and Wilson summered on this part of the Jersey Shore. In 1881, Garfield came to Elberon, desperately hoping that the Jersey coast salt air would help him recover from the gunshot wound he received from an assassin in Washington, D.C. Garfield, however, needed more than fresh air. He died 13 days after arriving.

Did you know that . . .

When it was announced that President Garfield would be convalescing from his gunshot wound in Long Branch in the summer of 1881, townsmen constructed a line of railroad track more than a half-mile long in less than a day so the president's car could be pulled right up to the porch of his summer house.

Today little of that original splendor remains, yet in towns such as Deal, Spring Lake and Sea Girt there is no shortage of wealth or million-dollar homes. But it's a different class of people who reside in such homes and frequent the beach and tennis clubs there. There is little real flaunting of wealth. Those who live in Deal and Spring Lake, for instance, prefer to keep their wealth behind the walls and shrubbery of their small estates.

Yet, despite the presence of such money on the North Jersey Shore, a place like Asbury Park gave rise to one of rock 'n' roll's greatest heroes, Bruce Springsteen. Singing about the woes of the working man, Springsteen and the characters in his songs symbolize the exact opposite of the grace and comfort of towns a few minutes north or south of Asbury Park.

But all this might very well change in the next few years. Towns like Asbury Park and Long Branch, both of which have suffered through decades of decline, appear ready to bounce back in a big way. Renovation work is already under way along Asbury Park's waterfront. Rock clubs and seedy seaside bars are being replaced with condominiums, health spas, restaurants and promenades. In Long Branch, an ultramodern, multistoried Hilton Hotel overlooks the ocean. Can casino gambling be far behind? Ocean Grove, with its tree-lined streets and Victorian homes, has become the Cape May of the North Jersey Shore.

Some of the contrasts found on the North Jersey Shore will never change, however. The residents of Sea Bright and Monmouth Beach, for instance, will always sweat out the frequent storms that hit the Jersey coast. The two towns are protected by a large stone seawall, but over the years even this hasn't been enough to keep the Atlantic Ocean from flooding streets and destroying homes.

Farther south in a town like Brielle, the greenery is enough to make you wonder if the ocean is really just a half mile or so away. Unlike Sea Bright and Monmouth Beach, which are built on the same skinny strip of sand that includes Sandy Hook, Brielle is located on more stable ground and has no worries about shifting sands and failing seawalls.

Because of North Jersey Shore beach erosion, especially in towns such as Sea Bright, the beaches above Asbury Park are not as wide as they used to be, nor are they particularly suited to handle the hordes of sun worshippers and swimmers that swarm through the area each summer. But what Long Branch, Asbury Park and Sea Bright lack in top-notch beaches, they more than make up for in nightlife. If it's dancing and good music you're after, Asbury Park, Long Branch and Sea Bright together offer a wide selection of clubs, crowds and sounds.

South of Asbury Park the beaches do get somewhat wider, and therefore, you'll probably find more room to lay your blanket on the sand. But not that much room. Belmar and Manasquan are often compared to Florida's Fort Lauderdale due to the inundation of college students during the summer months. If the beaches there get too crowded, you can always go fishing. Belmar has the largest party boat fleet in New Jersey; Manasquan has the Manasquan Inlet.

You won't find beaches in Spring Lake and Sea Girt quite as packed as Belmar's, and Manasquan's though. And back we go to the contrasts of the North Jersey Shore. Even if you don't choose to swim in Spring Lake or sun in Sea Girt because of limited food concessions and boardwalk entertainment, a Sunday bicycle ride through these two towns is highly recommended. The point is the North Jersey Shore is steeped in variety. And variety, they say, is the spice of life.

Sea Bright

Sea Bright sits just south of Sandy Hook. Because of the large stone and concrete seawall on its ocean side, visitors driving along Ocean Avenue, the town's principal thoroughfare, have no view of the beach. There's little beach to see, however. Erosion has been particularly cruel to Sea Bright. It's not unusual during a storm for waves to actually break on the seawall, which means that passing cars get hit with saltwater spray as seawater floods Sea Bright's streets.

Sea Bright is one of the Jersey Shore's narrowest towns. In some parts of it, the distance from the seawall to the Navesink and Shrewsbury Rivers on the town's west side is no more than a couple hundred yards. In between is Ocean Avenue and a small collection of side streets. Despite this, Sea Bright is a popular North Jersey Shore beach town. Virtually all available space has some sort of construction on it, be it summer homes, year-round homes, condominiums, restaurants, bars or beach clubs.

Did you know that . . .

Some scientists expect the Atlantic Ocean to rise 8 feet by the year 2100. That would mean Sea Bright and Monmouth Beach's seawall would need to be raised to a height of 41 feet before then in order to keep the ocean from washing away homes and roads.

Downtown Sea Bright consists of a number of shops and is a bustling area of activity in the summer. It's also a good place to eat. Check the **Sunflower Country Kitchen** (1125 East Ocean Avenue) for a delicious breakfast or lunch; the accent is on health food. The **Chuckling Oyster** (280 Ocean Avenue) is also recommended for supper or an evening drink. If it's a romantic view of the river you prefer, **McLoone's Rum Runner** (816 Ocean Avenue) has an outdoor patio on the Navesink and a scenic second-floor bar that regularly features some of the Shore's best bands on weekends.

Most of the town's nightclubs cater to the young, upwardly mobile set and, on the whole, are a bit classier than what you'll find farther south in Long Branch and Asbury Park. **Ichabod's** (1 East Church Street) and the **Good Side Cafe and Wine Bar** (10 East Ocean Avenue) are popular haunts that attract a lively, cocktail-lounge crowd.

On certain nights, **The Trade Winds** (1331 Ocean Avenue) becomes a teen club, which serves no liquor. Here you'll find a crowded, lively dance floor, an excellent sound system, and a disc jockey blaring out Top 40 tunes. Outside, there's a swimming pool and hot tub, which are part of the Trade Winds Beach Club.

Speaking of beach clubs, there are a number of good ones in Sea Bright. All of them, however, are private. In fact, there's only one public beach in town. But Sea Bright isn't the place to go to swim. It's best to drive up to Sandy Hook or down to Seven Presidents Park in Long Branch, where the beaches are public and wider. Come back to Sea Bright after the sun sets for supper and an after-dinner drink.

Monmouth Beach

Monmouth Beach is another beachclub town. If you're a local or a regular summer visitor who stays the season, membership in one of the clubs is the way to go. But for the day or weekend visitor to Monmouth Beach, the "members only" signs that can be found in front of the entrance to the clubs can be frustrating. You won't even be able to catch a glimpse of the ocean because the wooden platforms that are perched atop the seawall are private. There you'll find "No Trespassing" signs.

If you're driving through Monmouth Beach on your way to Sandy Hook to the north, or Long Branch and Asbury Park to the south, notice the juxtaposition of old and new. Old whitewashed summer homes stand next to eye-catching contemporary structures with large windows and skylights. The building that is now the Marine Police headquarters of the New Jersey State Police on Ocean Avenue used to be the area's Life Saving Service Station a century ago.

Long Branch

Though both claim the honor, it's difficult to say which town—Long Branch or Cape May—was America's first seashore resort. In the 1830s and 1840s, Long Branch was on its way to becoming a summer resort for wealthy New Yorkers. The draw, however, wasn't necessarily the ocean. Rather, it was the small gambling parlors and billiard halls that had begun to open in the town as well as the horse racing that went on, usually on the beach. For years thereafter, Long Branch attracted a particularly fast and lively crowd; society-types could be seen strolling the streets of Long Branch, and fashion and theater personalities were the objects of the latest gossip.

But it wasn't until the arrival of President Ulysses S. Grant in 1869, who decided to make Long Branch the summer capital of the nation, that the town began its Golden Age. It was then that the resort's political importance rivaled its social prestige. Over the next couple of decades, it was possible to see socialites such as Jim Fisk, Diamond Jim Brady and Lillian Russell on the same street as some of America's most important government officials and army generals such as Winfield Scott, George Meade and Philip Sheridan. American artist Winslow Homer sketched all this activity for publication in *Harper's Weekly.*

After Grant left office, Rutherford B. Hayes, James A. Garfield, Chester A. Arthur, Benjamin Harrison and William McKinley all summered, at one time or another, at Long Branch during their terms in office. Woodrow Wilson summered in West Long Branch when he was president.

In the meantime, Long Branch's reputation as a gambling mecca continued to grow. The Monmouth Park Jockey Club was begun in 1870; almost at once betting on horses proved wonderfully popular. Smoke-filled gambling houses were places where fortunes were won and lost over the course of a summer at Long Branch. Some people went so far as to call the town the "Monte Carlo of America."

Long Branch's era of splendor lasted until the early part of the twentieth century. Eventually, laws forbidding gambling stopped the flow of money on card and dice tables, which, in turn, stopped the flow of the rich and famous into Long Branch during the summer. After President Wilson, no other president used Long Branch as the country's summer capital. From then on, the eyes and ears of the nation turned elsewhere during June, July and August for its dose of political hearsay and social scuttlebutt.

Long Branch's decline as a major seashore resort was gradual but steady. Storms eroded its once fine beaches. Other resorts on the Jersey Shore now were more promising to summer visitors. By the late 1960s, elements of organized crime had settled into Long Branch, and not always surreptitiously. A couple of gangland murders seriously tarnished Long Branch's image. Urban blight, in the form of run-down buildings and shabby streets, and the problems associated with too many people on welfare tarnished its image even further.

Despite these problems, Long Branch has survived as a resort town. Families from northern New Jersey and New York still spend summers in bungalows that have been handed down from generation to generation. A boardwalk still attracts crowds to the beachfront at night. In the daytime, people still go to the beach to swim and sun.

The feeling in Long Branch is that if the town can hold out a little longer, it will experience a rebirth that could very well bring back memories of its glory days. Developers are seizing upon the opportunity to re-create a first-class resort that, hopefully, will encourage the return of the monied class in a big way. The presence of the large oceanfront Hilton Hotel in Long Branch could initiate the town's renaissance.

Things to Do

Spend the Day at Seven Presidents Oceanfront Park. Seven Presidents Oceanfront Park, named for the nation's chief executives who summered in the Long Branch area, possesses the best public beaches on the North Jersey Shore between Sandy Hook and Belmar. The 33-acre park is small, but it has three bathing beaches and three surfing/sailboarding beaches. There are sand dunes (not for walking on, though) and two usually crowded kiddie playgrounds filled with wooden apparatus and sand pits. In addition, shower and changing facilities are available and concession stands sell fast food and drinks.

Maintained by the Monmouth County Parks System, the park is meticulously kept and quite clean. During the week, the beach area is populated mostly by locals. However, during the weekends and especially on holidays, beach-blanket space can get scarce due to the arrival of those unable to get into Sandy Hook. Open year-round, there is an admission charge during the summer. The entrance to the park is at the intersection of Ocean and Joline avenues.

Sample the Shore's Best Hot Dogs. Funny that Long Branch, a predominantly Italian seaside community with more than its share of Italian restaurants and pizza parlors, should possess the two best places on the entire Jersey Shore for hot dogs. **Max's** is a veritable Long Branch institution. For years it was on the Long Branch pier. But due to a fire years ago, it moved a few blocks inland to Ocean Boulevard (not to be confused with Ocean Avenue) and opened for business where the Surf Lounge—a notorious mobster hangout—once stood. The hot dogs at Max's are long and tasty; the hamburgers are thick and delicious.

But the *tastiest* tube steaks and burgers are found a few blocks south of Ocean Boulevard at the **Windmill.** Here, the dogs taste as close to perfect as you'll get anywhere, and the sauerkraut is absolute tops. Charcoal-broiled hamburgers, California-style, are big favorites, too.

Competition between the Windmill and Max's is understandably keen. But Max's has the edge because it offers sit-down counter space and waitress table service. At the Windmill, you'll have to stand at the counter or else eat in your car. That can get awfully messy if you bring the kids along. Windmill diehards don't seem to mind the inconvenience, though.

Visit the Church of the Presidents. The history of Long Branch's Golden Age is recalled by memorabilia, photographs, documents and furnishings at the **St. James Chapel** (1260 Ocean Avenue). It is also known as the Long Branch Historical Museum. Open only by appointment, call (908) 229–0600 for reservations. While at the museum, visit the Garfield monument on nearby Garfield Terrace, which marks where the house stood in which the president was taken to recover from his gunshot wound. He died there on Sept. 19, 1881.

Visit the West End/West Long Branch Area. West End's shops carry a wide selection of contemporary fashions, popular with those students who attend Monmouth College in West Long Branch (see below). West End also has two of the more popular nightspots in the area: The **Inkwell** (665 Second Avenue), a former 1960s coffeehouse, still retains much of its original charm and is open until the wee morning hours. Delicious omelets are the Inkwell's specialty.

Did you know that . . .

Although Bruce Springsteen is widely associated with Asbury Park, he was born in Long Branch and raised in Freehold, a town 10 miles west of Asbury.

See Where the Movie *Annie* Was Filmed. West Long Branch's Monmouth College sits on perhaps the prettiest campus in New Jersey other than Princeton's. Once the Shadow Lawn Estate, which contained the Guggenheim Mansion and where President Woodrow Wilson ran the affairs of the nation during the summer, the building is now a historic landmark. Today it contains classrooms and offices. But for a few months a few years ago, it was taken over by the cast and crew of *Annie* as the mansion was transformed into the home of Daddy Warbucks.

Spend a Day Winning (or Losing) at Monmouth Park. Located in the nearby town of Oceanport on Oceanport Avenue, Monmouth Park features thoroughbred flat and turf racing Monday through Saturday during the summer. Those interested in observing the inner workings of Monmouth Park will want to take the free tram tour every Wednesday and Saturday morning during the summer. Tours begin as early as 7 A.M. and run for approximately two hours. Breakfast is served during the Saturday tour. Jockeys and trainers are frequently available to answer questions. For more information, call (908) 222–5100.

Deal

Driving south of Long Branch on Ocean Avenue, one might think he or she was suddenly transformed somehow to a millionaire's row in Newport, Rhode Island, or perhaps to the West Coast in the heart of Beverly Hills. On both sides of the road, you'll find colonial, seashore, Victorian and southern-styled mansions—most on large, immaculately kept, perfectly manicured pieces of property. The town is Deal, and if its residents could figure out a way to wall off the community and separate it from the rest of the world, they probably would.

Deal is one of the most private communities on the Jersey Shore as well as one of the richest. Because of this, there isn't much of a welcome for tourists, although do not forsake a drive along Ocean Avenue and through the town's equally impressive sidestreets for such lack of hospitality. There is a certain degree of snootiness, for sure. But then again, there is no need to lure tourists to Deal, say its residents. The town is well off without an influx of summer visitors each year, so they simply aren't encouraged to spend vacations there.

The *Deal Casino* is a private beach club, as one might have guessed, and it is extremely difficult to obtain membership. One has to be a resident, and, even then, the screening process is rigorous to say the least. Deal has no hotels and very few places to eat. Drive through Deal and admire its opulence. But if it's overnight or weekly accommodations on the North Jersey Shore you're looking for, you'll have to search elsewhere.

The same is fairly true for such neighboring communities as Elberon, Allenhurst, Interlaken, Loch Arbour and Rumson. One writer describes these towns as "straight out of *The Great Gatsby.*" He wasn't far off the mark.

Asbury Park

Fifty years ago Asbury Park was the pride of the North Jersey Shore. Its mile-long boardwalk was filled with strolling couples enjoying the clean, crisp air and perhaps some sticky saltwater taffy made in one of the nearby shops. **Convention Hall,** the boardwalk centerpiece, hosted such great names in big band music as Glenn Miller and Harry James, and on Saturdays the dancing went on until late at night. Beyond the boardwalk, the city's lovely lakes and parks were where families went to enjoy Sunday picnics, while the downtown section was crowded with shoppers on the other days of the week.

It was a well-planned city, too. The streets are wide and tree-lined and the churches large and impressive. Asbury Park was founded in 1871 by New York brush manufacturer James A. Bradley, who, a year prior, visited neighboring Ocean Grove and liked the area so much that he purchased 500 acres of land just north of the Methodist camp meeting colony. Bradley called his then undeveloped parcel of land Asbury Park, named for the first Methodist bishop in America, Francis Asbury. He forbade liquor and gambling, two vices, according to Bradley, that corrupted Long Branch. He also encouraged people with high religious and moral standards to populate the city and buy the homes he built. Many of the fine examples of Victorian and Queen Anne architecture in Asbury Park can be traced back to these formative years. Later these homes would stand side by side with those featuring Georgian and Art Deco designs, along with the traditional-styled seaside cottages that still dot the Jersey Shore.

Asbury Park's importance to the North Jersey Shore was unchallenged until the 1960s when the city suffered a rapid decline. Neglect, mismanagement and keen competition for tourists from other communities on the Shore took a heavy toll. Finally, race riots in the 1970s and the failure of businesses downtown due to the construction of shopping malls nearby stripped Asbury Park of much of its former glory.

During the 1970s, Asbury Park's character took on a strange new look. Its blue-collar beer joints and seaside bars nurtured a rock 'n' roll scene that was eventually to give rise to one of America's greatest rock performers, Bruce Springsteen (see below). In the 1960s Convention Hall was the North Jersey Shore's only auditorium that permitted large rock concerts. Bands like the Dave Clark Five, the Rolling Stones, the Jefferson Airplane and the Doors performed there, inspiring local rock 'n' rollers to develop their own brand of rock. By the time Bruce Springsteen had become an international rock 'n' roll hero, Asbury Park was generally considered a rock mecca and mentioned in the same breath as Memphis, Detroit and Liverpool.

Asbury Park's new status may be short-lived, however. A bold new renaissance is in the making that would all but end the rock culture that currently thrives in the city. Developers and investors such as country singer Johnny Cash have made a commitment to bring back Asbury Park's original splendor and renown as a first-class resort city. This will mean the construction of seasonal and year-round condominium complexes, widespread public improvements, such as the renovation of streets, parks and Asbury Park's downtown section, plus a compete overhaul of the city's beachfront. A $550 million redevelopment plan will give Asbury Park a chance to once again become a thriving community and make it practically unrecognizable in ten years to those who recall only neon lights and the all-night sounds of rock 'n' roll.

Already, part of Ocean Avenue is closed to traffic. Condominiums and hotels are being built where bars and pizza parlors once stood. Other nearby streets will be closed and a large public plaza is planned. Public parks adjacent to Deal, Sunset and Wesley lakes will be expanded and improved. Convention Hall is slated to be restored. Commercial development, the kind usually associated with beach resorts (novelty shops, amusement areas, arcades) will be contained to the south end of the boardwalk.

Asbury Park:
An American Rock 'n' Roll Town

In 1975, Bruce Springsteen's face graced the covers of both *Time* and *Newsweek*—in the same week. Rather than help his career, the instant notoriety nearly destroyed it. The pressure to live up to all the advance hype, plus the suspicions aroused in rock circles that Springsteen and his music were nothing *but* hype, proved heavy and unfair. Fortunately, the album that was released at the time, the classic *Born to Run*, was everything it was made out to be—and more. And looking back, Springsteen overcame his obstacles and rallied to become rock's greatest live performer and its most important artist since Bob Dylan and the Beatles.

The media blitz was tough on Springsteen, but it was just what the doctor ordered for Asbury Park and its music scene. Immediately after the appearance of the Springsteen *Time* and *Newsweek* cover stories, record companies sent scouts to scour the bars and rock clubs of Asbury Park in search of other Bruce Springsteens singing songs about lost, broken dreams and boardwalk love affairs. What they found was the house band at the Stone Pony, Southside Johnny and the Asbury Jukes, which went on to record a number of albums and garner critical praise for their earthy, rhythm and blues-influenced sound.

After the record company scouts came the fans. They had heard of places like the Stone Pony and hoped to catch a glimpse of Springsteen or members of his E Street Band sitting in with local groups on the club's stage. Others went in search of the places Springsteen wrote about like Madam Marie's, a boardwalk fortune-teller. All this brought much attention to Asbury Park and helped it to take its place in the rock 'n' roll history books.

Since Springsteen and Southside Johnny's rise to stardom, there have been other Jersey Shore, Asbury Park-based rock artists who have followed their paths. David Sancious, a former piano player with Springsteen's E Street Band, made a number of acclaimed jazz-rock albums in the mid- and late 1970s. Miami Steve Van Zandt, aka Little Steven, officially left the E Street Band in 1984 to pursue his own solo career. Superstar Jon Bon Jovi and members of his band began their careers at an Asbury Park club, The Fast Lane. Another big-time heavy metal band, Skid Row, cut their rock 'n' roll teeth in Asbury Park clubs. Although not Shore rock 'n' rollers per se (they're from Rhode Island), John Cafferty and the Beaver Brown Band were once regulars at the Fast Lane and Stone Pony before they got the opportunity to score the soundtrack for the rock movies *Eddie and the Cruisers I* and *II*. Other artists, although not as well known as those mentioned above but with Asbury Park in their rock 'n' roll veins, include Billy Chinnock, John Eddie, Glen Burtnick and Norman Nardini as well as the Smithereens and The Red House.

It's an ambitious project, to say the least, but town officials and developers are determined to see it become a reality. All of this will take years to complete, but already there is progress. Asbury Park's largest hotel, the Berkeley-Carteret on Sunset and Ocean avenues, has been completely renovated and now offers truly first-class accommodations. There are 254 rooms, elaborate conference centers, a ballroom and restaurant, and a decor that emphasizes elegance. In the lobby is the National Broadcasters Hall of Fame, which includes displays of old broadcasting microphones and photographs of radio personalities. Says a promotional pamphlet found in the lobby of the hotel, "All eyes will focus on this Grand Old Lady for she is the flagship that heralds Asbury Park into its future." That certainly seems to be the case.

Things to Do

Visit the Boardwalk Before Renovation Begins. Anyone interested in the rock culture of Asbury Park will want to visit **Madam Marie's,** the gypsy fortune-teller made famous by Springsteen in the song, "Fourth of July, Asbury Park (Sandy)." The tiny structure with the beaming eye painted on the side of it is where she stares into her tarot cards and predicts the future. Purchase a T-shirt at any of the boardwalk shops with the inscription "Greetings from Asbury Park, N.J.," the name of Springsteen's very first album, and the title of the city's most popular postcard, which also graced the cover of the record. Munch on some fudge or taffy. Asbury Park has the best selection of such sweets north of Atlantic City. Criterion Candies is the best shop on the boardwalk for such treats.

Go Swimming. Asbury Park isn't exactly known for its Class A beaches, but that doesn't mean one can't enjoy a day's worth of sun and surf at them. The beach area has been spared the worst effects of erosion due to the jetties that jut out into the ocean every hundred yards or so. Swimmers and sunbathers do take advantage of Asbury Park's relatively clean and rather safe beaches. But serious swimmers and body surfers might want to consider Seven Presidents Oceanfront Park in Long Branch as an alternative to Asbury's rather weak breakers.

Spend the Night Dancing at the Stone Pony. They call the Stone Pony the House That Bruce Built. "The Boss" is known to hang out and jam at the Pony when he's not on tour or in the recording studio. Those who make the pilgrimage to this legendary rock club aren't disappointed once inside, where they'll find photos of Springsteen, members of the E Street Band, Southside Johnny and the Jukes and other Asbury notables. Located at 913 Ocean Avenue, the Stone Pony is the most prestigious rock club not only on the Jersey Shore, but in all of New Jersey. A visit to Asbury Park would not be complete without visiting the Stone Pony. Few first-timers leave the Pony without purchasing one of the club's popular T-shirts.

Ocean Grove

Ocean Grove might very well be the most unique town on the North Jersey Shore. Unspoiled by mass development, Ocean Grove is a walk-in museum. When you enter the gate on Route 71, you step back in time—back to an era of lovely Victorian cottages and guesthouses, quiet summer evenings and peaceful strolls along the boardwalk. Teeming with tradition, Ocean Grove represents a most interesting slice of home-town America circa 1890, much the same way that Cape May does some 75 miles to the south.

Nestled between Asbury Park to the north and Bradley Beach to the south and flanked by Wesley and Fletcher lakes, Ocean Grove is not for everyone, however. Begun as a camp meeting retreat by Methodist in 1869, a strong sense of religious commitment remains in Ocean Grove. It's also a summer resort that attracts an unusually large proportion of senior citizens. And it's a dry town, to boot. so, if you come to the Jersey Shore to unwind, relax and simply slow down the pace of your life, then Ocean Grove is most appropriate. If, on the other hand, it's night-clubs and bright lights you want, best to stay elsewhere on the Shore. Asbury Park, Manasquan or Belmar would be good bets. But do make a point of spending at least part of a day walking around Ocean Grove and admiring its historic treasures. You won't regret it.

Ocean Grove's history goes back to 1870, the year the first Methodist Camp Meeting took place. Those who attended stayed in tents, listened to religious orators preach the Good Word and joined together in daily prayer meetings. Everything took place in tents or outdoors until the **Great Auditorium** was constructed in 1894. A huge, wooden Victorian structure, it was built to seat close to 7,000 people, and it is still used today.

Over the years, Ocean Grove's reputation as a summer retreat grew significantly. Hotels, guesthouses and summer homes replace the tents, although, to this day, there remains a summer tent colony around the Great Auditorium. Many of the nation's most noted religious leaders came to preach at the Great Auditorium. Billy Sunday, Billy Graham and Norman Vincent Peale have spoken from the auditorium's pulpit. President Ulysses S. Grant made frequent visits to Ocean Grove; his mother and sister had a cottage there. Future presidents James A. Garfield, Teddy Roosevelt and Woodrow Wilson also spent time in Ocean Grove. Stephen Crane, Enrico Caruso, William Jennings Bryan, Will Rogers and

Dr. W. E. B. DuBois spoke at the Great Auditorium, sat in the audience there or simply visited Ocean Grove during the summer. In 1970, President Richard Nixon gave a speech there in which he explained his plans to bring the Vietnam War to a halt.

Ocean Grove's heritage and history was directly influenced by the Camp Meeting Association. The association administered all government proceedings within the community. It was the association, for example, that directed the prohibition of liquor in the town. It also passed an ordinance that prohibited cars on the streets of Ocean Grove on weekends.

But in 1974, a court ruling ended the governing powers of the Camp Meeting Association. It was widely assumed that because of this, Ocean Grove would quickly move into line with the rest of the North Jersey Shore. Tradition, however, dies slowly in such towns where generations of families lived a life they thought righteous and most desirable. Today, despite the relaxation of some mores and the abolishment of some founding laws, Ocean Grove retains many of its original camp meeting customs. And for one week during the summer, the Ocean Grove Camp Meeting still meets as it did for more than a century. Sermons, prayer meetings, guest speakers and Christian socializing fill Sunday to Sunday; for many in Ocean Grove it still is the highlight of the year.

Things to Do

Visit the Great Auditorium and Auditorium Park. You may or may not want to partake in any of the religious gatherings that occur in the Great Auditorium, but a visit to it is certainly a must, since it is a Jersey Shore landmark. Constructed mostly of wood, the auditorium in known for its fine acoustics. If you're interested in attending a concert there, pick up a copy of the Ocean Grove Summer Program, which lists the events that take place in the auditorium during the summer. Choir groups, string ensembles and symphonies perform at the Great Auditorium June through August.

In front of the auditorium is the Beersheba Well. It was the first well dug in Ocean Grove; today the gazebo and fountain there stand as a monument to the first Methodists to attend camp meetings in Ocean Grove. Check out the statue of Ellwood Stokes nearby. He was one of Ocean Grove's first and most recalled spiritual leaders.

Visit Centennial Cottage. An excellent example of a typical Ocean Grove Victorian summer home, the cottage is now the town's museum. Built in 1874, the cottage has been fully restored and contains artifacts, photographs, furniture, toys and household items from Ocean Grove's Victorian era. The Centennial Cottage is located at the corner of Central Avenue and McClintock Street. Open only during the summer, there is a small admission charge. For more information, call (908) 774–0042 or (908) 775–0035.

Take a Self-guided Walking Tour of Ocean Grove. Pick up the pamphlet *Walking Tours of Ocean Grove,* which maps out three tours of the town. All three take you through picturesque Victorian streets that contain some of the finest examples of Victorian architecture found north of Cape May. Pamphlets are available at the Tourist Center at 64 Main Avenue, (908) 774–4736.

Stroll the Boardwalk. Ocean Grove's boardwalk is ideal for a leisurely early morning or evening walk. There are no concession stands, no amusements. It's you, the boards, some benches and the beach.

Go Swimming. Ocean Grove has some of the best swimming beaches in the area. Very family-oriented, they are clean, not as crowded as beaches in neighboring towns and guarded. Beach badges are required. For information and current rates, call (908) 988–5533.

Relax in a Rocker. Have you been itching to get through Tolstoy's *War and Peace*? Rent a room at the Pine Tree Inn (110 Main Avenue, 908–775–3264), the Innkeeper Hotel (19 Broadway, 908–775–3232), or in any one of Ocean Grove's many guesthouses and relax away an afternoon on a front-porch rocking chair with book in hand.

Have Lunch or Dinner at the Sampler Inn. Cafeteria-style dining—this is the place to eat if you're on a budget. Meals are priced incredibly low and are quite good, too. Big senior citizen gathering place. Located at 28 Main Avenue, (908) 775–1905.

Participate in a Sand Castle Contest or a Volleyball Tournament. Ocean Grove sponsors a number of community activities for both adults and children. In addition to the two mentioned above, there's an inner tube race, a biathlon, craft shows, kite-flying contests, scavenger hunt and puppet show. Write to the Ocean Grove Chamber of Commerce, P.O. Box 415, Ocean Grove 07756 for a calendar of events.

Visit the Ocean Grove Historical Society Museum. Located at 53 Central Avenue (908–774–1869), the storefront museum is open on Wednesdays and Saturdays. It contains an interesting Jersey Shore antique postcard collection and a prized horse from an old merry-go-round.

Bradley Beach

Many visitors to the North Jersey Shore drive right through Bradley Beach. It isn't difficult to do. Situated south of Ocean Grove, the town hardly possesses the type of tourist attractions found in Asbury Park or Long Branch—namely, large amusement areas, nightclubs or historic sites. What Bradley Beach does possess, however, is a comfortable, family-oriented atmosphere and beach area.

Bradley Beach is a middle-class resort. Most people who summer in the town have been doing so for years. Families rent the same summer house each season, or else have summer homes of their own there. Most of them are far from fancy; but they're all close to the beach and main shopping area on Route 71.

Aside from the beach, Bradley Beach has a mile-long boardwalk, good for jogging and walking, and a number of special events like weekly concerts at the **Boardwalk Band Shell,** located at Brinley and 5th Avenue on the boardwalk. The town also conducts local talent shows and a Little Miss Bradley Beach Contest. All of the events are small-scale, yet fun. For a list of summer activities and information pertaining to beach badges, contact the Borough Hall, 701 Main Street, Bradley Beach 07720.

Belmar

For many, Belmar means deep-sea fishing. The **Belmar Marina** on the Shark River and off Route 35 is home to more than 50 party and charter craft, all of which make daily trips out onto the ocean in search of blues, weakfish, blackfish, even albacore and shark. Many operate year-round. You won't find more fishing boats in one area anywhere else on the Jersey Shore.

The Belmar Marina also has five docks' worth of slips for private boats, a launch ramp, a fine bait and tackle shop called the **Fisherman's Den** and a small luncheonette where anglers sip hot coffee and swap fish stories. Just across the highway is **Pat's Riverview Diner,** which some folks say has the best menu of any of the Shore's diners, and the **Windmill**, a sister of the original and better-known Windmill in Long Branch, the place to enjoy the Shore's best hot dog. All of this makes the Belmar Marina and vicinity a pretty busy area during the summer months, especially on weekends and holidays.

Yet, others come to Belmar and never so much as bait a hook. This group of vacationers comes for Belmar's beaches and nightlife. The town has an interesting blend of families and college-age kids on its beaches each season.

The families come for the same reason families come to Bradley Beach each summer—affordable accommodations in the way of apartments, guesthouses and bungalows, and perhaps a bit of family tradition, too. The college-age crowd comes because Belmar permits group rentals. That means the limit on the number of people who can sleep and shower in one bungalow or beach house is greater here than in towns that do not permit group rentals. The more that stay, the tighter

Shark Fishing

Ever since the movie *Jaws*, no other fish has so captured the interest or imagination of sport fishermen as well as the general public as that so-called monster of the deep, the shark.

The shark hysteria that inundated America in the mid-seventies gradually wore off. But those who go out and specifically fish for shark still find it an immensely rewarding experience. As a result, today the shark is one of the most popular big game fish taken off the Jersey coast. Each summer boat basins in Brielle (Hoffman's Anchorage) and Point Pleasant Beach (Clark's Landing) sponsor shark fishing tournaments with thousands of dollars in cash prizes. The entry fees are rather steep (anywhere from $250 to $500 per boat), but the number of boats is usually limited, thus increasing one's chances of hitting the jackpot. Win or lose, the excitement level knows no bounds.

A number of sharks are regularly found off the Jersey coast. Blue, dusky and brown sharks are the most common. It's not unusual, however, to hook into a hammerhead or thresher shark. But the most prized shark is the mako. The mako is a classic fighting fish in every sense of the word, and a delicious eating fish, too; some people can't tell the difference between mako and swordfish.

The best time to fish for shark is June and July. Unlike other game fish that often require all sorts of specialized gear, sharking can be done using 30- or 50-pound class tackle. The preferred way to attract sharks is with a chum slick. The best bait: whole or chunks of bluefish.

Of course you'll have to go offshore to have any real chance of landing a mako (good news for swimmers, since makos have been know to attack humans). Spots such as the 28 Mile Wreck, the Mud Hole, and the shelf of the Hudson canyon are favorites with shark fishermen. One, however, need not confine oneself to just these three locations. Sharks can be found virtually anywhere 10 or 15 miles offshore with a good chum slick that includes plenty of blood.

Those not inclined or able to venture out in a boat can still enjoy shark fishing. The dogfish is a small shark that can be caught in the surf and large bays. Regular tackle and squid for bait can get anyone started in shark fishing.

Unlike the dogfish shark, which is harmless because it does not have teeth, the mako or any other shark caught offshore can cause serious problems for the fisherman who does not take the proper precautions once a shark has been landed. Take care to tie up securely the shark's jaw and tail even if the fish appears dead. Taking unnecessary chances miles offshore is foolhardy.

Since the growth in popularity of shark fishing, thousands of sharks have been hooked and killed needlessly. Those not interested in eating the fish (not all sharks make desirable dinners) and not wishing to keep, say, the jaw as a trophy (as many do), should consider tagging and releasing the sharks they catch. This helps marine biologists study the behavior and feeding patterns of the shark, a most mysterious creature. For more information on shark tagging, contact the American Littoral Society, Sandy Hook, Highlands 07732, or NMFS Co-operative Shark Tagging Program, NOAANMFS, Narragansett Laboratory, South Ferry Road, Narragansett, Rhode Island 02882.

the space, it's true. But the more that stay, the cheaper the rent, providing everyone kicks in. Wherever you find group rentals on the Jersey Shore, you're apt to find college-age kids. Lots of them.

And where there are college-age kids, there are nightclubs where the music is usually good and the scene quite lively. Belmar has a number of nightspots that cater strictly to the under-30 crowd. **Bar Anticipation** (703 16th Avenue) and **D'Jai's** (1805 Ocean Avenue) are particular favorites for those with music on their minds. Wear you dancing shoes. For the Irish and those who pretend to be Irish, there's **Ryan's Pub** (701 Main Street), which attracts a slightly older crowd. **Jason's** (1604 Main Street, South Belmar) is the Shore's number-one blues bar and home of the Jersey Shore Jazz and Blues Festival.

Belmar has a boardwalk, although the only amusements in town are found across the street from it at **Belmar Playland** (14th and Ocean avenues). There you'll find rooftop miniature golf and just enough video games and pinball machines to keep the addicted happy on nights they don't journey north to Asbury Park and Long Branch, or south to Point Pleasant Beach and Seaside Heights.

Spring Lake

They call Spring Lake the Irish Riviera. And with good reason. Whereas Deal is predominately Jewish, many residents of Spring Lake—year-round and seasonal—wouldn't be caught dead without green on each St. Patrick's Day. Neither would many in neighboring Sea Girt. You hear Irish in the last names: Kelly, O'Halloran, McManus. You see Irish at the bars: green beer parties, boisterous sing-alongs. And you feel a bit of Ireland in the air: an Old Country warmth permeates Spring Lake, a town where visitors can be made to feel like old friends.

There might be one or two better beaches on the North Jersey Shore than Spring Lake's beaches; they tend to become a bit smaller each year due to erosion, despite the presence of groins or jetties built to prevent the swiping of sand by fast currents and storms. But no North Jersey Shore community can boast a nicer boardwalk to walk or jog or bicycle on, especially in the early morning when most of the town is still asleep.

People come to Spring Lake for its boardwalk and sand-duned beaches, which are really a rarity in these parts of the Shore. But they also come for what lies behind all this, too. Walk a block or two away from the beach and the beautiful homes, the fancy, well-kept gardens and shrubbery, and the irresistibly quiet streets all give Spring Lake an extra special charm. Many of Spring Lake's stately old homes and seashore cottages have been restored. Most are private residences, but some have been made into delightful guesthouses and bed and breakfasts. Actually, no Jersey Shore town outside of Cape May offers a wider or finer selection of bed and breakfasts than Spring Lake.

The **Normandy Inn** (21 Tuttle Avenue, 908–449–7172) might be considered the cream of the Spring Lake bed and breakfast crop, especially if you're an admirer of beautiful nineteenth-century antiques, which can be found in each and every room to go with the distinctive Victorian ambiance throughout the 100-year-old mansion. Also on Tuttle Avenue, one of Springs Lake's prettiest streets, is the **Sea Crest** (19 Tuttle Avenue 908–449–9031) and the **Johnson House** (25 Tuttle Avenue, 908–449–1860). Neither possesses the extravagance of Victorian passion found in the Normandy Inn, but both the Sea Crest and Johnson House offer Spring Lake visitors comfort and hospitality plus in traditional-styled seashore colonial cottages.

The **Ashling Cottage** (106 Sussex Avenue, 908–449–3553) was built by George Hulett, the man responsible for many of Spring Lake's stunning late-nineteenth-century homes. He built Ashling Cottage with lumber from the dismantled Agricultural Exhibit of the Philadelphia Exposition of 1876. Eight other Hulett-constructed homes, similar in architectural design, are scattered about Spring Lake.

The **Stone Post Inn** (115 Washington Avenue, 908–449–1212), built in 1882, is one block from the beach and one block from the Spring Lake shopping district. The **Victoria House** (214 Monmouth Avenue, 908–974–1882) has an enticing wraparound porch with gingerbread accents, gothic shingles, floor-to-ceiling windows and stained glass. Other Spring Lake bed and breakfasts include **La Maison** (404 Jersey Avenue, 908–449–0969), the **Villa Park House** (417 Ocean Avenue, 908–449–9698) and the **Sandpiper** (7 Atlantic Avenue, 908–449–6060).

Lodging in Spring Lake can be a memorable experience. And if the town's bed and breakfasts don't meet your fancy, perhaps a few nights in one of Spring Lake's classic hotels might. The **Essex-Sussex,** one of Spring Lake's grandest hotels, is being made into a condominium/hotel in an attempt to generate revenue so it can be restored to its former elegance. Such elegance used to mean evening gowns for women and white coats and black ties for men, and uniformed doormen and graciousness beyond compare.

The Essex-Sussex Hotel might not have the 300 rooms it once had for public use, and it might have forever lost its grand tradition in the condominium conversion, but the Spring Lake seashore hotel charm can still be found in the other hotels in town. The **Shoreham** (115 Monmouth Avenue, 908–449–7100), for instance, is a large hotel that attracts a regular clientele; it has a terrific collection of rocking chairs spread the length of its long porch.

Did you know that . . .

The Milos Forman film, *Ragtime,* which starred James Cagney, was set in the Essex-Sussex Hotel. Other movies that have used Spring Lake as a setting include Woody Allen's *Stardust Memories* and Sergio Leone's *Once upon a Time in America,* which starred Robert DeNiro.

The **Warren Hotel** (Mercer and First avenues, 908–449–8800) has a lobby filled with wicker and antiques, while many of its 200 rooms have ocean views. Other landmark hotels in Spring Lake include the **Hewitt-Wellington** (200 Monmouth Avenue, 908–974–1212) and the **Colonial Ocean House** (First and Sussex avenues, 908–449–9090).

There are other things to do in Spring Lake besides go to the beach, walk the boardwalk or let an afternoon drift by sitting in a wicker rocking chair—although, for many of Spring Lake's visitors, this is all they need to be satisfied and all they really came for.

One can visit the **Spring Lake Historical Society Museum,** located on the second floor of the municipal building (5th Avenue and Warren Street). There you can view a collection of old photographs, furniture and memorabilia pertaining to Spring Lake's past. For more information, call (908) 449–0772.

The society also sponsors one of the most popular events in town, the Annual Spring Lake House Tour, which includes visits to a number of vintage homes, churches and public buildings. Often the tour culminates with lunch at the private and quite prestigious Spring Lake Bath and Tennis Club on Jersey Avenue. For more information on the tour, contact the Historical Society or the Greater Spring Lake Chamber of Commerce (P.O. Box 694, Spring Lake 07762, 908–449–0677).

Since Spring Lake is saturated with Irish culture, stop at the **Irish Centre** (1120 Third Avenue) and pick up a fine, imported woolen sweater or perhaps an Irish folksong record or two. A stroll around the willow tree-dominated paths and the gardens that hug the shore of Spring Lake, the body of water after which the town is named, is ideal for romantically inclined couples tired of the boardwalk. You can also board the Spring Lake Trolley and tour the town as it wends its way through some of Spring Lake's finest streets, down through the town center, and out along Ocean Avenue. The trolley runs daily during the summer until Labor Day.

The **Spring Lake Memorial Community House** (corner of 3rd and Madison avenues, 908–449–4530) is home to three theater groups. During the summer, musical productions are popular. During the Christmas season, an annual production of *Scrooge,* based on Charles Dickens' *A Christmas Carol,* is a routine sellout.

Finally, there's the highly popular annual five-mile run called the Spring Lake Five. Sanctioned by the Athletic Congress, the race attracts the best runners in the New York-New Jersey metropolitan area and even beyond. For this year's race date, write to The Spring Lake Five Mile Run, P.O. Box 534, Spring Lake 07762.

Sea Girt

Some of Spring Lake's charm and Irish heritage can be found in Sea Girt. Unlike Spring Lake, however, Sea Girt is almost exclusively a residential community. Sea Girt entertains no notions of becoming a tourist beach town, either. There are no public facilities near or at the beach. Parking is restricted.

About the only attraction in Sea Girt, aside from viewing its immaculately kept streets and expensive homes, is the Sea Girt Lighthouse on the corner of Ocean and Beacon avenues. Perched atop a traditional beach house, the light began beaming in 1896 and continued until decommissioned in 1955. It's recently been restored and is now owned by the borough of Sea Girt. It is not, unfortunately, open to the public on a regular basis. Lighthouse buffs, though, can usually arrange a tour of it by contacting the Sea Girt Lighthouse Foundation (P.O. Box 84, Sea Girt 08750).

The National Guard Training Center and the New Jersey State Police Academy are located in Sea Girt. It was here in a beautiful white mansion, dubbed the Little White House, that New Jersey governors summered, including the only one to eventually move to the *real* White House, Woodrow Wilson. The Training Center and Academy, however, are off-limits to tourists.

Manasquan

Each summer Manasquan swells with a crowd that's predominantly single, young and active. The rickety bungalows along Brielle Road and First Avenue, especially the north side of First Avenue, are sardine-packed with mostly the under-30 generation. Manasquan, like Belmar, is one of the few towns on the Shore that still permit group rentals. And in Manasquan, where it's possible to pass a beer through the window of one bungalow and into the hands of someone next door, the closeness of the bungalows often makes the town seem like one giant group rental.

On any given summer night, you'll hear hard rock, alternative rock, heavy metal or pop blaring from stereo systems as you walk down First Avenue. You might also catch the scent of a midnight barbecue in progress and see more than one Budweiser-can pyramid precariously erected on the edge of a bungalow porch. If the party is a private one, then walk over to the **Osprey** on the corner of Main Street and First Avenue, or to **Leggett's Sand Bar,** just a couple of doors south on First Avenue, and there'll be enough suds flowing and enough rock 'n' rolling to keep anyone well-stocked with fun.

Manasquan isn't overrun by the younger generation, however; there are family-style rentals in town, and you can find children digging in the sand on the beach. In fact, Manasquan does much to keep the family-resort image balanced with the perpetual party atmosphere on First Avenue and Brielle Road.

Did you know that . . .

The Manasquan Inlet marks the beginning of the Intracoastal Waterway, a waterway that stretches clear down to Florida. A boater can sail or motor along the entire passage without ever having to venture out onto the Atlantic Ocean.

The best way to get around Manasquan in the summer is by bicycle, especially if you plan to go anywhere near the beach. Manasquan has a severe parking problem, and nowhere is it more evident than on First Avenue and adjoining streets on the weekend. If you arrive at the beach early enough, you'll probably find space in a lot, but expect to pay dearly for the privilege. If you park illegally on the street, you're certain to get a ticket and perhaps even a towing bill.

First Avenue runs parallel with Manasquan's "boardwalk," an asphalt walkway, which everyone calls a boardwalk because it has almost everything a boardwalk is supposed to have except boards. Here, you'll find a small pavilion where one can sit and enjoy the view, day or evening.

You'll see all kinds of boat traffic in the inlet; pleasure boats, commercial fishing boats, racing boats, sailboats, Coast Guard boats (the white building across the inlet on the Point Pleasant Beach side is the Manasquan Inlet Coast Guard Station). Directly in front of the pavilion is Manasquan's fishing and surfing beach. The quality of fishing varies, but when the surf's up, nowhere on the North Jersey Shore possesses the power and hollow shape of Manasquan's waves. The famed "Manasquan Bowl" will test any surfer's abilities when the breakers are big. Due to the protection offered by the inlet jetties, the waves here are often glassy smooth when there's a southerly wind, which is most of the time, while in Point Pleasant Beach and Beaches south, the surf is choppy and difficult to ride.

If Manasquan's inlet beach is used mostly by surfers and surf fishermen, the Main Street beach is where the bulk of the beach action is. If you desire a little more peace and a bit more space, try Manasquan's north beach section. It is usually less crowded there, but parking, once again, is a big problem. Wherever you lay your blanket, you'll need a beach badge to do so. Badges can be purchased at the Manasquan Beach Police Headquarters on Main Street and the boardwalk. Day, week and season badges are available.

Rainy days in Manasquan can be spent sipping tropical drinks at **Casablanca Bar** (309 Fisk Avenue, 908–528–6466), a very popular, classy watering hole, due to its Moroccan design and yuppie atmosphere. **Doc Donahue's** (390 East Main Street, 908–223–1850) is another popular drinking hotspot.

Finally, shoppers shouldn't miss the **Circle Factory Outlet Center**—rain or shine. Located on Route 35 (on the Manasquan Circle), the Outlet Center consists of more than a dozen household and clothing outlets and more than 40 shops and stores that sell discounted goods (908–223–2300).

Brielle

Set back behind Manasquan, Brielle is a small town of shady streets and green lawns with little connection to the summer bustle that dominates its neighbor from Memorial Day to Labor Day each year. Brielle is a pleasant residential area, filled with fine homes sitting on the edge of the Manasquan River. It also has a beautiful country club and golf course and just enough restaurants to keep locals from having to deal with the summer crush at other area restaurants.

Boaters and fishermen, however, know Brielle for its fleet of party and charter boats and its excellent marinas. With the exception of **Bogan's Boat Basin,** which is located directly under the Manasquan River Bridge and is the most popular dock in the area for party boat fishing, all the other marinas are located east of the bridge on Ashley and Green avenues. There you'll find the **Brielle Yacht Club,** the **Brielle Marine Basin** and **Hoffman's Anchorage.** The latter two run charter boats out onto the Atlantic. The Brielle Marine Basin also contains a complete marine shop and boat repair facilities. The Yacht Club's restaurant and bar are open to the public; it's a good place to have a drink, take in the sights on the river, and chat with local sailors. Hoffman's Anchorage is noted for its quality charter boats, experienced captains and annual fishing tournament. Located adjacent to Bogan's is the *River Queen,* a Mississippi riverboat replica that cruises the Manasquan River. Cocktails and dinner are served on board. For departure times and reservations, call (908) 528–6620.

If you continue along Green Avenue, you'll come to Brielle Road and a picturesque old drawbridge that's still in operation. The setting in the harbor, which is known as the Glimmer Glass, is postcard perfect, especially in spring and fall when cars don't crowd the bridge. Right next to the bridge is a good restaurant called, fittingly enough, **The Draw Bridge** (361 Brielle Road, 908–223–8434). If you cross the bridge, pass the restaurant and continue down Brielle Road, you'll come to the Manasquan beachfront.

One of Brielle's biggest events—Brielle Day—is held every September, usually a weekend or two after Labor Day. It's a popular event that attracts not only Brielle residents, but tourists, too. There is a "fun run" to enter, a crafts show to browse through, and plenty of good things to eat.

Where to Eat on the North Jersey Shore

Brielle Yacht Club, 1 Ocean Avenue, Brielle, (908) 528–7000
Price Code: Expensive   Menu: Continental
Romantic, candlelit dining on the Manasquan River. Italian dishes are best.

Casa Comida, 336 Branchport Avenue, Long Branch, (908) 229–7774
Price Code: Moderate   Menu: Mexican
The most popular Mexican restaurant on the North Jersey Shore. Loud, zesty atmosphere. Big helpings. For dessert, try a piece of Kahlúa pie, no matter how stuffed you might be.

Evelyn's, 507 Main Street, Belmar, (908) 681–0236
Price Code: Moderate   Menu: Seafood
Practically an institution when it comes to Jersey Shore seafood restaurants. Basic seafood menu with all the expected trimmings.

McLoone's Rum Runner, 816 Ocean Avenue, Sea Bright, (908) 842–2894
Price Code: Moderate   Menu: Continental
Classy ambiance along the Shrewsbury River with gorgeous views of nearby Rumson. Varied, "can't-go-wrong" menu. Entertainment and lively bar action.

The Old Mill Inn, Old Mill Road, Spring Lake Heights,
(908) 449–1800
Price Code: Expensive   Menu: Classic American
Good food, jacket-and-tie atmosphere and occasional ballroom and big
band dancing.

The Stadium, 504 Station Plaza, Sea Girt, (908) 449–1444
Price Code: Moderate   Menu: Continental
Popular eatery with North Jersey Shore locals and businessmen. Lunch
and dinner. Entertainment on weekends.

Tuzzio's, 224 Westwood Avenue, Long Branch, (908) 222–9614
Price Code: Inexpensive/Moderate   Menu: Italian
Long a favorite with Long Branchers, Tuzzio's dining room is set back
behind the bar in a bland setting. But appetizers like hot mussels and
steamed clams and the veal scallopine and veal marsala make up for the
drab surroundings.

Union Landing, 622 Green Avenue, Brielle, (908) 528–6665
Price Code: Moderate   Menu: Seafood
Located on the Manasquan River just a few blocks from the beach.
Above-average seafood dishes and appetizers. Good repeat business.

Yankee Clipper, 1 Chicago Boulevard, Sea Girt, (908) 449–7200
Price Code: Moderate   Menu: Continental
Gorgeous view of the ocean gives whatever you order an extra special
touch. Excellent Sunday brunch with live light jazz.

3

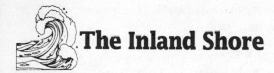 The Inland Shore

While the North Jersey Shore, which is actually the Monmouth County coastline, provides the visitor with beaches, boardwalks and resort towns that range from extravagant (Spring Lake) to economical (Bradley Beach), the inland part of the county offers the visitor something entirely different.

The Inland Shore, or western Monmouth County, is an area of green rolling hills, winding country roads, lazy rivers, vegetable and fruit farms, sleepy towns with general stores and corner malt shops, and an ambiance that is a far cry from what one finds closer to the ocean.

The Inland Shore is also steeped in colonial and revolutionary war history. Towns such as Freehold and Englishtown still retain a colonial charm, which often reminds visitors of areas in Vermont and Massachusetts. Many old farmhouses date back to the eighteenth century, some of which are open to the public and well worth visiting. A crucial revolutionary war engagement, the Battle of Monmouth, was fought just outside Freehold. Today, Monmouth Battlefield State Park tells the story of the battle—the only one in which the leader of the American forces, Gen. George Washington, met the leader of the British forces, Gen. Henry Clinton, in combat.

Speaking of parks, Allaire State Park is one of New Jersey's best. Few state parks anywhere have more things to do and see. The Monmouth County Parks system is also superb, quite possibly the best county parks system in New Jersey. Turkey Swamp offers some of the finest camping in the area and many of its most interesting hiking trails. Deep-cut Park is a horticultural center; it consists of over 450 acres of gardens and greenhouses. Longstreet Farm is a turn-of-the-century working farm. It's especially popular with young children because they can take part in farm chores. In all, there are more than 20 county parks in Monmouth with a total of more then 5,000 acres.

The Inland Shore is also famous for its flea markets, antique shops, horse farms, stables and racing facilities. Freehold Raceway features harness and thoroughbred horse racing. Raceway Park and Wall Stadium offer drag and stock car racing, respectively. Englishtown, Collingwood and Howell are first in everyone's mind when it comes to flea-market bargains. When one includes the activities and area of the North Jersey Shore (chapter 2) with those of the Inland Shore, it's easy to see why Monmouth County is the most alluring of all Shore counties, perhaps the prettiest, and certainly the most varied.

The Inland Shore is a perfect alternative to the typical beach attractions. When people vacation at the Shore, often they think of the area as nothing *but* sand and sun. The decision to go to the beach today and the boardwalk tonight, then back to the beach tomorrow is all too common. Rainy days or dull, cloudy ones do provide respite. But more times than not, the day not spent on the beach is dedicated to poker games on the front porch of the bungalow or late mornings in bed.

Now, nothing is wrong with these pleasant passings of time—provided that is indeed what one wants to do. But many shore visitors simply don't realize that a 15- or 20-minute drive due west—whether it be Monmouth County's Inland Shore or Ocean County's Pine Barrens (see chapter 6)—unveils a whole set of exciting things to do and see.

Few people who vacation at the Shore actually rent accommodations inland. For one thing, there aren't nearly the number or variety of lodgings, in say, Englishtown, that you'll find in any of the beach towns. For another, during the months of July and August, when more visitors come to the Jersey Shore than at any other time, it can get uncomfortably hot inland. The best time to visit the Inland Shore is on those cloudy, nonbeach days, or during the fall when not only is it cooler, but the area's farms are busy harvesting and the scenery is spectacular.

Matawan

Cheesequake State Park. Located just off the Garden State Parkway (Exit 120), Cheesequake State Park is often overlooked by Shore visitors on their way to points farther south. Although the park doesn't possess the number of things to do and see that Allaire State Park (see below) or Island Beach State Park (see chapter 4) offers visitors, a morning or afternoon visit is, nevertheless, worthwhile.

Begin your tour of Cheesequake at the Nature Center. Swamp and pine forest exhibits, a saltwater aquarium and a slide show of rare wildflowers found in the park are Nature Center highlights. The park naturalist conducts tours from the center. Call (908) 566-3408 for more information regarding tours and special exhibits.

Cheesequake has three main hiking/nature trails, each of which is interesting and quite easy to walk. The park is known for its valuable salt- and freshwater marsh areas, and trail guides available at the park office or Nature Center help explain the flora and marsh activity you'll see on your walk. The Green Trail is the longest trail in the park (3½ miles) and has the widest range of plantlife. You'll pass through a white cedar swamp and an extreme northern reach of the Pine Barrens forest and view a most interesting variety of vegetation. This is possible because Cheesequake is located where the state's northern vegetation zone ends and the southern one begins.

As for the marsh area, hikers might come upon numerous kinds of birds (pick up a copy of the handout "Birds of Cheesequake" before you set out) as well as small animals found in the park. Marshland is the earth's second most productive ecosystem. Only the underwater coral reef contains more life and produces more nutrients that plants and animals feed on. The Cheesequake marshland is particularly valuable to central New Jersey ecology because it acts as a water purifier in an area where rapid commercial and residential development has often endangered water supplies.

Despite its interesting hiking trails and marshlands, Cheesequake is far more popular in the summer for its swimming and picnicking facilities. Hooks Creek Lake is a small swimming hole and it does get crowded, but it's an ideal place for families with young children. There's no threat of swift currents or punishing breakers that frighten toddlers at ocean beaches. A bathhouse for changing and showering and a concession stand are on the premises. Nearby is a play and ballfield area.

Cheesequake's picnic facilities are well used in the summer, too. Most sites have tables and grills or stone fireplaces. A number of sites, though, are quite close to the Parkway. If you desire a site set away from the sights and sounds of passing cars, ask the ranger at the entrance gate to suggest a more peaceful spot.

Few people realize it, but Cheesequake also has a camping area. There are 52 campsites in the park and 2 large group camping areas. Once again, ask a ranger to recommend a site so that you're away from civilization, if that's what you wish. Some campsites are a stone's throw away from an apartment complex that is adjacent to the eastern boundary of the park.

With the exception of Allaire State Park farther south, there are no other camping areas on the North Jersey Shore that are as close to the beaches and resort areas as Cheesequake is. The few private camp-grounds in the area are found farther west in Freehold, as are such county parks as Turkey Swamp, which also has camping.

Cheesequake is a fine place to bicycle, too, especially during the autumn when the leaves are changing colors. Its roads are well paved and usually void of traffic in the off-season. It's impossible to lose your way on the park's road system, as it is well marked and simple in design.

For information on special park activities and camping reservations, call (908) 566–2161 or write Cheesequake State Park, Matawan 07747. Admission is charged during the summer months.

Holmdel

Garden State Arts Center. The Garden State Arts Center, the large amphitheater located in Telegraph Hill Park just off the Parkway at Exit 116, is one of New Jersey's most impressive performing arts venues. Each season, from June through September, the Arts Center plays host to an incredible array of performers and special events. Singers such as Liza Minnelli, Connie Francis, Tom Jones and Peter Allen; rock bands like Crosby, Stills and Nash, the Allman Brothers Band, Santana, and Southside Johnny and the Jukes; symphonies such as the London Symphony Orchestra and the New Jersey Symphony Orchestra; and special events such as an evening with Mikhail Baryshnikov, Itzhak Perlman, the Boston Pops or even Bill Cosby make the Garden State Arts Center one of the premier cultural centers, not only in New Jersey, but in the entire mid-Atlantic region.

In addition to all this, the center also sponsors annual heritage festivals, which celebrate the ethnic roots of Italians, Poles, Ukrainians, Jews, the Irish, Germans, Scots and Slovaks among others. The festivities include a number of exhibits and displays, plus various forms of live entertainment and music. Most of the festivals occur in either June or September, before or after the summer lineup of main events.

Finally, there are many free daytime programs sponsored by the Garden State Arts Center Foundation and Cultural Fund aimed specifically at children, senior citizens and the handicapped. For information about what free events are scheduled for this year, call (908) 888–5000.

The Garden State Arts Center seats 5,200 while another 4,000 are permitted to purchase "lawn tickets" and, with a blanket, sit on the grassy knolls that surround the amphitheater. Tickets for Garden State Arts Center events go very fast. Thus, it's to your advantage to check the season calendar as early as possible. The *Asbury Park Press,* the Shore's largest newspaper, usually publishes the calendar Memorial Day weekend. You can request specific information pertaining to concerts and such listed on the calendar by calling the main number listed above, or by stopping at the Arts Center ticket office.

Veteran concertgoers to the Garden State Arts Center usually purchase all their tickets at once before the season opens, thereby guaranteeing them seats for the show of their choice. The Arts Center has a habit of adding more shows as the season progresses, so it's a good idea to check periodically with the ticket office to see if anything that's been added appeals to you. The price of tickets varies with the performer and seat location. Lawn seats usually cost between $15 and $17.50.

Holmdel Park. Aside from being a delightful county park with all the standards—hiking trails, fitness trails, picnic areas, a fishing and skating pond and open playfields—Holmdel Park has the Longstreet Farm, a 300-year-old "living history" farm that has been restored to its 1890-1900 period. Owned by the Longstreet family, one of the very first Dutch families to settle in the area, the farm was a prosperous one from the mid-1700s to the 1920s.

Today, visitors can wander through the old barns and sheds and watch park personnel dressed in 1890 farmer's garb perform farm duties the way Monmouth County farmers would have done them nearly a century ago. Chickens, pigs, goats, sheep, cows and geese inhabit the pens and pastures, although it should be noted that Longstreet Farm is not a petting zoo.

Open to the public is the Longstreet Farmhouse, restored to its late Victorian period and furnished appropriately. Guided tours of the house are available. In addition, Longstreet Farm provides a number of educational programs that deal with the history of the farm and the task of running it. "Down on the Farm," for instance, is a popular special event that caters to visitors wishing to experience firsthand such farm chores as milking cows, feeding hogs and planting a garden.

As you tour the farm and farm buildings, pay special attention to the collection of turn-of-the-century machines and carriages; much of these were actually used by those who worked the fields and barnyard at Longstreet. The Longstreets, being "gentlemen farmers" and quite wealthy, rarely dirtied their hands doing chores. Hired help and tenant farmers performed the duties of running the farm.

Holmdel Park and Longstreet Farm are open year-round and are free. They are located on Longstreet Road, a few miles west of the Parkway, Exit 114. For information pertaining to Longstreet Farm's special programs, call (908) 946–3758.

Holmes-Hendrickson House. A few hundred yards up Longstreet Road is the Holmes-Hendrickson House. Built about 1754, the house contains a compromised architectural style, taking from both Dutch and English eighteenth-century designs. This is proof, say historians, that by the mid-1700s, Dutch and English settlers were accepting and even integrating elements of each others' customs. Prior to this, much tension existed between the two groups of settlers. The English controlled the government of the New Jersey colony and hoped the Dutch settlers would assume English traditions. For years the Dutch stubbornly resisted, preferring instead to isolate themselves from the English whenever possible.

The Holmes-Hendrickson House has been restored and contains furnishings from the mid-eighteenth century, the kind that might have been in a farmhouse of this type. The kitchen area contains displays dealing with the way Dutch settlers prepared food. Information on the uses and types of furniture in the bedroom and sitting area is presented by the house guide. Once can also see antique farm tools on the second floor.

The Holmes-Hendrickson House is run by the Monmouth County Historical Association. It is open May to October. Small admission charge. For more information call (908) 462-1466.

Middletown

Deep Cut Park. Gardeners, horticulturists and ordinary people who appreciate fine flowers will be interested in Deep Cut Park and its Horticultural Center. Nestled in one of Middletown's nicest areas, this 40-acre Monmouth County park of gardens and greenhouses, walking paths and water lily ponds, is especially nice in spring when many plants and flowers are beginning to bloom. Deep Cut, however, is open year-round and usually has something of interest in the greenhouses to warrant a visit during the other three seasons.

Before you stroll through the gardens, stop at the Visitor Center and pick up brochures and pamphlets relating to Deep Cut's gardens. Guided tours of the gardens and greenhouses are available for groups, provided reservations are made in advance. There's a horticultural reference library on the premises as well as volunteers who conduct the day-to-day activities at the center.

At Deep Cut, you'll find perennial gardens, a shade garden, a winter garden, a vineyard and vegetable garden, a butterfly and hummingbird garden and a special greenhouse where endangered orchids are cared for.

Deep Cut also conducts a number of seminars and classes designed to improve horticultural appreciation and awareness, and home gardening. It also has a Horticultural Hotline (908-671-6906) manned by trained horticulturalists who will answer any home gardening questions you might have. Deep Cut is located 1½ miles east of the Garden State Parkway on Red Hill Road, just across from Tatum County Park. No admission charge. For more information, call (908) 671-6050.

Marlpit Hall. Marlpit Hall was, at different times in its history, the home of two influential politicians in colonial Middletown. The house was originally a tiny Dutch dwelling built in the late seventeenth century by James Grover, Jr., a justice of the peace and gristmill owner. Later when John Taylor, a merchant and also justice of the peace, purchased the house, he enlarged it considerably, using plans drawn from the Georgian architectural style, so popular with English settlers. Thus, like the Holmes-Hendrickson House in Holmdel, Marlpit Hall possesses both Dutch and English architectural features.

Marlpit Hall has been restored so that it resembles the 1700-1820 period of the house's history. Inside, you'll find numerous examples of eighteenth-century furniture, including drop-leaf and tilt-top tables, chests and a dressing table, Windsor chairs and the Taylor family clock, which was made in Monmouth County and listed in the 1818 inventory of the house.

Located at 137 Kings Highway, Marlpit Hall is open May through October. Admission charge. For more information, call (908) 462–1466. Marlpit Hall is under the supervision of the Monmouth County Historical Association.

Englishtown

Englishtown Auction. You'll find everything from antiques to zories (rubber beach sandals), from hubcaps to bargains on houseware items, from fresh produce to homemade apple pies, and from plants to peanuts at the Englishtown Auction. Even if you're not looking to buy anything, an early Saturday morning sojourn to Englishtown is an experience you're not apt to forget quickly. This 50-acre, nationally known flea market and auction is packed solid with well over 700 vendors each Saturday and Sunday morning, year-round. Those with things to sell arrive as early as 4 A.M. to get a strategic selling spot and set up before the first buyers arrive at 7 A.M.

Don't be fooled by the flea market environment; not everything sold is used merchandise or junk that's often discarded if its owner can't unload it. Many of the vendors, especially those with inside stalls, sell brand new merchandise, usually at prices below what you can expect to pay at retail stores. Of course, there are hustlers at Englishtown, and you'll have to check thoroughly whatever you buy for damages, stains or scratches. Sometimes damaged goods are sold at Englishtown. But more times than not, you'll go home with a bargain you couldn't possibly find anywhere else.

Those wishing to sell instead of buy or browse should contact the Englishtown reservation office, (908) 446–9644. Once you have a reservation, plan to arrive early enough to secure the best space available.

If it's antiques you're looking for, be prepared to get to Englishtown when the sun comes up. You'll want the first crack at anything of value that might have come out of granny's attic and be considered junk by an unknowing seller. Be advised that other antique hunters will surely arrive when you do, thus any "steals" go quickly.

Saturdays are often better than Sundays for both buyers and sellers. Parking can be a problem and so can crowds, especially during the holiday season. Englishtown Auction is located at 90 Wilson Avenue, off Routes 9 and 527.

Old Bridge

Raceway Park. Some of the finest drag racing on the Eastern Seaboard occurs at Raceway Park, which straddles the Englishtown-Old Bridge boundary on Route 627. During July, the four-day National Hot Rod Association Summer Nationals are held here and attract thousands; it's the biggest racing event from Maine to Florida. Race categories include funny cars, dragsters and pro stock.

Regular racing at Raceway Park takes place on Wednesday nights from April to October and on Sundays from March to November. Mostly time trials are held on Wednesday nights and Sunday mornings. Sunday afternoons are the eliminations and finals on the quarter-mile drag strip. Motocross and truck races are also popular at Raceway Park. These events take place throughout the racing season.

The Raceway Park season schedule is published in February. To get a copy, send a self-addressed, stamped envelope to Raceway Park, Pension Road, Englishtown 07726. Raceway Park's Information Hotline is (908) 446–6331.

Shrewsbury

Allen House. The Allen House stands on what once was a Lenni Lenape Indian trail and later a highway used by Dutch and English settlers to get from the settlement of Shrewsbury, one of the very first on the Jersey Shore, to Middletown. The Allen House was built by Judah Allen in the late seventeenth century. A subsequent owner turned it into a highway tavern. Called the "Sign of the Blue Ball," the tavern catered to travelers and provided the area with an important meeting place.

During the revolutionary war, a skirmish between surprised Continental soldiers and attacking Tories (those loyal to the British crown) led to the death of two soldiers and the capture of nine others. The incident was referred to as the "Allen House Massacre."

The Allen House has been restored to the period in the mid- and late eighteenth century when it operated as a tavern. Because the building was in such bad disrepair, little of the original house remains. The two-floor structure has since been furnished with period furniture, and tours of the house are conducted by Monmouth County Historical Association guides.

The Allen House is located on one corner of what is known as the Historic Four Corners of Shrewsbury. On the other three corners stand the **Quaker Meeting House,** built in 1816; **Christ Church,** built in 1769; and the **Presbyterian Church,** built in 1821. The Four Corners is at the intersection of Route 35 and Sycamore Avenue.

You can visit the Allen House from May through October. For more information, call the Monmouth County Historical Association at (908) 462–1466.

Fort Monmouth

Army Communications-Electronics Museum. Fort Monmouth is the home of the U.S. Army's Communications Electronics Command, the main research center for further development in the field of military-related communications. It was here, back in the 1930s, that army scientists and technicians developed radar (many experiments were conducted at Sandy Hook, see chapter 1), and where the U.S. Army Signal Corps had its communications school until it relocated to Georgia in 1976.

The Army Communications-Electronics Museum depicts the history of Fort Monmouth from its origin in 1917 to the present and traces the development of communications and electronic military equipment. The museum also contains communications relics that date as far back as the Civil War when the U.S. Army Signal Corps was created; foreign military communications equipment from the armies of France, Germany, Japan and North Vietnam, among others; and special exhibits like President John F. Kennedy's White House telephone, which he used on the first satellite telephone call between the United States and Africa, and a scale model of the type of radar used in Hawaii at the outbreak of World War II.

To get to the museum, enter Fort Monmouth's Main Gate on Route 35 in Eatontown. Proceed down Avenue of Memories to Building 275, aka Kaplan Hall. The museum is located on the first floor. Admission is free. For more information call (908) 532–2445.

For those interested in visiting another museum while on the base, there is the **U.S. Army Chaplain Museum.** This small museum traces the history of the chaplain branch of the U.S. Army and includes a special exhibit on the role of religion in warfare from the Battle of Jericho in biblical times to the present. Located in Watters Hall (Building 1208), the museum is open to the public by appointment only. For reservations, call (908) 532–3487.

Colts Neck

Delicious Orchards. No trip to inland Monmouth County would be complete without a stop at Delicious Orchards. And at no time is a stop more worthwhile than in the fall when the apples are ripe, the cider fresh and the pies oh so tasty. Located on Route 34 (Box 4, Route 34, Colts Neck 07722), this large, popular country market is full of fresh Jersey produce, baked goods, cheese and homemade breads and contains more than enough proof of why New Jersey is known as the Garden State.

Delicious Orchards is quite popular on weekends in the fall when people seem to make a day of shopping at the market. You can buy your Halloween pumpkins here and bushels of apples. Many people order pies for the holidays. In addition to the delicious apple pies, be sure to try some apple donuts and apple cake. And don't leave without a gallon of New Jersey apple cider in your arms.

Delicious Orchards is open Tuesday through Sunday, from 10 A.M. to 6 P.M. For more information, call (908) 542–0204.

Lincroft

Monmouth Museum. Located on the Brookdale Community College Campus (Newman Springs Road, Exit 109, Garden State Parkway), the Monmouth Museum likes to call itself a Museum of Ideas. Unlike the Monmouth County Historical Association Museum in Freehold (see below), which deals with Monmouth County history, the Monmouth Museum has no permanent collections and no historical exhibits. Instead the museum is concerned with ideas and concepts stemming from the world of art, science, nature and human culture. Revolving exhibits might include watercolor paintings done by local artists, a display centered on the theme of migration, an overview of customs, mores, dress and folk art of a particular people or a natural history exhibit, such as Dino Might, a collection of 14 robotic dinosaurs designed to teach children about the prehistoric creatures.

In the Junior Gallery, children are encouraged to touch as well as look. One of the gallery's most popular exhibits is one that deals with land planning. The exhibit encourages youngsters to build their own communities—and then confronts them with problems like pollution and waste disposal.

Open year-round, six days a week, (closed Mondays), the Monmouth

Six Pick-Your-Own Fruit and/or Vegetable Farms

Battleview Orchards
R.D. #1, Wemrock Road
Freehold, 07728
(800) 662–3075
(apples, peaches, pumpkins, gourds, blueberries, strawberries, sour cherries)

Casola Farms
Route 34
Colts Neck, 07722
(908) 946–8885
(strawberries, plum tomatoes, pumpkins)

Crest Fruit Farm
R.D. #5, Thompson Grove Road
Freehold, 07728
(908) 462–5669
(apples, peaches, plums, pumpkins, strawberries)

Eastmont Orchards
Route 537
Colts Neck, 07728
(908) 542–5404
(apples and peaches)

Menzel Brothers
Route 34
Holmdel, 07733
(908) 946–4135 or (908) 946–3060
(broccoli, cauliflower, lettuce, peas, pumpkins, spinach, strawberries, tomatoes)

Shwahla Farm
R.D. #4, Fort Plains Road
Howell, 07731
(908) 462–7587
(blueberries)

Museum provides a vastly interesting alternative to the historical museums in the area. For more information on current exhibitions and guided tours, call (908) 747–2266. There is an admission charge.

Freehold

Monmouth County Historical Association Museum. The Monmouth County Historical Association oversees upkeep, tours and special exhibits in four county historical houses—the Holmes-Hendrickson House (Holmdel), Marlpit Hall (Middletown), the Allen House (Shrewsbury) and the Covenhoven House (Freehold, see below). In addition, it also runs the main museum and library at 70 Court Street in Freehold.

The museum contains paintings, ceramics and furniture from the colonial era, many of which, as one might expect, have a direct relationship to Monmouth County history. Its collection of 23 pastels of Monmouth County Dutch colonial farmers by the noted artist Micah Williams is the toast of the museum along with Emmanuel G. Leutze's famous painting *Washington at Monmouth.* Leutze (1816-1868) also painted *Washington Crossing the Delaware*, which hangs in the New York Metropolitan Museum. Another exquisite piece is a locally built Wainscot chair, which is the oldest major piece in the museum's collection. It was built in 1695. Upstairs in the museum's attic is a potpourri of relics, curiosities and toys donated to the museum but not on formal display.

A guide will take you around the museum, sketching out a capsule history of Monmouth and pointing out the significance of the displayed items and paintings. There is an admission charge.

The association also sponsors a number of excellent annual events, including the American Decorative Arts Lecture Series, various folk art workshops and a popular Christmas exhibit at the museum. For more information, call (908) 462-1466.

Covenhoven House. William Covenhoven was a well-off Dutch farmer, whose house was built in 1753, although it is believed the kitchen area dates back as early as 1710. The house is significant not only because of its age and its blend of Dutch and English architecture but because British Gen. Henry Clinton occupied the house and his troops plundered it just prior to the Battle of Monmouth. Because of this, the house is often referred to as Clinton's Headquarters.

Considered a mansion by eighteenth-century Monmouth County standards due to its unusually large size, the house is in excellent condition and is furnished according to a 1790 inventory of Covenhoven's property taken after his death. The inventory also included furnishing plans, so the Monmouth County Historical Association was able to furnish the house upon restoration with pieces the Covenhoven family might have used (the originals were destroyed or stolen by the British) and placed precisely where they would have stood in the house in the late eighteenth century.

As you tour the house, notice that it contains closets, even a large, walk-in one. In the colonial era, closets were taxed as if they were rooms and rarely constructed because of this. Clothes and such were kept in drawers and chests. It's suspected that Covenhoven chose to have closets in his house despite the additional tax to show off his wealth.

There are two floors to tour, which a guide will take you through, and an attic where there's a display of the material and tools used to build the house and a photographic story of its restoration by the Monmouth County Historical Association.

The Covenhoven House is located at 150 West Main Street and is open from May through October. There is a small admission charge. For more information, call the Monmouth County Historical Association at (908) 462-1466.

Freehold Raceway. Harness Racing at Freehold Raceway began in 1853 and has been a major source of gambling entertainment in New

Jersey ever since. In 1984, a fire destroyed the grandstand, but it has since been rebuilt with better views of the 11 races that are held Monday through Saturday from August to the end of May. Post time is 1 P.M. except during daylight saving time when it is moved back to 12:30 P.M.

Freehold Raceway's biggest race is the James B. Dancer Memorial Race with a $350,000 purse. Held every September 1st, the race commands widespread attention in the racing world. Guided tours of Freehold Raceway are available to groups provided reservations are made in advance. The tour includes an overview of prerace stable activities and preliminary nonbetting races. Call (908) 462–3800 for more information on the races as well as reservations for the guided tour. The Raceway is located at the Freehold Circle, where Route 9 and Route 33 intersect.

Did you know that . . .

The only daytime harness racing in the United States is at Freehold Raceway.

Turkey Swamp Park. Set in western Monmouth County, yet only 35 minutes from the beach resorts of the North Jersey Shore, Turkey Swamp Park is the only county park at the Inland Shore to offer camping. It has 64 campsites, 32 of which can be reserved, while the remaining 32 are taken on a first-come, first-serve basis. In addition, there's also a wilderness camping area, but it's mainly used for youth-group camp outings.

As might be expected, the park has five very good hiking trails of various degrees of length and difficulty. They all wind through the pine forest at Turkey Swamp and pass by swamps and bogs, wild blueberry patches and other plantlife associated with the Pine Barrens. Guided nature walks are led by park naturalists providing reservations are made in advance. There is also a 17-acre lake that's stocked with catfish, sunfish and bass, and fishing, of course, is permitted. Canoes, rowboats and paddleboats can be rented, too.

Turkey Swamp Park is noted for two popular annual events: Turkey Swamp Park Day, held in early October, consists of a special set of activities related to the park's ecology, plus a small fair and a crafts show; and the Jersey Devil Hunt, also held in the fall, is just that, a fun-filled search for that legendary creature of the Pine Barrens. Reservations for the Jersey Devil Hunt are mandatory. (For the story of the Jersey Devil, see chapter 6.)

Turkey Swamp Park is located on Georgia Road, off Route 524, and is open year-round, although camping is only permitted March through

November. There is no fee to enter the park, although there is a camping charge. For further information call (908) 462–7286.

Monmouth Battlefield State Park

On June 28, 1778, a pivotal revolutionary war battle raged just outside Freehold between the Continental forces of George Washington and British regulars under Gen. Henry Clinton. The confrontation gave Washington's troops the desperately needed confidence to continue fighting for America's independence from England after the brutal, demoralizing winter spent at Valley Forge.

Washington's battle plan was formulated after receiving word that General Clinton's forces were en route from Philadelphia to New York City through New Jersey. Clinton feared the arrival of a French fleet off America's shores and wanted his troops in New York City, where they would be better able to withstand an attack or siege.

Washington and his army left Valley Forge on June 19. He ordered Gen. Charles Lee to head an advance unit and attack Clinton's supply wagon train and rear guard. For some still unexplained reason, Lee did not follow the orders Washington gave him until the very last moment thus losing valuable time. He finally did attack on June 28 but retreated when told of approaching British reinforcements from Clinton's main force. Clinton regrouped his army and immediately went on the offensive.

By this time, Washington and his troops had arrived at the scene of battle. Angered at Lee for not following his orders, Washington assumed command and regrouped the American forces. The British attacked; each time they assaulted the American positions they were repelled.

The shooting subsided when darkness overcame the battlefield, and during the cover of night, Clinton and his troops escaped from the American grasp. They went to Sandy Hook, where they boarded ships, crossed New York harbor, and made it to lower Manhattan without further incident.

Both sides suffered heavy losses at the Battle of Monmouth, yet both claimed victory. Washington had much to rejoice over; his men, once he rallied them, performed admirably in the field, taking the British head on and standing their ground. Clinton, on the other hand, fulfilled his objective of getting to New York City and managed to outfox Washington when it seemed he and his men were doomed.

A visit to Monmouth Battlefield State Park is a return to that day in June when Washington's Continental Army battled the British to what really amounted to a draw. The park sits on land where much of the fighting occurred. The Visitor Center contains the full, detailed story of the battle, using displays and an electronic map of the battlefield that depicts troop movements while a narrator reveals the day's heroics. A gift shop in the building sells books and pamphlets relating to the battle for those wanting even more information on what some historians consider one of the turning points of the war.

Monmouth Battlefield State Park is located on Route 33 and is open year-round. Admission is free. For further information, call (908) 462–9616.

Things to Do

Take a Walk Around the Battlefield. Paths around the park give a good overview of the battlefield. Before you wander around the grounds, however, listen to the account of the battle in the Visitor Center. Then gaze out at the fields and imagine Washington's troops holding back waves of British soldiers as they attempt to rout the Americans. Let your imagination go even further and hear the boom of cannon and the pop of muskets.

Have a Picnic. The battlefield grounds have two picnic areas with a total of 60 tables. Spring and fall or early and late summer are the best times to picnic at the park. The midsummer sun often makes it too hot to enjoy fully the scenery and sense of history all around you.

Take the Kids Fishing. If your children are under 14 years of age, they're permitted to fish in the Liberty Grove Pond, which is conveniently located between the two picnic areas.

Attend the Annual Battle of Monmouth Reenactment. Each year on the weekend closest to the battle date, volunteers don the red coats of the British and the blue of the Continental Army and act out the battle. It's a grand affair, certainly the highlight of the park's summer season. This is a popular event, so do expect crowds. Bring a hat along and wear cool, comfortable clothing as you'll be standing in the sun most of the day.

Visit the Craig House. John Craig was the Paymaster for the Freehold area militia and fought with Washington at the Battle of Monmouth. During the strife, British troops took control of his farm after his family fled and used the farmhouse as a temporary hospital. To get to the Craig House, one has to leave the main area of the park, make a left on Route 33 and head to the Freehold Circle, where Route 33 and Route 9 meet. Head north on Route 9 to Schibanoff Road. The Craig House is located on that road, west of Route 9. Call (908) 462–9616 for more information.

Visit Molly Pitcher Spring. Molly Pitcher, well placed in revolutionary war history and legend, is said to have drawn water from the spring on Wemrock Road to quench the thirst of her husband, a gunner with the Continental forces, during the heat of battle. When he went down with a wound and could no longer man his cannon, Molly Pitcher took his place. For her bravery and duty to her country, General Washington made her an honorary officer in the American army. View the marker near where Wemrock Road intersects Route 522.

Visit the Owl Haven Nature Center. Although not under the jurisdiction of Monmouth Battlefield State Park, the center is on park property. Owl Haven is run by the New Jersey Audubon Society and is situated on Route 522, just up from Molly Pitcher Spring. Owl Haven's exhibits pertain to local wildlife, especially owls. The center often has live owls on the premises; these have been injured somehow in the wild and are nursed back to health by Audubon members. Owl Haven sponsors a series of special birding outings throughout the year. For more information, call (908) 780-7007.

Visit Old Tennent Presbyterian Church. The church is not on park property but is related to the battle and is just a couple miles away from the Molly Pitcher Spring and Owl Haven Nature Center. Located on Tennent Road off Route 522, the church was built in 1751 with the generous financial support of William Covenhoven, owner of Covenhoven House (see above). On June 28, 1778, the church was used as a hospital for Americans wounded during the battle.

Although the church isn't open to the public except on Sundays when religious services are still held there, a walk through the oldest sections of the cemetery will reveal a number of barely legible markers. In the graves are the remains of American and British soldiers killed during and immediately after the battle, including one Lt. Col. Henry Moncton, a British officer whose sword hangs on display at the Monmouth County Historical Association Museum in Freehold (see above).

Visit Battleview Orchards. Not many out-of-staters are truly convinced that New Jersey is indeed the Garden State, but regulars to such pick-your-own farms and orchards as Battleview Orchards know better. Each year, from May through October, Battleview, which borders Monmouth Battlefield State Park on Wemrock Road off Route 33 (hence the name), offers pickers a chance to select some of the area's best fruit. More than 40,000 bushels of apples, its specialty, in addition to 10,000 bushels of peaches, 100,000 quarts of strawberries and blueberries, pumpkins, sour cherries and gourds are harvested annually. All fruit picked is sold by the pound and weighed in the orchards. Battleview supplies containers. Purchase a Battleview Pick-Your-Own Club Membership Card for $1 and you'll receive a newsletter containing regular announcements concerning harvests and best picking times as well as special discounts and canning and freezing information.

Battleview Orchards consists of 100 acres of apples (McIntosh, Red Delicious, Golden Delicious, Stayman Winesap and Rome Beauty), which are harvested from September through October; 70 acres of peaches, which are harvested from mid-July to mid-September; 12 acres of strawberries from late May through late June; 12 acres of pumpkins and gourds, from mid-September through October; 10 acres of blueberries and 3 acres of sour cherries, both of which are harvested in July.

Battleview Orchards Country Store sells its special blend of delicious apple cider (comparable to Delicious Orchards cider, see above), which is pressed on the premises and contains no preservatives. Also sold are cider donuts, homemade pies, jams and jellies, local honey, produce, and of course, all fruit harvested but not picked by pickers. You can even buy canning, freezing and jelly-making supplies, too.

For more information, call (908) 462–0756. For weather and picking conditions, call (800) 662–3075.

Wall

Wall Stadium. Each Saturday night from April through September, stock car racing fans gather at Wall Stadium to watch finely tuned, revved-up cars driven by professional and amateur racers. There are heats, consolation races, finals and featured races, and you can rest assured that the action is heavy and the excitement hot when the checkered flag is lowered.

The four divisions of stock car racing at Wall Stadium are Modified (the fastest, most expensive cars), Modified Affordable Division or M.A.D. Stock (restricted modified cars in terms of cost and equipment), Modern (six and eight cylinders) and Street Stock (street cars). First heats begin at 7 P.M. The night's racing ends when the last of the featured races is over.

Many of the race slots in the various divisions are filled by professional circuit racers from the Mid-Atlantic region (New Jersey, New York, Pennsylvania). But anyone with a properly equipped car can enter. One needs a Wall Stadium Pit License, which costs $50 but is good for the entire racing season; one must also pay a small fee to use the pit on the night one races.

Wall Stadium is also host to a number of special racing events, including popular demolition derbies that are held four or five times a year. There's plenty of fun, and the crack-ups are incredible. Just as incredible are the relatively few serious injuries suffered by drivers in these "you smash me, I'll smash you" contests.

Wall Stadium is located on Route 34. For more information on races and demolition derbies, call (908) 681–6400.

Farmingdale

Collingwood Auction and Flea Market. Many of the same things you're apt to find on a vendor's table at Englishtown can also be bought at the Collingwood Auction & Flea Market. There are indoor and outdoor vendors at Collingwood, just as at Englishtown, but usually not as many at the former. Regular flea marketeers say, however, that good to excellent bargains on used items can be found at Collingwood. Books, dishes, glassware, automotive parts and household items are best bets.

Collingwood is open on weekends and Fridays throughout the year. It's located at the intersection of Routes 33 and 34, south of the U.S. Naval Weapons Station at Earle. For information on selling space at the flea market, call (908) 938–7941.

Allaire State Park

From 1674, when the first New Jersey blast furnaces began smelting ore, until little more than a century and a half ago, the Shore iron industry was a vital part of the local economy. The Central and South Jersey coastal plains possessed large, rich iron ore deposits, the result of decaying vegetation in the many low-lying swamp areas. Many Shore settlers worked in the industry—either smelting the iron ore by running large furnaces or by crafting iron products.

On what is now Allaire State Park stand the remains of Allaire Village, once a profitable iron ore community that was self-sustaining to the point of issuing its own currency to be used in the village. It began in 1822 when James P. Allaire of New York purchased the Howell Works, the original ironworks on the land, from Benjamin Howell of Philadelphia. Under Allaire, the big furnaces turned out quality iron castings for such household items as caldrons, pots, kettles, stoves and piping. It was a prosperous operation indeed; more than 450 workers and family members inhabited Allaire Village during its heyday in the early to mid-nineteenth century. In addition to iron workers, the village provided employment for carpenters, millers, harness makers, coach drivers, a baker, even a schoolteacher to educate the village children and a minister to preach at the Allaire Chapel on Sunday mornings.

Allaire's bog iron business and the community that grew up around it thrived until 1846, when things turned bad for the New Jersey bog iron industry. By then coal had been discovered in Pennsylvania's Allegheny Mountains. Allaire, Batsto (see chapter 6) and other New Jersey bog iron foundries burned charcoal from pitch pine to fire their furnaces. Coal, however, was cheaper to use than charcoal. Allaire suffered severe financial difficulties and in 1848 was forced to quiet its furnace forever. When it did, Allaire Village became known as the Deserted Village.

Many buildings remain from the village's heyday, and one can visit them here at Allaire State Park. Buildings such as the carpenter's shop (1835), where wooden utensils were repaired and wagon wheels made; the blacksmith's shop (1836), where tools were made and horses shod;

the bakery (1835), which later served as the village school; the General Store (1835), where villagers did their shopping and gossiping; and the foreman's cottage (1827), where the foreman of the iron furnace and his family lived, have all been restored, along with other village buildings. Together, they provide an interesting glimpse back to the days when bog iron was king in these parts.

During the summer, Allaire Village and its surroundings are a beehive of activity. Blacksmiths, weavers and quilters work on the premises, depicting methods used 150 years ago. On some weekends, craftspeople set up displays, usually in front of the bakery, and sell their work. You'll find all sorts of lace and hand-sewn items, carved wood pieces such as duck decoys, handmade brooms, and watercolor paintings of local scenes.

Of all the parks at the Inland Shore, none is as popular as Allaire. The park is approximately 20 minutes away from the beach towns of Belmar, Spring Lake, Sea Girt and Manasquan and is the closest state park to the ocean that offers camping. There are 55 sites, which are open all year, and it's no secret that many more are needed to meet the demand. If you plan to camp at Allaire during the summer, expect to find few, if any, sites left by late afternoon. From June 15 to Labor Day, one-third of the sites may be reserved for 7-or 14-night periods. The remaining two-thirds of the sites are available on a first-come, first-serve basis. Campers usually queue up early in the morning to secure a site. For more information on camping and camping reservations, call (908) 938–2371.

Allaire State Park is open year-round. During the peak summer months, there is an admission charge. The park is located in Farming- dale on Route 524, just three miles from the Parkway South Exit 98.

Things to Do

Visit Allaire Village. A self-guided map of Allaire Village is available at the Visitor Center. Be sure to visit the blacksmith shop, general store and the chapel. Church sessions are held there on Sunday mornings from July to Labor Day. Notice that the steeple is located in the back, rather than the front, of the church. To make your visit even more re- warding, select a day when one of the many seasonal special events is held. Each year Allaire Village publishes a Calendar of Events, which lists the times and dates of all shows and special activities. To request a calendar, write to Allaire Village, Allaire (Farmingdale) 07727, or call (908) 938–2253.

Ride the Pine Creek Railroad. The Pine Creek Railroad is located adjacent to the Allaire Village. Children and train buffs will enjoy a ride on either the coal-burning or diesel-powered locomotive that winds its way through a scenic area of Allaire. Passengers sit in antique rail cars and board at Allaire Station, where there's a small museum.

The volunteers who operate the Pine Creek Railroad also stage three events each year that are worth investigating. In June there's the Great Locomotive Chase, a Civil War reenactment; in September the Railroad sponsors Railroader's Day, a celebration of America's railroad heritage; and in December, The Christmas Express brings Santa Claus to Allaire. For more information on these, call (908) 938-5524.

Take a Wagon Ride Through Allaire. A horse-drawn wagon takes visitors on a lazy ride over one of the park's horse trails. Fun for the kids. Wagons depart from the Visitor Center throughout the day in the summer and on weekends in late spring and early fall.

Go Fishing at Lower Mill Pond or on the Banks of the Manasquan River. Lower Mill Pond is stocked with fish each April so youngsters under the age of 14 can enjoy participating in a Junior Fishing Contest. (Call park for details.) Adults are permitted to fish the Manasquan River, which is also stocked weekly—with trout. The Manasquan runs throughout the park's interior and offers better than average fishing during trout season. There are no bait-and-tackle shops in the area; bring all the gear you need with you.

Canoe the Manasquan River. Contrary to popular belief, Allaire does not rent canoes or any other small boats. But there are areas on the river bank to launch canoes, providing you bring your own. The scenery is quite nice and the water calm. A good way to spend a summer afternoon.

Go Hunting. Allaire is the only park at the Inland Shore that allows hunting. A specified hunting area is in the south section of the park. Permits and licenses are required; only deer hunting is permitted.

Hike Allaire's Nature Trails. A number of fair hiking trails wind throughout much of the park's 3,000 acres. Much of Allaire's wilderness area is thick forest that contains a fine representation of northern Pine Barrens plantlife. If you take the Green Trail, which begins at Lower Mill Pond at the entrance to the Deserted Village, you'll come to the Allaire Nature Center a quarter mile into your walk. There you'll find exhibits dealing with Allaire's natural history. Naturalist-led nature walks are held during the summer seasons. Guides are informative and interesting.

Go Horseback Riding. Monmouth County has more than its share of riding stables and academies. Many of them permit horses to be brought to Allaire by trailer, or the stables themselves actually sponsor rides in the park on the well-marked, easy-grade horse paths. Allaire does not rent horses. The horse trails are turned into cross-country paths in the winter.

Have a Picnic. Like all county and state parks on the Jersey Shore, Allaire has a picnic area, complete with tables and stoves. To keep the kids occupied, there is a playground just beyond the picnic area and pony rides (which tend to be expensive and short, however). Picnicking is a popular activity at Allaire, so expect the tables around you to be occupied as well. If it's privacy you prefer, take your lunch into the woods and eat on the trail. No fires of any kind are permitted in the wooded area (strictly enforced), and do bring out what you brought in, meaning any and all trash.

Play Golf. Allaire has the only state-owned golf course. The 18-hole, par 69 Spring Meadow Golf Course has its own entrance on Route 524, a few hundred yards west of the park's main entrance. Included on the premises—a clubhouse, which offers meals, and a Pro Shop.

Howell

Howell Antique Village and Flea Market. Yet one more worthwhile flea market to visit is the Howell Antique Village and Flea Market, which features much of the same merchandise found at Collingwood and Englishtown, although you'll probably find more produce and eggs and better bargains here than at the other two markets. As for antiques, you'll find them at Howell, but don't expect too many deals or steals. These days the demand for antiques has increased dramatically. This has driven up prices and forced even amateur collectors to search even harder for good buys. Howell is open weekends. Located at 2215 Route 9. For further information, call (908) 367–1105.

Where to Eat at the Inland Shore

Battleground Country Club, Route 527 (Millhurst Road), Tennent, (908) 462–7575
Price Code: Expensive   Menu: Continental
Fine dining in classic American atmosphere. Tasty lamb and veal dishes. Reservations required.

Colts Neck Inn, Routes 34 and 537 (Freehold Road), Colts Neck, (908) 462–0383
Price Code: Moderate/Expensive   Menu: Continental
A good place for smorgasbord dining and Sunday brunch. Horse-farm ambiance.

The Farmingdale House, 105 Academy Street, Farmingdale, (908) 938–7951
Price code: Expensive   Menu: Northern Italian
Pleasant atmosphere, excellent main entries and desserts. Jackets required, reservations suggested.

The Fromagerie, 26 Ridge Road, Rumson, (908) 842–8088
Price Code: Expensive   Menu: French
Delightfully rich sauces, exquisite veal dishes. Routinely voted one of the top restaurants in New Jersey by area critics.

Koh's Shanghai Wok, Route 35 and Deal Road, (Middlebrook Shopping Center), Ocean Township, (908) 493–8118
Price Code: Moderate   Menu: Chinese
The best Chinese restaurant in the area—Szechuan, Cantonese and Hunan cuisine. Excellent service.

Little Kraut, 115 Oakland Street, Red Bank, (908) 842–4830
Price Code: Moderate   Menu: German
Wonderful German dishes such as wiener roastbraten and sauerbraten in small, comfortable setting.

Margaux Country Dining, 29 Route 34, Colts Neck, (908) 431–7595
Price Code: Expensive   Menu: French
Innovative French is the best way to describe the menu. Expensive, yes, but worth it.

The Pear Tree, 42 Avenue of the Two Rivers, Rumson, (908) 842–8747
Price Code: Expensive   Menu: Northern Italian and French
Quiet, romantic setting to enhance gourmet entrees and mouth-watering desserts. A great place to celebrate a special occasion.

The Shadowbrook, Route 35, Shrewsbury, (908) 747–0200
Price Code: Moderate/Expensive   Menu: Continental
Yet another of Monmouth County's elegant country restaurants. Set in a Georgian mansion on a 20-acre estate. Veal and duck dishes are recommended.

Shiki Japanese Steak House, Route 35 North, Middletown Township, (908) 671–9500
Price Code: Moderate/Expensive   Menu: Japanese
Steaks and exotic seafood dishes cooked tableside, sushi bar, Polynesian drinks.

4

 The Barnegat Peninsula

A funny thing about the Barnegat Peninsula—technically speaking, it's an island. It *used* to be a peninsula, before the Point Pleasant Canal was dug, linking the Manasquan River with Barnegat Bay. Since then, the long, narrow barrier beach has been cut off from the New Jersey mainland. Manasquan Inlet, which is part of the Inland Waterway, and the Manasquan River are to the north. Barnegat Inlet is to the south. The Point Pleasant Canal and Barnegat Bay are to the west. To the east, of course, is the Atlantic Ocean.

There are, however, five bridges that connect the 22-mile island with the rest of the Jersey Shore. The Manasquan Bridge spans the Manasquan River and connects Brielle and Manasquan and the rest of Monmouth County with Point Pleasant Beach and Ocean County via Route 35. The Point Pleasant Canal has two bridges across it; one crosses on Route 88 and connects Point Pleasant with Point Pleasant Beach, and the other crosses a half mile south and links Point Pleasant with Bay Head.

The final two bridges are farther south. The Mantoloking Bridge goes across Barnegat Bay as does the Thomas B. Mathias Bridge. The former joins Bricktown with Mantoloking and is the most centrally located of the bridges. The latter brings cars from Toms River to Seaside Heights and Island Beach State Park via Route 37.

During the summer months, the Barnegat Peninsula (we'll use "peninsula" to be consistent) becomes one of the most popular sections of the Jersey Shore for vacationers from the New York–northern New

Jersey metropolitan area. The island is quite long as already noted, but only in Point Pleasant Beach and parts of Island Beach State Park is the land mass any wider than a mile. Then, take away 10 miles for Island Beach State Park at the southernmost part of the peninsula. That means the many thousands who vacation here from June to September crowd themselves onto a 10-mile strip with only one very congested artery, Route 35, running from top to bottom of the peninsula.

Why then would people want to buck the traffic that inevitably backs up all the bridges each summer? And why would people want to come to a part of the Jersey Shore whose resources are taken to the limit beginning Memorial Day Weekend? Because of its beaches, its boardwalks, the bay and the ocean.

The Barnegat Peninsula's beaches, from Jenkinson's in Point Pleasant Beach to the sand-dune dominated stretch in Island Beach State Park, are, in a word, outstanding. Unlike those beaches to the north that are narrower and constantly falling prey to erosion, the beaches of the Barnegat Peninsula are wider and spacious.

Jenkinson's Beach compares favorably with the beaches of Wildwood, generally considered to be the state's biggest and best beach area (see chapter 8). There is one major difference, though. Jenkinson's is a privately owned public beach, which means a private corporation owns the beach but opens it to the public—for a fee, of course. Wildwood, on the other hand, is municipally owned and free.

Bay Head and Mantoloking's beaches are privately owned, too. But unlike Point Pleasant Beach, Bay Head did not permit access to the public, until the mid-1980s when a court order forced the town to sell a certain number of beach badges to those living outside the town. The whole idea of who has the right to beach access—and who doesn't—has been a very sticky affair, especially in Bay Head. More about this later on.

Heading all the way south to Seaside Heights, the beaches are private, but the restrictions to beach access vary. Membership in beach clubs, ownership of a summer cottage, or rental of one, usually entitles you to use of the beach, providing you purchase a beach badge. But the day visitor who wishes to lay his or her towel on the sand without paying some sort of beach fee will find that's not possible.

If it all sounds quite restricting, it is. But somehow everyone is accommodated in the end. Seaside Heights and Point Pleasant Beach's public beaches would probably remain the most popular beaches with day visitors even if the restrictions were loosened. These two towns have boardwalks and nightlife and naturally attract the largest number of vacationers. And then there's always Island Beach State Park, which, of course, has public beaches—beaches that are undoubtedly the prettiest on the peninsula and perhaps the entire Jersey Shore.

As for boardwalks, the Point Pleasant Beach boardwalk is entirely family-oriented; it has a little of everything, which pleases both kids and adults. The Seaside Heights boardwalk is a smaller version of the one in Wildwood (see chapter 8). Wildwood has piers full of amusement rides, some of which are the wildest and fastest on any boardwalk anywhere. Seaside Heights isn't quite as spectacular, but it comes close. No boardwalk north of Wildwood can match Seaside's arcades, amusements and action.

Seaside Park, Lavallette and Bay Head also have boardwalks, but they're strictly for strolling. No rides or games of chance, just wooden planks to walk on and wonderful views of the beach and ocean.

Finally, there's the bay. The Barnegat is a water playground for the central Jersey Shore. On any given summer weekend, it is dotted with colorful sails latched to the masts of sailboats and sailboards. Yacht clubs in Bay Head and Mantoloking regularly sponsor regattas that attract sailors from around the country. In addition, there are water-skiers pulled by wake-creating motor boats, jet skiers, fishermen and crabbers in rowboats and those out in all sizes of pleasure boats soaking up the sun and scenery.

You don't even need your own boat, sailboard or jet ski to enjoy Barnegat Bay. Seaside Heights and Ortley Beach, for example, have rental facilities for all of the above. You can also fish on the edge of the bay without even getting your feet wet, or throw a crab trap over the side of one of the many fingerlike lagoons in Ocean Beach. About the only thing people don't do in the bay in large numbers is swim. It's a bit dangerous with all the boat traffic, and besides, the ocean is only a few blocks to the east.

The towns on the Barnegat Peninsula cover the full range of resorts. Point Pleasant Beach is the largest town on the north end of the peninsula and possesses a small town center, excellent restaurants and a large fishing fleet to go with its fine beaches and boardwalk. It's a family resort, to be sure, with summer cottages and midpriced motels the main means of lodging.

Bay Head and Mantoloking are wealthy communities in comparison. They have glorious beaches, an Ivy League ambiance, and some of the most stately beachfront mansions that you'll find on the Shore. Except for Bay Head's couple of hotels and its bed and breakfasts, there is little in the way of other accommodations available. Mantoloking offers less than that.

Much of Normandy Beach, Ocean Beach (Units 1, 2 and 3), Lavallette and Ortley Beach consists of well-maintained summer homes and row after row of brightly painted, tightly packed summer bungalows. The latter are rented by the week, month or season, or owned outright by families who have been coming to this neck of the Jersey Shore for years. People here enjoy the proximity to Seaside Heights and to the restaurants in Point Pleasant Beach.

Seaside Heights has the nightclubs and the night action. Bars there stay open until early in the morning and almost always feature loud music and dancing. Wheels of chance on the boardwalk spin until the last bettor goes home. Seaside Park is more residential, a striking contrast to its neighbor. It acts as a nice buffer between the Heights and Island Beach State Park, where nature rules and early morning walks along the beach provide serenity and solitude.

Point Pleasant Beach

Like the town of Highlands, Point Pleasant Beach likes to call itself the Seafood Capital of New Jersey. Proclamations such as these are difficult to prove, especially on the Jersey coast, where virtually every town has its share of seafood restaurants, clam bars and fish markets. Point Pleasant Beach can flex its seafood muscles a bit more than most though, because it is home to one of the four commercial fishing fleets in the state. (The other three are located in Belford on the Bayshore, Barnegat Light on Long Beach Island and Cape May.) What this means is that the fishing and restaurant industries in Point Pleasant Beach work hand in hand, which results in lots of delicious, fresh seafood on your dinner plate.

If you ride along Channel Drive and then around Inlet Drive, you'll see the commercial fishing trawlers, co-op fish markets and warehouses, repair shops and party and charter boats. Places like **Garden State Seafood** and **Fishermen's Co-op** sell fish that were probably pulled from the sea only hours before they're filleted and set on ice. Virtually any piece of equipment an angler or boater will ever need can be found in one of Channel Drive's supply stores. On Broadway and Inlet Drive, you can do your own fishing. **Gull Island County Park,** a tiny section of land on Broadway, permits fishing in the shallows of the Manasquan River, while anglers who go to Inlet Drive can cast their lines in the Manasquan Inlet. Due to strong tidal currents, however, be sure to use heavy sinkers and metal lures. Try to fish on the outgoing tide, it's then that fish look to feed on whatever comes their way from the Manasquan River backwaters.

It's also on Channel Drive and Inlet Drive that you'll come across Point Pleasant Beach's—and the Barnegat Peninsula's—best seafood restaurants. (See end of chapter for addresses and telephone numbers of restaurants.) The **Lobster Shanty** is well known and remains the area's most popular restaurant. But Jack Baker's **Wharfside,** located right across the street from the Lobster Shanty, **Barmore's Shrimp Box** on

Inlet Drive and **Spike's Fish Market** on Broadway also offer delicious seafood dishes. These restaurants often have waits up to an hour or more in the summer, especially on weekends, so plan your dinner date accordingly. For those wishing simply to share a pot of steamers or a tempting shrimp cocktail in the evening, try Jack Baker's **Patio Bar,** behind the Wharfside Restaurant. It has a splendid view of the Manasquan River and possesses an informal, relaxed atmosphere.

So Point Pleasant does indeed have a valid claim to the Seafood Capital of New Jersey title. But, strangely enough, the town also has a superb selection of Italian restaurants—better, perhaps than any other Shore resort town north of Atlantic City. Add the two together and the odds are that if you're on the Barnegat Peninsula and wish to dine in a fine restaurant, you'll wind up in Point Pleasant Beach.

Filomio's, Tesauro's and **Alfonso's** are the best choices. The former is located next to the Manasquan Inlet Coast Guard Station. All the portions served are large and savory, and the menu is far from just a list of the standards. Tesauro's is located on Broadway and has a large, loyal clientele who have been dining at the restaurant ever since it was a mom-and-pop eatery on nearby Ocean Avenue. Alfonso's is really in Point Pleasant, not Point Pleasant Beach. But it's so close to Point Pleasant Beach—and so good—that it deserves mention. A big favorite with locals, the sauces are zesty and the pasta is cooked just right. You'll find yourself returning to these three restaurants whenever you're in the area.

Speaking of food, there are two other establishments in Point Pleasant Beach that should not be missed. If you enjoy submarine sandwiches, consider it a must to sample one at **Jersey Mike's Sub Shop** on Arnold Avenue in Point Pleasant. With the notable exception of the White House Sub Shop in Atlantic City, you won't find a tastier hero on the Shore.

Jump from subs to ice cream. **Bob Hoffman's** on Route 35 is a Point Pleasant Beach landmark. All the ice cream is homemade; no matter what flavor you choose, it's bound to be rich and creamy. Bob Hoffman's is the only place on the Barnegat Peninsula worth waiting 15 minutes or more on a summer night for that ice-cream sundae or float.

On to less fattening things. If you're an antique collector or mere browser, Point Pleasant Beach is rapidly becoming one of the best places on the Shore to find that turn-of-the-century vase, lamp stand, chest or coat stand. The **Point Pleasant Antique Emporium** (908–892–2222) on the corner of Bay and Trenton avenues is, by far, the largest antique center in the area. Open seven days a week, the Emporium has over 100 dealers under its roof. Everything from exquisite Victorian furniture to pocket watches and rare books can be found here.

Across the street from the Emporium on Bay Avenue are **Pleasant**

Times (908–295–0005) and **Lion's Head Antiques** (908–295–0017). The latter shop specializes in linens and vintage clothing. On Arnold Avenue, Point Pleasant Beach's main shopping street, check the **Snow Goose** (908–892–6929) for good antique buys and its unique collection of sleighs. On River Avenue, visit the **Doll Den** and **Doll's Museum,** where on display, are nearly 1,000 antique dolls, some of which are for sale. You must make an appointment to visit the museum. Call (908) 892–7855 for reservations.

Even though Point Pleasant Beach has fine restaurants and antique shops, it is still best known for its beaches and boardwalk. Of them all, Jenkinson's is the most popular. It's large enough to accommodate even the biggest Fourth of July crowds and still have room for volleyball, Frisbee or touch football games. It's also the only place where you can ride an old-fashioned beach train from one end of the beach to the other.

Seasonal beach badges or daily beach tags are required to gain entry on all Point Pleasant Beach beaches. Any of the booths situated on the boardwalk at the entrances to the beach have daily tags for sale.

Did you know that . . .

Author Robert Louis Stevenson is said to have visited the Point Pleasant Beach area in the late 1800s and was inspired to write *Treasure Island* when he sat on the mainland viewing Osborne Island in the Manasquan River. The island is west of the Manasquan bridge, just opposite Point Pleasant Hospital. For years, locals have referred to the island as Treasure Island in Stevenson's honor.

As already mentioned, the boardwalk, like almost everything else in Point Pleasant Beach, is family fun. Ten years ago, boardwalk bars like the Hoffman House and the Riptide featured live music and drew a large, young, rather lively crowd to the boardwalk. But today there are condominiums where the Hoffman House stood, and the Riptide is now called **Park Place** and features only the softest rock. These days, the college-age crowd heads to boardwalk clubs like Jenkinson's Pavilion and Martell's Tiki Bar, where you can dance to everything from Jamaican-flavored reggae music to hard rock.

Families with children ultimately wind up at **Jenkinson's South,** home of the boardwalk's last kiddie-amusement-ride area. The boardwalk is also lined with wheels of chance, food-concession stands, arcades and shops. On the north end of the Point Pleasant Beach boardwalk are excellent views of the Manasquan Inlet and more concession stands.

On Thursday evenings during the summer, the town sponsors fireworks on the beach. The best place to view the aerial display of colors is the boardwalk or on a boat just offshore. You'll see many party boats and private craft, their lights twinkling 100 yards from the beach, and their horns honking in appreciation of a truly fine fireworks show.

Most of Point Pleasant Beach's motels, guesthouses and other accommodations can be found on three main thoroughfares: Broadway (motels), Ocean Avenue (bungalows, some motels), and Arnold Avenue (motels, guesthouses). Although the town has no information or welcome center, visitors can stop at the Chamber of Commerce (517 Arnold Avenue, 908–899–2424) and pick up a Guide Book, which lists and describes the various accommodations in town.

Those who come to Point Pleasant Beach to fish usually wind up staying at any of the motels on Broadway, because just about all of them are a stone's throw from the party-boat docks. Anglers have a wide selection of party boats to choose from. Some boats specialize, for instance, in weakfish or fluke fishing; others concentrate on bluefish. Competition for business is keen among boats. You'll see mates standing on Broadway and Channel and Inlet drives waving you into their boat's parking lot. A good place to find out about different boats and the places they fish offshore is the **Cottage,** a luncheonette and breakfast nook at Ken's Landing (corner of Broadway and Inlet Drive). Here, you'll find local fishermen grabbing a bite to eat and talking fish year-round. Any of the other luncheonettes along Broadway are also good spots to pick up fishing tips.

Two events in Point Pleasant Beach should go on the vacationer's calendar. In July, the **Ray Catena Offshore Grand Prix** is held off the waters of Point Pleasant Beach and other Shore towns. The large powerboats are usually on display the week prior to the race, as are the Budweiser Clydesdale horses, a throwback to the days when giant parades highlighted the week of race festivities.

The Ray Catena Offshore Grand Prix is the largest powerboat race in the Northeast; it brings top racers from around the country to Point Pleasant Beach. The best place to view the start of the race is at Manasquan Inlet, as the boats pass through it on their way to the ocean course.

The other event is known as the **Festival of the Sea** and occurs in September after the summer season is over. The town sponsors a seafood festival, a street fair, a five-mile run, an arts and crafts show and the hilarious Tube Race and parade. Contestants compete in a mile-long inner tube race off Jenkinson's Beach for the charity of their choice. It's a fun affair for spectators and participants alike and is a great way to end the summer.

Bay Head

New Jersey Monthly once claimed that Bay Head possessed the "snootiest" beach on the Jersey Shore. On the outside looking in, *all* of Bay Head might appear uppity. Most who summer in Bay Head are well off and regard the town as a special place indeed. And it *is* special. Think of Nantucket. Think of Martha's Vineyard. If Bay Head could somehow be moved to either of these famous Massachusetts summer retreats, few there would take notice. Bay Head contains virtually the same qualities that make these two islands off Cape Cod the pride of New England.

Consider the following. On Sunday mornings, the tiny town center of Bay Head is cluttered with Mercedes and Jaguars vying for parking spaces. Yachtsmen from the nearby **Bay Head Yacht Club** dressed in bright green or pink pants and polo shirts can be found at **Mueller's Bakery** or the **Bay Head Gourmet Deli** picking up buns and the *New York Times.* Nannies push carriages down the tree-lined streets, past cedar-shingled summer cottages nearly a century old.

Out on Barnegat Bay, a Bay Head Yacht Club-sponsored regatta might be getting under way. The club's tennis and squash courts are surely full. Doctors and lawyers team up against stockbrokers and company executives. On Twilight Lake, novice sailboarders are taking their first lessons. Meanwhile, teens head to the beach dressed in the latest swimwear. Such is life in Bay Head on a summer Sunday morning.

Bay Head's beaches aren't necessarily any better than the other beaches on the Barnegat Peninsula—except that they're less crowded, and when you turn your back on the ocean, you see million-dollar mansions instead of a boardwalk overrun with amusement rides and arcades. The Bay Head beach is owned by the Bay Head Improvement Association, which, for years, offered membership and beach badges only to those who lived in Bay Head. Beachgoers in communities such as Point Pleasant and Bricktown cried discrimination and went to court to fight for the right to buy Bay Head beach badges. After a long, drawn-out battle, they won. Now Bay Head must sell badges to out-of-towners, too.

If you wish to stay in Bay Head in the summer, you'll have to rent a cottage (very expensive), rent a room in one of its two classic, wooden hotels (the **Grenville,** 345 Main Avenue, 908–892–3100, and **The Bluffs,** 575 East Avenue, 908–892–1114; expensive) or stay in one of its bed and breakfasts (not exactly cheap).

Conover's Bay Head Inn (646 Main Avenue, 908–892–4664) is widely regarded as one of the best bed and breakfasts in the area; the warm hospitality and coziness found in the rooms are unequaled. The **Bay Head Sands** (2 Twilight Road, 908–899–7016) is quite cheery and will take young children. The **Bentley Inn** (649 Main Avenue, 908–892–9589) is very popular with young couples. The **Bay Head Gables** (200 Main Avenue, 908–892–9844) is noted for its art deco and rooms with views of the ocean. The **Gray Goose Inn** (676 Main Avenue, 908–899–0767), a 16-room mansion built in the 1890s, is an easy walk to the beach and nearby shops.

Nightlife in Bay Head is quite limited. Only **The Bluffs,** a hidden bar under **The Bluffs Hotel** on East Avenue, offers spirits and social play. The bar used to be a speakeasy during the days of Prohibition and has lost little of the atmosphere that made it a popular watering hole on the Peninsula 60 years ago.

Bridge Avenue, which intersects Route 35 midway through town, is Bay Head's village center. **Dorcas of Bay Head,** the corner cafe (Bridge and Lake avenues), is where you can get an outside table, eat lunch, and people-watch. The old Bay Head theater is now the **Shopper's Wharf;** it houses a collection of shops that cater to the Bay Head visitor. **Bay Head Books,** farther up Bridge Avenue, will take care of your summer reading needs, while the **Bay Head Cheese Shop** serves customers with a wide variety of imported and domestic cheeses. On nearby Mount Street, local artist Dick LaBonte has a small gallery, **Anchor & Palette,** that features his paintings and prints (908–892–7776).

Even if you don't spend the weekend or even just a night in Bay Head, a stop or drive around this most picturesque of Shore towns is well worth it. Bay Head has a rare charm, one that should be experienced by all Barnegat Peninsula visitors.

Mantoloking, South Mantoloking, and Normandy Beach

Driving south on Route 35 through Mantoloking, you can't help but be awed by the magnificent homes that sit majestically overlooking the ocean and bay. Mantoloking is as private and low-key as Deal is farther up the coast. There are no hotels, no restaurants, nothing for the visitor to do except drive on through and admire such stately summer homes. The beaches are beautiful in Mantoloking, but the parking regulations are even more restrictive than in Bay Head. If you don't have a driveway in which to park, you're pretty much out of luck.

South Mantoloking and Normandy Beach also have great beaches and beautiful homes though not as spectacular as those found along Mantoloking's bay and oceanfronts.

The Ten Most Commonly Asked Questions about Sailboarding

Although sailboarding (often called Windsurfing, after the trademarked Windsurfer craft) is a relatively new sport, created in 1967, there are more than a half million board-sailors in the United States and close to three times that many world-wide. Within the past few years, the sport has outgrown its cult status, become an Olympic event, and has evolved into a legitimate recreational water activity that people of all ages can enjoy.

One of the best places to sailboard on the Jersey Shore is Barnegat Bay. A fair breeze usually blows there in the afternoon, and because it is not wide open like the ocean to the east, yet still wide enough to have fun, the bay has excellent sailboarding conditions. In addition, the water is usually calm, so the novice can learn the basics quickly. Of course, those who want to take the art of sailboarding a step or two further can sailboard in the ocean, where the advanced practice of wave jumping can be enjoyed.

Question:
What exactly is sailboarding?

Answer:
Sailboarding is a hybrid water sport that emphasizes the thrills of surfing and the finesse and grace of sailing. A board, much like a traditional surfboard, skims along the water as wind fills the sail, which is attached to a mast. The mast is at-tached to the board by way of a ball joint that enables it to move in all directions.

Question:
Can anyone learn to sailboard?

Answer:
Almost anyone. You need to be in fairly good physical condition. You need to know how to swim. You need to be patient. There are no other limitations, not even age.

Question:
Is it a good idea to take lessons?

Answer:
Yes. Learn the proper way and avoid acquiring bad habits. An instructor from a reputable sail-boarding shop like Windsurfing Bay Head (76 Bridge Avenue, 908–899–9394) will often begin with a lesson or two on land. He or she will explain to you the basics and help you get the "feel" of the board underneath your feet before you venture out onto the water.

Question:
How long will it take before I'm a capable sailboarder?

Answer:
That depends. Like anything else, some people pick up sailboarding quicker than others. How much you practice is another factor. Generally speaking, some initial lessons, perhaps 5 hours' worth, followed by 30 hours of practice on your own is enough for the

novice to feel fairly confident on a sailboard. With three months of regular practice, one should be able to handle all but the most challenging bay conditions.

Question:
Must I purchase a sailboard right away?

Answer:
No. You can rent one to get started and make sure you enjoy the sport. But eventually you'll want your own equipment. Ask for advice before sinking money into a sailboard and related equipment. They come in many different lengths, weights and styles. A newcomer to the sport should consider a board that's approximately 12 feet long and 40–45 pounds in weight. As for sails, you'll want a large sail, which is best for light winds. The average sail size for a beginner is about 60 square feet. Later on, you'll want to own other sails to meet specific wind conditions.

Question:
How much must I spend?

Answer:
Once again, that depends. You can expect to spend anywhere from $700 to $1300 for a board, sail, mast and boom. Buy only from a reputable boardsailing shop. Don't rule out used equipment, but know what you're buying.

Question:
Is sailboarding dangerous?

Answer:
Any water sport can be dangerous if proper precautions aren't taken. Generally, the worst that will happen to you is falling into the water. Good water safety is imperative, as is a basic knowledge and respect for wind, wave and water conditions and, as already noted, an ability to swim. One important safety rule for novices: Never sail alone.

Question:
When is the best time to sailboard at the Jersey Shore?

Answer:
The best seasons are spring and fall, when the wind is most consistent. Sailboarding, however, is most popular during the summer, when the air and water temperatures are warmest. You'll see, however, more and more boardsailors out on Barnegat Bay year-round.

Question:
How do I find out about contests and regattas?

Answer:
By checking with local shops in your area and subscribing to the sailboarding magazine *Wind Rider*. The N.J. Boardsailing Association sponsors contests in the summer and fall. Write to the association at P.O. Box 1558, Cranford, NJ 07016 for a contest calendar.

Ocean and Chadwick Beaches

These tiny communities with matchbox-size bungalows on miniature lots, sardine-packed in row after row of narrow lanes and one-way streets, are a far cry from what is found a mile or two north in Normandy Beach and Mantoloking, where many homes sit on large lots. These summer-only communities are bustling with activity June through September, but afterwards they become ghost towns. Along the northbound section of Route 35 are fast food eateries, laundromats, surf shops, shell shops, pizzerias and lots of real estate offices. In the late afternoon, when everyone is returning from a day at the beach, traffic is backed up while crossing guards halt cars to let pedestrians get across the highway. The southbound section of Route 35 is less congested because it's less commercialized. Barnegat Bay activities such as fishing, crabbing, sailboarding and boating originate here.

Surf's Up!

Although surfers populate the entire coastline of New Jersey and surf waves from Sandy Hook to the tip of Cape May, it's here on the Barnegat Peninsula where they ride the biggest and most challenging waves. Dozens of surf spots along the peninsula handle all types of swells. Many of the "spots" are "beach breaks," meaning a location where the waves are formed on sandbars and break fairly close to the beach. The waves of Island Beach State Park and those in Lavallette and the Seasides hit sandbars and form especially neat, cresting curls, ideal for all levels of surfing.

Perhaps the only place on the entire peninsula not suited for surfing is Point Pleasant Beach. Years ago, Point Pleasant Beach used to have top-notch surfing. Today, most of what is there now is known as "shore break," waves that curl right on the beach, thus leaving no room in which to ride them. Due to the loss of its offshore sandbars, its relatively deep water and the reconstruction of the nearby Manasquan Inlet jetty, the only swell that produces ridable waves in Point Pleasant Beach is one from the northeast.

Bay Head usually has one or two beaches with waves that are quite good. But, once again, due to shifting sandbar patterns, it's difficult to say which beach will be the best for surfing each year. Check with local surfers for the latest surf report. From Mantoloking down to Lavallette, the sandbar situation improves dramatically. One theory why the sandbars are so pronounced at this section of the peninsula is because there is no inlet or man-made jetties to disturb the currents and natural flow of sand. Therefore, waves in Lavallette are apt to be much more consistent than farther up the peninsula.

Lavallette and Ortley Beach

Lavallette possesses some of the cottage culture that comprises small beach towns like Chadwick and Normandy to its north. But it has a bit of a year-round population and a pleasant shopping district on Grand Central Avenue (Route 35 South) that makes the town something more than a summer-only community. Lavallette takes advantage of both the bay and ocean sides of town, perhaps more so than any other on the peninsula. Unlike communities such as Bay Head and Mantoloking, Lavallette has not permitted residential development of most of her bayshore. Instead, there's a wonderful waterfront park that provides all the activity space one would need for fishing and crabbing (two piers), boating (two launch ramps) and even swimming (there is a guarded beach).

As for Lavallette's beaches, they are very good for bodysurfing, since the offshore sandbars are out far enough to prevent waves from curling

In the Seasides, the best waves are found by the amusement pier, as already noted. During and immediately after storms or low pressure fronts, powerful waves often roll in on both sides of the pier, creating challenging conditions for surfers. You'll see the area's best surfers gliding down the faces of waves here, cranking radical turns and cutting off the lip of the curl.

The biggest problem surfers encounter on the Barnegat Peninsula is not lack of waves, but the permission to get to them. Due to private ownership of the beach and restrictions on those public beaches, surfers are often denied access during the day in the summer months. Some towns do designate certain beaches as "surfing beaches" (Bay Head and Lavallette, for instance), but such beaches don't necessarily produce the best waves.

Fortunately for surfers, surfing conditions along the Jersey Shore are best in the early morning hours and in late afternoon, so surfers and swimmers usually keep out of each other's way, and badge checkers are either not yet on duty or have gone home for the day. It's also during the early morning and late afternoon that the wind is most likely to be offshore, which makes for the best-shaped waves.

The best place to find out about up-to-the-minute surfing conditions (wind, tide, swell direction, wave size) is at a surf shop. The Barnegat Peninsula has four major shops that can give the visiting surfer advice as to where the best waves are and what the beach restrictions might be. Many of the shops also sponsor surf contests, as does the Eastern Surfing Association. Check surf shop bulletin boards for details and entry blanks.

on the shoreline as they do, say, in Point Pleasant Beach. Lavallette's waves break just right for catching a wave with just a few flaps of finned feet, or a few swift paddles while riding a raft, boogie board or surfboard. At the same time, children can frolic in the white water that gently washes ashore—the end product of the outside breakers—with little fear of being hit by one and knocked down.

Beach badges are available throughout the summer at Borough Hall (Grand Central and Washington avenues). One can purchase a badge for the season, half season, week or weekend. Badge fees are quite reasonable.

Ortley Beach is the next town south and is merely an extension of what is found in Lavallette. Its most noted landmark is **Joey Harrison's Surf Club** (1900 Ocean Avenue). With its extra large dance floor and its nightly live entertainment in the summer, it is one of the most popular nightspots in the area.

Seaside Heights

Seaside Heights' boardwalk is nearly as famous as its South Jersey Shore counterpart in Wildwood. Although the Wildwood boardwalk is longer (2½ miles as opposed to 1 mile in Seaside) and contains more amusement rides (five piers' worth as opposed to one in Seaside), the summer Saturday night thermometer (if such things existed) would certainly register as high in Seaside as it would in Wildwood.

The biggest reason for the parity is Seaside's intense concentration of activity. Seaside is a small town, so the moment one enters it, one has a strong sense of being surrounded, even overwhelmed, with flashing neon lights, blaring music, traffic, hustle, shrieks echoing from the Casino Pier as the roller coaster races downward and the alternating smell of salt air, pizza, caramel popcorn and amusement-ride grease.

Seaside is a fast, lively, action-packed town from June through August. It's a place where summer loves are won and lost and where families from North Jersey come, as they always have, for their annual two-week vacation at the Shore. At Seaside they spend the day on the beach, but the night belongs to the boardwalk. Like a religious ritual, families will live out a tiny part of the American Dream by spending and splurging and treating themselves to one thrill after another.

The boardwalk is like a large magnet that attracts visitors the moment they find a parking space—something that can be quite rare in the summer. Once you're on the boardwalk, though, it's just a matter of what appeals to you most—the rides, the wheels of chance, the arcades or the fast-food stands.

If it's the amusement rides, head straight to the Casino Pier, where the best ones are found. Here are some of the newest, fastest, most spine-tingling and stomach-shaking amusement rides north of Wildwood. Yet, despite all this, Seaside is most proud of the **Casino Pier Carousel.** Located in the **Casino Arcade,** between Grant and Sherman avenues on the boardwalk, the 80-year-old Carousel is truly a piece of Americana. A night spent on the boards wouldn't be complete without at least one ride on it. It is an antique amusement ride and certainly a classic; of the more than 10,000 carousels made during the golden age of carousels at the turn of the century, only 200 still exist. The wooden, brightly painted figures were handcarved, and the military band music you hear as you approach the carousel comes from an authentic Wurlitzer Band Organ built in 1923.

Carousel buffs from all over come to ride and photograph the Casino Pier Carousel. There's even a tiny gift shop where you can purchase figures, books and even albums of military music. One can only speculate how long the carousel will remain in Seaside Heights. Each year there's talk of breaking it down and selling the wooden horses, which can command up to $15,000 per horse at auctions.

If it's the wheel of chance you prefer, you can lay bets on a name or number for as little as a dime or as much as a dollar. The old saying "You get what you pay for" certainly applies here. A dime placed on a winner will get you a towel, a box of candy or, worse, a small plastic doll. But if it's a buck you're willing to bet, it's possible to win video cameras, bicycles or cassette players. The competition for your bet will be keen, whether it be a dime or a dollar, so expect to be hawked and hollered at as you pass by the many stands.

You can find skeeball and pinball and the latest selection of video games in any of the many arcades on the boardwalk. **Lucky Leo's** and **Sonny's and Rickey's** are popular haunts. The **Central Arcade,** the **Royal Arcade, Funtown Arcade** and **Big Top** are also worth exploring.

Finally, everyone succumbs to a boardwalk dinner at least once during their Seaside vacation. That might mean something as simple as a plain pizza or as complex as sausage-and-meatball sandwich smothered in tomato sauce and topped with melted cheese, peppers and onions. For dessert, there's candy apples, cotton candy, caramel popcorn or all of the above.

Seaside's beaches are wide (as wide as Jenkinson's in Point Pleasant Beach), usually clean, and open to the public on a day or season basis. Tags or badges can be purchased on the boardwalk at the entrance to the beach. You'll find excellent surfing on either side of the Casino Pier (but especially on the north side) and one of the best surf shops in all New Jersey in neighboring Seaside Park. Called **Grog's Surf Palace** (910 Central Avenue), the shop boasts a broad selection of the latest state-of-the-art surf equipment and the latest fashionable surfwear.

Seaside is also the unofficial waterslide capital of the north and central Jersey Shore. The **Water Works** complex across from the Casino Pier on Ocean Terrace is an incredible maze of water tubes and tunnels and corkscrew turns that will leave watersliders gasping for air. The big thrill, though, is to slide down the five-story Freefall and come splashing into a wading pool. Less adventurous types can opt for an inner-tube float down the Lazy River. In all, Water Works has 27 different slides, flumes and pools in the complex.

Aside from the boardwalk, there are four other main thoroughfares in town; each one runs north and south and gets very congested on weekends and holidays. Ocean Avenue and Ocean Terrace run parallel to each other and are closest to the boardwalk. Here can be found most of the bathhouses and pools, for those not inclined to sandy their feet or test the ocean's waters. The Boulevard contains the bulk of Seaside's nightclubs with **Club Masquerade** and **Temptations** (612 Boulevard) standing out among the others.

Central Avenue is where you'll find many of the hotels in Seaside Heights. You'll notice rather quickly that your choice of lodgings is limited. Motels, apartments or bungalows are essentially it. Seaside, in other words, has no bed and breakfasts or higher-priced luxury hotels. For a free list of accommodations and rates, write the Greater Toms River Chamber of Commerce (which includes Seaside Heights), 611 Main Street, Toms River, NJ 08753, and request a copy of the Central Ocean County, NJ, Visitor's Guide.

Recommended Barnegat Peninsula Surf Shops

Brave New World
1208 Richmond Avenue
Point Pleasant Beach 08742
(908) 892–9833

Grog's Surf Palace
910 Central Avenue
Seaside Park 08752
(908) 793–0097

Grog's Surf Palace on Broadway
210 Broadway
Point Pleasant Beach 08742
(908) 899–0003

New Image Surf 'N' Wear
Route 35 & West Osprey Avenue
Lavallette 08735
(908) 793–4822

Ocean Hut Surf Shop
3111 Route 35 North
Lavallette 08735
(908) 793–3400

Seaside Park

Although a neighbor of Seaside Heights, Seaside Park is much quieter and less hectic. It draws mostly summer residents who own bungalows or rent them for the season. Those who spend their summers there are in the enviable position of being within a short distance of Seaside Heights' boardwalk excitement and nightlife and of Island Beach State Park (see below).

Seaside Park's beaches are less crowded and take less abuse than those in Seaside Heights. The town's boardwalk has no amusements or concession stands, but it doesn't really need any of this, being so close to Seaside Heights. On the bay side of Seaside Park, sailboarding and sailing are quite popular.

Island Beach State Park

The most frequently asked question of park rangers by first-time visitors to Island Beach State Park is a good one: Where is the island? The fact is Island Beach State Park is not an island; it's situated at the south end of the Barnegat Peninsula. But remember too, Barnegat Peninsula is not really a peninsula. It's an island. So, technically speaking, Island Beach State Park is *located* on an island but is not an island in itself.

To make matters even more confusing, Island Beach was *once* an island. Back in 1720 during a particularly powerful storm, the ocean and bay met in what is now Ortley Beach; the two colliding bodies of water cut off Island Beach from the rest of the Barnegat Peninsula. The same storm closed New Inlet farther south. The new waterway was called Cranberry Inlet and quickly became a primary route for ships coming into or leaving Barnegat Bay. Historians tell us that pirates also valued the inlet and used it to enter Barnegat Bay.

Did you know that . . .

The summer mansion of the governor is located in Island Beach State Park.

In 1812, however, another heavy storm hit the Jersey coast and this time closed off Cranberry Inlet. Thus, Island Beach lost its island status, despite repeated attempts by man to reopen the waterway. Only one other time did Island Beach actually become island again. That was in 1935 when the bay met the ocean in what is today Island Beach State Park. This time locals wanted it closed and filled in the new inlet. Area rumrunners and bootleggers didn't like the idea much because they, like privateers and pirates years earlier, recognized the strategic value of such a link with the ocean. In 1962, the famous March Storm temporarily cut Island Beach into 11 separate islands, and every now and then during winter storms, a new inlet will be formed somewhere in Island Beach State Park. But as soon as the storm subsides, so does the water.

Island Beach might never have become a state park had Henry Phipps, a steel-making magnate and contemporary of Andrew Carnegie, realized his 1926 dream of making the area a grand beach resort for the wealthy. Phipps envisioned seashore mansions and bayside marinas filled with yachts. Fortunately for future visitors to Island Beach, Phipps' dream was shattered after the stock market crash in 1929.

In the years following the crash, little thought was given to other schemes that would have exploited Island Beach's vast natural beauty. People did reside on Island Beach in small beach shanties until World War II, when the Army came in and used the area to conduct experiments in antiaircraft rocketry. Immediately after the war, however, the Army gave up its interest in Island Beach. In 1953, the state purchased Island Beach from the Phipps Estate and, six years later, made it into a state park.

Today, Island Beach State Park is a vivid reminder of what the rest of the Barnegat Peninsula looked like prior to development. The park's precious sand dunes and such vegetation as red cedar, beach plum, American holly and wild black cherry, once common on the peninsula, are now just little more than a memory everywhere else.

Island Beach is not a large state park; it's approximately 10 miles long and less than a mile wide. The width varies, depending on where you are in the park. In some areas, it's barely more than 1,000 feet from bay to beach; in the southern part of the park, it's more than a mile wide. The park's main artery is the two-lane road that extends from the entrance gate to Central Avenue down almost, but not quite all the way, to Barnegat Inlet. Virtually all of the bay side of Island Beach State Park is off-limits to visitors. That's because Island Beach is as much a wildlife sanctuary and natural preserve as it is a day-use area for people.

Despite this restriction, Island Beach has plenty to offer. You'll find no place in New Jersey with more beautiful beaches. Long stretches of white, driftwood-dotted beaches with great sand dunes perched atop them make for a truly splendid setting. Behind these dunes is a secondary dune system overrun with dense thicket and berry bushes, which attract many different types of birds and small rodents.

During the summer, Island Beach is an exceedingly popular day-use area. It's quite common for the park to fill up its 2,400 parking spaces as early as 10 A.M. and therefore close Island Beach to vehicles. If you plan to visit the park, simply plan to get there as early as possible. Earlier than that on holidays. There is an admission charge year-round, although the fee is reduced in the off-season. Bicyclists and hikers are always admitted free.

Did you know that . . .

Eel grass, which once grew in abundance in Barnegat Bay, was dried out and used for house insulation to protect against cold winter winds the same way fiberglass insulation does today. Eel grass has the added advantage of being odorless and non-flammable. The Governor's Mansion in Island Beach State Park is insulated with eel grass. Unfortunately for the eel grass industry, a blight wiped out the bay's eel grass and ended harvesting of the plant. Today, however, eel grass, say marine biologists, is making a gradual comeback.

Things to Do

Spend the Day on the Beach. Island Beach has both guarded *and* unguarded beaches. If you wish to escape the crowds and venture off on your own, you can. But be advised, the currents offshore are tricky and often swift. No one should swim alone in unguarded waters. The guarded beaches—Ocean Bathing Units #1 and #2—have changing rooms, lockers and showers as well as concession stands. Skip the fast food and enjoy a beach picnic. Island Beach is one of the precious few state beaches where you are allowed to bring food onto the beach and barbecue as long as the fire is at least 50 feet east of the dunes. This is one of Island Beach's biggest selling points in the summer, and many people take advantage of the liberal park policy.

Visit the Aeolium. Approximately a mile south of the park's entrance is the Aeolium, a welcome center of sorts that includes displays pertaining to the history of Island Beach and the fragile ecological balance of the park. You'll also see exhibits that point out the various forms of wildlife that live in the park, and you can pick up a park map and information on such topics as bird-watching and beachcombing.

Walk a Self-guided Nature Trail. The trail that begins near the Aeolium is a good one to hike. Stay *on* the trail. If you walk through the brush and wander about on your own, you're certain to come into contact with poison ivy, damage plant life, and injure sand dunes. The dunes are any barrier island's most treasured resource. They protect the land from ocean storms and waves and beach erosion. The grass that grows on the dunes prevents the sand from being blown or washed away. To trample on it is to kill it. This seriously threatens the life of the sand dunes. If the sand dunes are threatened, then so is the very existence of the barrier island. (For more information on sand dunes, see chapter 8.)

For those who prefer guided tours, park naturalists conduct daily tours during the summer. Each tour lasts approximately an hour, is limited to some 25 people and usually originates at the Aeolium. Check at the Aeolium for times and types of tours available.

Go Bird-watching. Like so many other natural areas on the Jersey Shore, Island Beach is located on the Atlantic Flyway. Thus, in April and May, and then again in September and October, the park is filled with resting migratory birds. Either spring or fall is a good time to bird-watch at Island Beach. The number of people visiting the park is low, the birds are usually plentiful and the dreaded mosquito has not yet readied itself for its summer onslaught, or else has hopefully finished up its bloody business.

Island Beach also hosts bird-watchers in summer and winter. A number of nesting birds are in the thicket during the months of July and August, although much of this area is not open to visitors for obvious reasons. In the winter, you can travel down to the southern tip of the park and search out sea birds like the kittiwake and gannet. You can also find snowy owls there, as Island Beach seems to be one of their favorite haunts.

Go Scuba Diving. Scuba diving is permitted off Island Beach providing divers have proof of underwater diving training in the form of a valid certification card. Also, divers must adhere to certain rules in the park and waters offshore. Upon arriving, ask a park ranger for Island Beach's Diving Policy and Procedures Sheet.

Go Surfing. Island Beach offers experienced surfers the opportunity to enjoy their sport under the challenging conditions and with beautiful backdrops of sand dunes and beach thicket. Only seasoned surfers should surf Island Beach due to its strong currents. The waves are of the beach break type and usually best during a south swell.

Ride a Horse on the Beach. Island Beach is open to horses and horseback riders before and after the peak summer season, namely, from October 15 to April 15. Reservations must be made in advance by calling (908) 793–0506, as there are only a limited number of horses allowed on the beach at any one time. There is no extra charge for horses. Of course, horses are *not* to be ridden on sand dunes. There is a beach access path for riders to use. Ask a ranger for directions.

Go Beachcombing. Island Beach is an excellent place to walk on the beach and search for natural treasures. One can usually find an interesting assortment of shells and driftwood. Island Beach is also a particularly good place to find seahorses during the late summer and early fall. Once dried, the seahorse, like the starfish, is considered a prized find. During the winter, one might find what's known as *frost fish*. Frost fish are usually whiting that have either jumped out of the water onto the beach or have been beached by a wave. In any case, when the temperature is very low, these fish freeze almost instantly. Those who collect frost fish do so for eating purposes. Frost fish supposedly taste better than fish hooked and then frozen because the chemical interactions within the fish, which changes the taste of the fish, do not occur when the fish freezes to death.

Go Surf Fishing. Island Beach offers the angler some of the finest surf fishing on the Jersey Shore. Anglers are even permitted to take four-wheel drive vehicles on the beach. Taking advantage of this will only enhance the fishing trip because you'll be able to follow bluefish and striped bass runs down the beach. These occur in autumn, when mullet are found in large numbers just offshore. Mullet are what bring the blues into the surf. Some fishermen use metal lures, but the best bait, say experienced anglers, is exactly what the blues are looking to eat—mullet. Fishermen can get four-wheel drive permits at the front gate, provided they show proof the vehicle will be used for fishing purposes only. In other words, you must have fishing equipment on hand. Three-day permits, good for three *consecutive* days, and annual permits are available for a fee. Island Beach is open to fishermen 24 hours a day. Those who prefer to fish off a jetty rather than off the beach can do so at the very end of the park, where the north jetty of Barnegat Inlet is located.

If You Have a Boat. The bay side of Island Beach offers excellent crabbing. Beware, though, of very shallow water and the change of tides. One of the best places to snorkel on the Jersey Shore, believe it or not, is on the bay side of Island Beach. The water at Tice's Shoal is amazingly clear and full of marine life. Boaters also come to Tice's Shoal for a day of "boat parties." Often referred to as "Cocktail Cove," a number of boaters drop anchor here and spend the day sunning and sipping cocktails. Note: There is no boat launch at Island Beach State Park.

Where to Eat on the Barnegat Peninsula

Alfonso's, 1001 Arnold Avenue, Point Pleasant, (908) 892–4121
Price Code: Moderate   Menu: Italian
Alfonso's has a legion of locals who swear it's here you get the area's best pasta and Italian meat dishes.

Barmore's Shrimp Box, 75 Inlet Drive, Point Pleasant Beach,
(908) 899–1637

Price Code: Moderate   Menu: Seafood

Seafood of the traditional sort: stuffed flounder, lobster, fried clams. Waterfront dining. Almost always a wait in the summer.

The Bluffs, 575 East Avenue, Bay Head, (908) 892–1114

Price Code: Expensive   Menu: Continental

Dining on the oceanfront. Lamb and veal dishes are recommended. Pricey, but nice atmosphere.

Crab's Claw, 601 Grand Central Avenue, Lavallette, (908) 793–4447

Price Code: Moderate   Menu: Seafood

A reputable restaurant for seafood. Ideal for those vacationers in the Lavallette-Seaside area who don't wish to drive to Point Pleasant Beach for dinner.

Filomio's, 17 Inlet Drive, Point Pleasant Beach, (908) 892–2723

Price Code: Moderate/Expensive   Menu: Italian

Filomio's lasagne is legendary, but the real gems on the menu are the seafood dishes. Save room for dessert.

The Grenville Hotel, 345 Main Avenue, Bay Head, (908) 892–3100

Price Code: Expensive   Menu: Continental

Creative, gourmet dishes make the Grenville the talk of the Barnegat Peninsula. Jacket and tie; reservations a must.

Lobster Shanty, 83 Channel Drive, Point Pleasant Beach,
(908) 899–6700

Price Code: Moderate   Menu: Seafood

One of New Jersey's most popular seafood restaurants. Nautical decor, set on the Manasquan River. Buffet is a best bet.

The Southern House, Route 35 North and Washington Avenue,
Point Pleasant Beach, (908) 899–7427

Price Code: Moderate   Menu: Ribs

Family restaurant that serves the best barbecued ribs this side of Texas.

Spike's Fish Market and Restaurant, 415 Broadway, Point Pleasant Beach, (908) 295–9400

Price Code: Moderate　　　　　　　Menu: Seafood

Small restaurant on the Manasquan River that boasts big servings and the best Key lime pie on the Jersey Shore. Friendly atmosphere.

Tesauro's, 402 Broadway, Point Pleasant Beach, (908) 892–2090

Price Code: Moderate　　　　　　　Menu: Italian

Standard Italian menu; a favorite eatery with tourists and locals alike.

Wharfside, 101 Channel Drive, Point Pleasant Beach, (908) 892–9100

Price Code: Moderate　　　　　　　Menu: Seafood

Wharfside has its loyalists; so does the Lobster Shanty. Both are on Channel Drive; both are Jack Baker creations. Take your pick.

5

Long Beach Island

Long Beach Island is appropriately named. It is an island, a barrier island, which sits some four miles off southern Ocean County, connected
to the mainland by only a causeway, which stretches across lower
Barnegat Bay and Little Egg Harbor. Long Beach Island is indeed long—
some 18 miles long from the northern tip of Barnegat Light State Park to
the southern edge of the Holgate National Wildlife Refuge—not to mention skinny. Nowhere is it more than a mile wide. In fact, in many sections of the island, it's barely a half mile from beach to bay. And finally,
Long Beach Island is mostly beach—some of the finest beach found on
the Jersey Shore.

But what the name of the island doesn't do is reflect the intangibles,
such as Long Beach Island's unique character. Long Beach Island has little in common with its neighbors. There's virtually no resemblance to
the bright lights and fast pace of Seaside Heights to the north, for example, or to the glamor and gaudiness of Atlantic City to the south. There's
even little to suggest any sort of relationship to southern Ocean County
towns like Tuckerton and Manahawkin, which lie just across the bay,
other than one of necessity.

Perhaps because it is an island somewhat removed from the mainland and is somewhat isolated from the rest of the Jersey Shore (there
is only one way on and off the island—the Manahawkin Bridge), Long
Beach Island has an identity all its own. Some claim it's similar to that
found on Cape Cod. As on the Cape, those who vacation on Long Beach

Island usually return year after year. Most stay for weeks, rather than weekends or just the day. Some stay the summer.

On Long Beach Island, people know their summer neighbors and frequently socialize with them. It's a family-oriented island; except on weekends and holidays, it's strangely quiet and even a touch tranquil, especially in northern island towns like Barnegat Light and Loveladies. Long Beach Island has no boardwalks, just sand dunes peppered with beach grass and cottages that snuggle up behind them. There are few bars and nightclubs, but the island does have some fine restaurants. There is only one amusement area, and it's a small one at that.

To spend a week or so on Long Beach Island is to sample a wonderful sense of community that's rare in beach resort towns during the summer months. To spend a month or longer on the island is to actually become a part of that community. What's amazing is that it's as strong as it is, despite the influx of people onto Long Beach Island each summer. The island possesses a winter population of approximately 10,000. In the summer, that figure swells to 10 or 12 times that size.

Did you know that . . .

Because Long Beach Island is approximately four miles from the mainland, it is relatively free of pollen. Those who suffer from hay fever will find Long Beach Island much to their liking.

The island's main artery is Long Beach Boulevard, an asphalt ribbon that extends the length of the island. It loosely connects the string of beach towns, some of which have the most unusual of names (Ship Bottom, Harvey Cedars, Loveladies). On the boulevard is where you'll find many of the island's eateries, its specialty and gift shops and the stores that provide just about all of the essentials for one to remain on the island the *entire* summer. That means never *once* having to go over the Manahawkin Bridge and onto the mainland. It's no secret that islanders value their self-sufficiency, even if it doesn't run as deep as some would believe.

Venture to either side of the boulevard and you'll discover the most splendid collection of summer houses found on the Jersey Shore. In communities like Ship Bottom and Surf City are streets and lanes of white-washed cottages and well-kept beach bungalows. Down in Beach Haven and up in Barnegat Light, Victorian mansions remain from a century ago. In Harvey Cedars and Loveladies, you'll come across a dazzling assortment of luxurious, contemporary ocean and bay front homes. Most of them were constructed after the now legendary 1962 March

Storm, which decimated much of the island. All these homes were built on pilings to prevent in the future the millions of dollars in flood damage suffered during that memorable storm.

In between all this, two cultures coexist side by side, much as they do, once again, on Cape Cod. The most obvious of the two is the beach culture, which permeates every aspect of day-to-day Long Beach Island living. People come to Long Beach Island, first and foremost, to enjoy its excellent beaches and the activities that revolve around them.

In July and August, everyone sports a golden tan on Long Beach Island because a sunny day doesn't go by in which *some* time isn't spent on or near the beach. Long Beach Island has more than its share of sun bums. But it also supports very hearty surfing, bodysurfing, sailboarding, water skiing, jet skiing, and sailing crowds. And after the sun has gone down, surf fishermen, beachwalkers and beachcombers armed with metal detectors take over the beach along with kite-fliers when there's a decent breeze.

Over on the bay side of Long Beach Island is just as much activity. Some of the best clamming and crabbing waters north of Chesapeake Bay lie between the island and mainland towns like Tuckerton, Manahawkin, Barnegat and Waretown. Lower Barnegat Bay and Little Egg Harbor (which, together, are often known simply as "the bay") are dotted with tiny green islands that provide shelter and nesting areas for waterfowl and migratory birds.

Because of the bay's shallow waters, boat navigation can, at times, prove tricky. There are a number of hidden shoals. But these potential hazards don't prevent all sorts of pleasure craft and their crews from enjoying the bay's waters in spring, summer and fall. Charter and party boats are docked up and down the bay side of Long Beach Island, and the sails of sailboarders and sailboats fill out the scenery with their color. Water-skiers and jet-skiers zip across the water's surface at a fast clip, negotiating around the fishermen, crabbers and clammers in their rowboats. It all makes for a very busy bay.

The beach culture of Long Beach Island extends itself away from the Water's edge, too. Surf shops, shell shops, bait-and-tackle shops and a wide range of seafood restaurants can be found practically anywhere on the island. Clothing boutiques feature the latest surf 'n' sail fashions. Virtually every store, be it a grocery store or pharmacy, sells beach chairs, suntan lotion, bellyboards and children's sandpails. Even the names of the streets—Lagoon Drive, Beachview Street, Bay View Avenue, Nautilus Drive, Marina Boulevard, Sand Dune Drive—reflect Long Beach Island's beach culture.

But another culture thrives on the island in the summer, too. It's a bit less obvious than the island's beach culture and more refined and urban-influenced. It's one that enables such Long Beach Island institutions as Beach Haven's Surflight Theatre, which stages musicals and comedies throughout the season, and the unusually large number of art galleries to do more than simply survive.

Long Beach Island possesses museums, historical societies and cultural groups that sponsor lectures and seminars on island legend and lore, weekly outdoor concerts, poetry readings, art and sculpture instruction and dance classes. Artists show and discuss their work at the Long Beach Island Foundation of the Arts and Sciences. In short, the availability of beach alternatives makes Long Beach Island more than just an island of sun, surf and sand.

During the off-season, Long Beach Island is not nearly as busy or as crowded as it is during the summer, but it's just as inviting. Like anywhere on the Jersey Shore, September is an excellent time to visit Long Beach Island. The weather is usually gorgeous—warm days and cool, sweater nights—and the water temperature in the ocean is the warmest of the year. It's not unusual to swim in 75-degree water in early autumn on Long Beach Island.

Many restaurants, guesthouses and bed and breakfasts remain open throughout the fall. This is the time to go surf fishing, beachwalking and surfing. Bird-watchers make a point of getting down to the Holgate section of the Edwin B. Forsythe National Wildlife Refuge at least once during the fall. It's also a good time to visit the island's antique shops and other specialty shops, as many of them offer solid bargains on merchandise left over from the summer season.

Activity on the island slows down to a trickle in winter, but, by mid-March, summer is on many people's minds. Boaters are busy readying their boats for summer. Home owners are patching roofs and painting porches. Families from Philadelphia and West and North Jersey begin their search for a summer bungalow to rent. This continues until Memorial Day, when many islanders settle in for the summer.

The easiest way to get to Long Beach Island is via the Garden State Parkway (Exit 63) and Route 72 East. Once you leave the Parkway and get on Route 72, you'll pass through Manahawkin and drive over a causeway. This will take you over the lower reach of Barnegat Bay and Cedar Bonnet and Bonnet Islands. If you look to your left (north) as you ride over the causeway and Manahawkin Bay Bridge, you'll get a view of the Barnegat National Wildlife Refuge and the many tiny islands and marshland coves that it comprises.

The first thing you should do before beginning your visit or vacation on Long Beach Island is to stop at the Information Center, located on Ninth Street in Ship Bottom, just a few hundred yards from the Manahawkin Bridge. It's open seven days a week, year-round. Here, you can get up-to-the-minute information on lodging and a calendar of events that will list times and places for such things as fishing tournaments, fairs, surfing contests and lifeguard competitions. Also available are copies of Long Beach Island's three weekly newspapers. The *Sandpiper, Beachcomber* and *Summer Times* are all free and provide excellent coverage of island life and activities.

You can also pick up information on weekly and season beach badge fees. Badges, however, are not sold at the Information Center. Instead, they're available at the municipal offices of the towns of Long Beach Island. Prices for beach badges on the island are quite cheap, especially when compared to the prices of badges sold at other Jersey beach resorts. Expect to pay less than $15 for a full season badge, no matter what municipality you purchase it from. Badges are not required for children under 12, and some Long Beach Island towns offer special discounts to senior citizens. Badges are good only in the town where they are purchased.

Once you get your bearings (don't forget to pick up a free map of the island at the Information Center), you'll have to decide which part of Long Beach Island you plan to explore first. The town of Ship Bottom sits almost in the middle of the island. If you make a left on Long Beach Boulevard, you'll head north and go toward Barnegat Light State Park and such beach communities as Harvey Cedars and Loveladies. A right turn on the boulevard will take you in the direction of Beach Haven and Holgate.

Barnegat Light State Park

At the northern tip of Long Beach Island lies Barnegat Light State Park, home of **Old Barney,** the famous lighthouse. Barnegat Light is New Jersey's smallest state park; it consists of only 36 acres. Nonetheless, it's a very popular park, mostly because of the lighthouse, which is easily Long Beach Island's most noted landmark. Over the years, Old Barney has become one of the most photographed and painted lighthouses in America.

Old Barney, though, isn't the original lighthouse to beam a light from the top of Long Beach Island. The first was quite smaller than Old Barney and much less sturdy. It was constructed in 1834; in 1856 it collapsed after a storm.

Old Barney was begun in 1857 and completed a year later. Designed by Gen. George Gordon Meade, the Yankee Civil War hero known for his victory at Gettysburg, the new lighthouse was built to last. Meade constructed it so that its stability was "nine times stronger than is required

A Short History of Long Beach Island

The Dutch were the first Europeans to sight and then settle on the spit of land that came to be known as Long Beach Island. But it was New England whalers who were the first to exploit the island's chief natural resource, namely, its proximity to migratory whale routes. As a result, whaling was the first real industry begun on Long Beach Island.

There were three known whaling stations on the island. With crews on land ready to launch whaleboats from the beach the moment a whale was sighted, and other crews aboard whaling ships offshore, the whaling industry was a thriving one. Most people living on the island in the eighteenth century were connected to whaling in one way or another.

Whaling, however, began to die out on Long Beach Island in the early part of the nineteenth century. What essentially followed was the growth of tourism, which, today, is still the island's number-one source of revenue. Hunters frequented Long Beach Island in search of ducks and birds, and fishermen caught plenty of fish, both in the shallows of the bay and in the ocean's surf. The earliest Long Beach Island guesthouse, built at the beginning of the 1800s, was for hunters and fishermen. Another one was built in 1822. Known as the Mansion of Health, it stood on land in what is today Surf City.

By the mid-1800s, a stagecoach route was begun by enterprising Philadelphians to bring outdoorsmen and their families from the city of Brotherly Love and nearby Camden to the bay town of Tuckerton. From there, island-bound visitors were taken across the bay in a boat.

Tourism picked up substantially when a railroad bridge was completed across Barnegat Bay. A rail line was also established in Beach Haven; it ran north to Barnegat Light and was a main means of transportation on the island for years. During this time people stayed at the Harvey Cedars Hotel, the Engleside and the Spray Beach Hotel. By the end of the century, Beach Haven established itself as the island's main tourist town. In addition to staying in hotels there people began building Victorian summer homes and seaside cottages and stayed the summer.

While tourism was being developed on Long Beach Island, there was another, shall we say, "alternative" means of making a living, at least according to local legend. Those involved were known as Barnegat Pirates or "wreckers" and "mooncussers," as David J. Seibold and Charles Adams III tell it in their delightful little book, *Legends of Long Beach Island.*

According to the authors (who also wrote *Shipwrecks Near Barnegat Inlet,* another book dealing with Long Beach Island history and lore), "The wreckers waited until a moonless night . . . the lights of the ships offshore were visible, as they sailed the busy shipping lanes north and south of New York. These ships tried to cut their sailing times and distance by coasting as close to the shore as possible, avoiding any of the navigational hazards that could bring a voyage to an abrupt and tragic halt."

The Barnegat Pirates knew all about such shortcuts. Accordingly, these shady characters would tie a lantern to a mule or ox and walk it up and down the shoreline. Occasionally a passing sea captain would spot it and think the light to be from a nearby ship. He might have ordered his ship toward it, hoping to get a better view of it and gain a route even closer to the shore. It was too late when he realized the dastardly trick that was played on him. Usually the ship was wrecked on the shoals or else broken into pieces by waves and ultimately beached. The pirates then looted the ship, which most likely carried valuable cargo.

There's little to prove convincingly that such acts of piracy and sometimes murder did indeed occur, as Seibold and Adams carefully point out. Chances are, however, some of this did go on. Similar stories circulate of pirates performing the same evil deeds on Cape Cod and Cape Hatteras. And there have been a lot of shipwrecks off Long Beach Island. But until more research is done on the subject, the truth about the Barnegat Pirates will remain shrouded in mystery.

Despite such grim tales, Long Beach Island continued to prosper as a summer tourist resort. The Barnegat Lighthouse, affectionately known as Old Barney, became increasingly popular with visitors. Bird-watchers and boaters enjoyed the bay side of the island. By the 1950s sunbathers and swimmers filled the island's beaches.

But it was the construction of the Manahawkin Bay Bridge and the completion of the Garden State Parkway that brought even more people to Long Beach Island in the summer. These two factors, coupled with the widespread reputation the island possessed (and still does) for its all-around beauty, today make Long Beach Island one of the Shore's most prized possessions.

to resist the maximum force of the wind," that element of nature that helped cause the destruction of the original lighthouse.

Old Barney's white beam, derived from a kerosene lamp of 16,000 candlepower, could be seen nearly 30 miles out at sea. It provided a reliable point of reference for ships offshore and remained in operation for 69 years. In 1927, a lightship stationed off the coast forced it into retirement. But then during World War II, Old Barney was taken over by the U.S. Coast Guard. It was used as a lookout tower for surfacing German U-boats. The vigil staged by the Coast Guard atop the lighthouse wasn't entirely successful, however. In 1942, two tankers were sunk off Barnegat Light by German torpedos.

Visitors are permitted to climb the 217 steps that lead to the top of the lighthouse. The lens, however, is no longer there. It's on display at the Barnegat Light Historical Museum, located a half-mile south of the park on Central Avenue in the town of Barnegat Light. Still, the climb to the top is well worth the effort. From there, one is treated to a sweeping view of Barnegat Bay, Island Beach State Park and virtually all of Long Beach Island.

Enter the park on Broadway Avenue. In the summer, there is a small admission charge. The park is open year-round, although the lighthouse closes sometime in October.

Things to Do

Climb Old Barney. One doesn't have to climb all the way to the top to enjoy the vista. Small rest areas on the stairwell have portholes. But climbing to the second and third porthole will give the visitor a pretty good idea of just how narrow Long Beach Island really is. Along with Twin Lights and Mount Mitchill in the Highlands, Old Barney offers the best bird's-eye view of the Jersey Shore.

Go Swimming. In front of the lighthouse is a small beach area. Due to the shifting nature of sand, a small sandbar formed during a winter storm a few years ago, which makes the water wonderfully calm—perfect for small children and senior citizens. Lifeguards are on duty during the summer. Bathhouses, showers and lockers are available.

Have a Picnic. Picnic tables are situated on the rim of Barnegat Inlet. The view is that of Barnegat Bay and neighboring Island Beach State Park.

Boat Watch. During the summer and on weekends in the spring and fall, Barnegat Inlet is filled with boats. You'll see both pleasure craft and commercial fishing boats as well as the occasional Coast Guard cutter. Despite its popularity, the inlet is one of the most dangerous inlets to navigate on the coast. In bad weather, it's downright dangerous to pass through due to its many shoals and strong currents.

Beach Walk. You're not apt to find anything unusual on a July weekend, save a few odd pieces of driftwood. But after a storm, all sorts of things wash ashore here.

Go Fishing. Anglers have the choice of fishing from the inlet jetty, where weakfish and occasional stripers are hooked, or from the beach, where fluke, bass and bluefish are commonly caught.

Barnegat Light

Directly below Barnegat Light State Park is the town of Barnegat Light. Known as Barnegat City until 1948, it has some of Long Beach Island's best beaches, a number of old Victorian homes, some of which were once owned by local sea captains, one of the island's two museums and a large portion of the area's commercial fishing industry.

Barnegat Light's main historical significance, of course, is its connection to Old Barney. But an incident in the revolutionary war occurred here in 1782 that has also secured Barnegat Light a place in New Jersey history. In what has been labeled the Long Beach Massacre, Capt. Andrew Steel and his band of men, who slept on the beach after taking ashore cargo from a grounded British vessel raided by American privateers, were murdered by Tory sympathizer John Bacon and his men. Twenty-one American patriots were killed in the darkness, and the mass murder has haunted the island's history ever since. A plaque commemorating the event and honoring the Americans killed is in Barnegat Light State Park.

There are only two main thoroughfares in Barnegat Light. One is Long Beach Boulevard (called Central Avenue in Barnegat Light), which leads visitors to the entrance of the park. The other is Bay View Boulevard, which meanders along the bay side of Barnegat Light. After a visit to Old Barney and the park, a drive along Bay View Boulevard is recommended. It's here where the town's string of small marinas can be found. Docked in them are charter fishing boats, private craft and small boats that can be rented by the day. **Kubel's Bar** on Seventh Street and Bay View is a favorite hangout for local anglers, commercial and amateur alike, and a great place to trade fishing information.

Farther south on Bay View, past the Barnegat Coast Guard Station, is Viking Village, home of Barnegat Light's tile fishing fleet. Barnegat Light is called the Tile Fish Capital of the World. The bright-colored, speckled bottom fish, which taste something akin to red snapper or grouper (some even say lobster, but that's stretching it a bit) and used to go by the name leopard fish, was brought back into fish markets by local fisherman Lou Puskas. Almost singlehandedly, he resparked a demand for the fish that had all but disappeared years ago.

Some of the world's prime tile fishing grounds are located in the huge underwater canyons (Hudson, Veatch and Oceanographer) that lie off the Mid-Atlantic coast of the United States and within reach of Barnegat Light fishermen. Puskas, and later other local fishermen, began bringing in tile fish after Russian fishing trawlers practically destroyed the living they made fishing for cod. Puskas and other Barnegat Light fishermen hauled the tile fish catch up to New York's Fulton Fish Market and the demand for the fish grew in the 1970s and 1980s.

You can purchase fresh tile fish at **Cassidy's Viking Village Fish Market** (18th Avenue and Bay View Boulevard), which buys the fish directly from the dozen or so tile fish boats that call Viking Village home.

Also in Viking Village is a small group of shanties where nautical items, antiques, beach bric-a-brac and paintings are sold and where visitors to the island can sign up for a **whale-watching cruise** aboard the *Miss Barnegat Light*. This 95-foot catamaran, which doubles as a party fishing boat on days when whales haven't been spotted offshore, makes all-day trips out some 50 miles offshore, where humpback, finback and minke whales are frequently sighted. Don't be surprised if you also spot schools of dolphins to and from whale-sighting spots. For reservations and more information on the *Miss Barnegat Light* whale-watching cruises, call (800) 325–SEAS. Walk-on tickets for the cruise can be purchased at the Whale-Watching Shanty next to Cassidy's Fish Market in Viking Village.

Over on Central Avenue is the **Barnegat Light Historical Museum** (5th and Central avenues). The former one-room schoolhouse is a small museum, but those interested in local history will find a visit rewarding. An exhibit depicts life from Long Beach Island's Victorian past, and any number of old photographs show the island's Life Saving Service crew in action. But the museum's biggest attraction is the original lens of Old Barney. Also, a number of relics, photographs and documents trace the history of the lighthouse and the museum's attempt to track down and obtain the lens after it was removed from the structure some years ago.

The **Edith Duff Gwinn Gardens** are located behind the museum and are cared for by friends of the fondly remembered local environmentalist and botanist. No admission is charged to either the museum or gardens, although the former has a very limited schedule in the summer and fall and is not open in the winter or spring. Check with the Information Center in Ship Bottom for opening and closing times, or else call (609) 494–3407.

Loveladies

Most people who visit Long Beach Island are amused by the peculiar names of some of its towns. The name Loveladies is indeed unusual. But unlike Ship Bottom, which has as unusual a story of how the town was so named as the name itself, Loveladies was simply named after a hunter, Thomas Lovelady, who used to hunt ducks in the area.

Loveladies possesses an altogether different kind of charm from her neighbor, Barnegat Light. Because the town bore such a large part of Mother Nature's wrath in the 1962 storm, virtually all traces of Loveladies' past were swept away by the ocean. Residents and newcomers to the town rebuilt it, and in Loveladies today you will see the most thorough display of contemporary seashore summer homes found anywhere on the Jersey Shore.

Most of these summer homes are examples of bold, even spectacular architectural design. The shapes and sizes of the structures vary tremendously. Some are truly grand and most beautiful to look at with their strange angles, extraordinary curvatures and sweeping views of the ocean. Others could only be described as extreme, depending, of course, on one's taste and architectural fancy.

Loveladies is mostly residential; there are really no places for the weekend visitor, for example, to rent a room. Those wishing to stay in the Loveladies area will have to look in Barnegat Light or Surf City and Ship Bottom for lodging.

While visiting or merely passing through Loveladies, a stop at the Long Beach Foundation of the Arts and Sciences (120 Long Beach Boulevard) is recommended. The foundation is the hub of cultural activity on the northern part of the island. Aside from the various courses in art, yoga and even marine biology that are open to summer and year-round residents, exhibits and lectures are also presented as well as an annual Seashore Open House Tour that is especially popular. Many of the events and activities sponsored by the foundation have fees, but they are quite reasonable. Stop by the foundation office for a calendar of events; you'll notice that something's going on practically every day.

Harvey Cedars

Today, the name Harvey Cedars is a misnomer. No red cedars are left, although in the nineteenth century, many of these stood tall on this part of the island. That explains at least where the *Cedars* part of the town's name comes from. As for *Harvey*, the town was originally known as Harvey's Whaling Quarters. Legend has it that a cave dweller named Daniel Harvey was one of the area's first inhabitants.

Some of Long Beach Island's earliest settlers—whalers from New England—settled here. From the shore, whales would be spotted by lookouts and the hunt would begin. Unfortunately, very little remains in Harvey Cedars that recalls its whaling heritage. (Some relics and tools can be found, however, in the Long Beach Island Historical Museum in

Beach Haven.) Storms accounted for much of the area's destruction over the years.

About the only prominent building that remains from those days is the Harvey Cedar Hotel, located on the bay side of town. Today it's known as the **Harvey Cedars Bible Conference Center.** Another old building, the headquarters of the Long Beach Island Fishing Club, was once a Life Saving Service Station. It's located on Long Beach Boulevard.

Surf City

No, the Beach Boys' Brian Wilson didn't compose the classic 1960s pop song, "Surf City," for singers Jan and Dean with this Long Beach Island town in mind. He could have, though. Surf City has all the elements of the surf town Jan Berry and Dean Torrence sang about, with the possible exception of "two girls for every boy."

Surf City also possesses a whaling history as strong as Harvey Cedars, but once again, due to storms, few reminders of its past can be found except what's in the Long Beach Island Historical Museum. Originally, the area where Surf City now sits was known as the Great Swamp. Its name was then changed to Long Beach City and, finally, Surf City. The term *City,* though, is really misleading. Fewer than 500 residents live in Surf City year-round, although the population bulges to perhaps 10 or 15 times that during the summer.

A small shopping area in Surf City caters to those who summer on the north part of Long Beach Island. Stores carry a full line of beach essentials, and there's also lodging and a number of places to eat here. Almost everything is located on or very near Long Beach Boulevard.

Not only does Surf City have excellent beaches on the ocean, but there's a delightful bay beach at the end of 16th Street that is just right for small children. The water there is shallow and calm and the beach filled with families. It's also a great place to watch the sun set each evening as well as boat-watch on the bay.

Ship Bottom

Ship Bottom, one of the largest year-round communities on Long Beach Island, is also the commercial center of the island. As already noted, the legend behind the name Ship Bottom is a strange one. It seems that sometime in the early 1800s, a bottom-up boat washed ashore, a victim of the dreaded Barnegat Shoals. When islanders went to investigate the shipwreck, they heard a frantic knocking from within the hull. Immediately they broke a hole through it and found a beautiful Spanish-speaking woman inside, the ship's only survivor.

Treasure Hunting

Beachcombing, or "treasure hunting," as it's also called, has become increasingly popular over the past few years. By slowly skimming sections of the beach with a metal detector, treasure hunters often find coins, rings, bracelets and other pieces of jewelry, as well as silverware and other valuable trinkets buried beneath the sand. They also find bottlecaps, nails and an assortment of other useless pieces of metallic junk. As any treasure hunter will admit, "you take the good with the bad."

Few beachcombers or treasure hunters expect to strike it rich. But it's the thrill of possibly discovering that diamond ring or sixteenth-century Spanish coin, in addition to the relaxation and gentle form of exercise that accompanies it, that makes treasure hunting so popular at the Jersey Shore.

What You'll Need: A metal detector (prices range from $150 to as high as $1,000) plus accessories, such as headphones, a sand scoop, sifter, prober and patience.

How to Do It: Locate a section of the beach where crowds normally congregate. Turn on the metal detector and walk across the sand, moving it in a slow, wandlike manner. Plan out the area you intend to beachcomb so as to be sure the same stretch of beach isn't covered twice. When you hear a beep, or if your meter indicates something metallic underneath your metal detector, scoop up the sand, let it filter through your sifter and see what you've found. Experienced treasure hunters might simply stick their prober into the sand and determine whether or not the object is worth scooping out.

When to Go: The best time to treasure hunt with a metal detector is immediately after a storm or after an unusually high tide, if you're most interested in finding things that wash up onshore. Those looking for lost jewelry and money should wait until late afternoon or dusk after the beach has emptied. Weekends are better than weekdays. Longtime treasure hunters like to take out their metal detectors just after sudden thunderstorms when people scurry from the beach seeking cover from rain and lightning. They're not as apt to be careful packing up their belongings, and they often drop into the sand things of value.

Beach Haven

The southern half of Long Beach Island is dominated by Beach Haven. It is the busiest beach town on the island during the summer because it contains the most accommodations, the island's only amusement area, lots of restaurants, nightclubs and fine beaches.

A balanced blend of old and new exists in Beach Haven; the town boasts a historical district in which you'll find the bulk of its remaining Victorian seashore homes as well as its bed and breakfasts and guesthouses. Yet, there are also a number of newer homes and commercial establishments in town and a definite commitment to tourism.

Like all other Long Beach Island towns, Long Beach Boulevard is Beach Haven's principal thoroughfare, although it's called Bay Avenue in Beach Haven. On it can be found many of the town's shops and restaurants and **Fantasy Island Amusement Park** and the **Pier 18 Mall.** Centre Street and Engleside Avenue are important streets, too. They intersect Bay Avenue in the town's center. The east or ocean side of these two streets contains much of the Beach Haven historical district. These streets and those adjoining them are delightfully kept; many of them have lawns and white picket fences and possess a quality not unlike what you'll find in Bay Head on the Barnegat Peninsula (see chapter 4).

In this section, you'll also find the **Long Beach Island Historical Museum,** the **Surflight Theatre, Bicentennial Park** and some of Beach Haven's excellent beaches. There are bicycle lanes on Bay Avenue and Atlantic Avenue. By renting a bike or riding your own, you'll be able to get much more than a glimpse of the nicest section of Beach Haven.

Things to Do

Visit the Long Beach Island Historical Museum. Housed in an old church, a number of fine exhibits pertain to Victorian Long Beach Island, its commercial fishing industry and the golden age of whaling. But what seems to capture the attention of most visitors to the museum is the collection of photographs and charts that vividly tell the story of the March 1962 storm. Aerial photographs show the astonishing amount of beach erosion that occurred and the number of homes that were washed away by waves and high tides. There are even photos of two naval warships grounded on the beach. On a rainy or cloudy day, expect to find the museum fairly crowded. Young children can play in a special hands-on, kiddie corner where they can learn a bit about island history at the same time. The museum is located on Engleside and Beach avenues and has an admission charge. For museum hours, call (609) 492–0700.

Take a Walking Tour of the Victorian Historical District. After visiting the Long Beach Historical Museum, purchase the pamphlet, *Walking Tour of Beach Haven,* available at the curator's desk. The museum sits smack in the center of the historical district; therefore, the tour begins right outside the museum. Actually, there are two walking tours to choose from. One includes 16 homes; the other, 27. All the homes on both tours were built prior to 1900 and are fine examples of Victorian and traditional seashore colonial homes. Because all the houses are privately owned, the tour doesn't include entrance into any of them.

Homes of particular interest in the walking tour include the island's first **Life Saving Service Station,** built in 1848 in Harvey Cedars and later brought down to its present location at 509 Old Dock Road; the only **salt box home** on Long Beach Island at 114 Second Street; and the **Magnolia House** at 215 Centre Street, one of the island's oldest boarding houses and presently a bed and breakfast.

Attend a Historical/Cultural Lecture. Each summer the Long Beach Island Historical Association sponsors a number of superb programs that do much to keep the Shore's culture and heritage alive as well as to entertain vacationers and year-round residents alike. Lectures such as "Spools, Ghoulies, and Things that Make Noise in the Night," "The History of the Life Saving Service" and "The Wreck of the *Fortuna*" attract enthusiastic crowds. Most of the presentations are free and occur during the evening. The association also sponsors a Victorian Porch Party, a garden party, craft shows and flea markets. For complete information on this summer's programs, contact the Historical Association at P.O. Box 232, Ship Bottom 08008.

Attend a Play at the Surflight Theatre. The Surflight Theatre is a Long Beach Island institution. Its predecessor, the Joseph P. Hayes Surflight Summer Theatre, was founded more than 40 years ago by Hayes, an aspiring actor and stage impresario. It was Hayes' intention to bring first-rate theatrical entertainment to Long Beach Island during the summer. Almost from the beginning, his little theater succeeded beyond his expectations. A number of soon-to-be-famous actors and actresses performed on the Surflight stage, including Joan Crawford and David Hartman.

Hayes died in 1976, but his theater lives on. Plays used to be held in a hot, converted mechanic's garage on sticky summer nights. The audience sat on stiff, metal folding chairs. Today, productions are staged in a modern, air-conditioned theater next door to Hayes' old theater. Located on the corner of Engleside and Beach avenues, Surflight now operates from March through December and presents some 15 shows a year, not including children's productions of classics such as *Peter Pan, Snow White and the Seven Dwarfs,* and *Cinderella.*

New York actors and actresses audition for positions in the Surflight Company; those selected move down to Long Beach Island for the season and perform in most of the productions. Walk past the theater patio area on any given morning or early afternoon, and you're almost certain to find actors and actresses wrestling with new lines and song lyrics.

For reservations and a copy of the Surflight's production calendar, call the box office at (609) 492–9477, or write to Surflight Theatre, P.O. Box 155, Beach Haven, NJ 08008.

Have a Hot-fudge Sundae and Watch Another Show. Next to the Surflight, on Beach and Centre streets, is the **Show Place** (609–492–0018), Long Beach Island's most popular ice-cream parlor. From Memorial Day

Weekend through Labor Day Weekend, college-age waiters and waitresses will bring you your favorite ice-cream dish and sing and dance a few numbers, too. Sometimes patrons are asked to join in, and that's when the fun really starts rolling. Expect a line to get in on weekend nights, but the wait is well worth it.

On your way home, stop in at **Seafarin' Sweets,** located behind the Show Place, and pick up a bag of famous Fralinger's saltwater taffy, the only place on Long Beach Island where you can get the chewy treat. Adjacent to both the Show Place and Seafarin' Sweets is the **Alliance for a Living Ocean** shop, which sells T-shirts, sweatshirts, mugs, posters and other gifts with ecological themes. The Alliance for a Living Ocean is a nonprofit organization dedicated to saving the ocean and Long Beach Island's beaches from pollution and misuse. Shop profits fund numerous environmental awareness programs sponsored by the Alliance.

Attend an Outdoor Summer Concert. Every Saturday evening, weather permitting, the Beach Haven Bicentennial Park Association sponsors a free concert in **Bicentennial Park** (Beach Avenue, between Engleside and Amber streets). Dixieland jazz, big band, orchestral music and Pine Barrens folk music are usually heard from the bandshell throughout the season. The concerts run from mid-June through the end of August.

Take the Kids to Fantasy Island. Long Beach Island's only amusement area is small and aimed at kids under 12. The park boasts a dozen amusement rides, a casino arcade, a miniature golf course, some wheels of chance and a Victorian ice cream parlour. Next to Fantasy Island is the **Thundering Surf Water Slide,** also a popular attraction for kids. There is no admission charge to Fantasy Island, though there is one for Thundering Surf.

Go Shopping in the Pier 18 Mall. Located on the corner of Bay Avenue and Third Street, the Pier 18 Mall contains more than 50 shops and fast-food stands. You can buy anything from a hot dog smothered in onions to fresh cherrystone clams on the half shell. You can also purchase clothes, beach accessories, nautical knick-knacks and much, much more. A great place to spend a rainy summer afternoon.

Did you know that . . .

Tucker's Island is frequently called the Jersey Shore's Atlantis.

Take a Boat Trip to Atlantic City. One of the more popular attractions on the bay side of Beach Haven is to step aboard a party boat called the *Black Whale III* for a fun ride to and from Trump Castle in Atlantic City. There you can spend the day playing blackjack or stuffing

Tucker's Island

Tucker's Island *used* to be an island; today it is under the Atlantic Ocean, as good an example of the unpredictable nature of barrier islands as you're apt to find. Back in the late 1800s, Tucker's Island, also known as Sea Haven, Short Beach and Tucker's Beach, played an important role in the rescue of hundreds of people from the frequent shipwrecks that occurred off Long Beach Island.

The island was inhabited by members of the U.S. Life Saving Service and their families. The Tucker's Island crew performed rescue operations for some 200 shipwrecks between 1869 and 1915. There was a 50-foot lighthouse at the Life Saving Service Station, which, with Old Barney on the north end of the island, provided valuable beacons for ships passing in the night.

At one time, Tucker's Island was actually part of Long Beach Island. But nor'easters gradually created what is today known as Beach Haven Inlet, and Tucker's Beach became Tucker's Island. From that point on, it was just a matter of time before the ocean began eating away the island. By the turn of the century, beach erosion was so great that the inhabitants were forced to leave and resettle on the mainland. One by one, the buildings on Tucker's Island fell into the sea. In 1935, the life saving station, which was the last building standing on Tucker's Island, was destroyed by storm waves. In 1955, the whole island disappeared under the Atlantic.

nickels or quarters into slot machines or just plain stroll the famous Atlantic City boardwalk. The *Black Whale III* is moored at the Beach Haven Fishing Center on the bay at the end of Centre Street. Reservations are highly encouraged. For information, call (609) 492–0333.

The Holgate Section of the Edwin B. Forsythe National Wildlife Refuge

This 2½-mile stretch of barrier beach and tidal saltmarsh sits at the southern tip of Long Beach Island. Along with a small portion of Barnegat Light State Park, Holgate is the only undeveloped barrier-beach tract on the island.

Because it's designated primarily for the survival of wildlife, there are no basic amenities like bathrooms or a visitor center, even though the public *is* encouraged to visit Holgate. Wildlife Refuge officers patrol the beach in four-wheel drive Jeeps. They'll answer any questions you might have about Holgate's delicate ecosystem. They'll also hand out a summons to anyone who disobeys rules that prohibit walking on the sand dunes and disrupting the nesting sites of birds. **Note:** Holgate is closed to visitors from April through August to preserve the nesting sites of the endangered piping plover.

Things to Do

Bird-watch. Three birds on New Jersey's Endangered Species List— the piping plover, the black skimmer and the least tern—nest at Holgate and can be seen (with binoculars) beyond the fence when Holgate is closed to pedestrian traffic during the summer. Many other migratory birds use Holgate as a rest-and-feed stop in the fall and then later in the spring. Other birds one might see during the summer: the snowy egret, peregrine falcon, great blue heron, American oystercatcher, glossy ibis and great black-backed gull. For a complete list of birds that frequent Holgate, stop at the Visitor Center of the Edwin B. Forsythe National Wildlife Refuge Area one mile east of Route 9 in Oceanville.

Walk the Beach. A walk from one end of Holgate to the other will un- doubtedly tire most people's legs; it is, after all, a five-mile round trip in soft sand. But for those who enjoy early morning beachwalks or walks at dusk, Holgate is the very best place to walk and you don't have to walk *all* the way to the end of the refuge.

Treasure Hunt. A number of Spanish coins have been found on the beach here over the years. There are tales of buried treasure, but it's more likely that the coins are from sunken Spanish galleons off the coast. The best time to sift the sand is immediately after a storm.

Go Surfing. Some of the best waves found on Long Beach Island are at Holgate. Be advised, however, that there are no lifeguards on the beach and currents can be a problem. Swimming is not recommended here for the very same reason, although experienced bodysurfers do go into the water at their own risk.

Go Boardsailing. When the wind is right, boardsailors find Holgate quite exciting, especially if there is a small swell running which allows for wave jumping and wave riding.

Where to Eat on Long Beach Island

Bayberry Inn, 13th Street and Long Beach Boulevard, Ship Bottom (609) 494–8848
Price Code: Moderate   Menu: Continental-American
One of the more popular restaurants on Long Beach Island. Especially enticing are the crab and lobster dishes.

Harvey Cedars Shellfish Company, 7904 Long Beach Boulevard
Harvey Cedars, (609) 494–7112
Price Code: Moderate   Menu: Seafood
More than one Long Beach Islander will tell you this is the island's best restaurant, seafood or otherwise. Informal dining, large portions, almost everything is delicious.

Octopus's Garden, 414 Long Beach Boulevard, Surf City
(609) 494–8191
Price Code: Moderate   Menu: Mostly seafood
An interesting menu, friendly service and specialties such as scallops sautéed with artichoke hearts make the Octopus's Garden one of Long Beach Island's culinary delights.

Owl Tree, 7908 Long Beach Boulevard, Harvey Cedars
(609) 494–8191
Price Code: Moderate   Menu: Continental-American
House specialties include grilled swordfish and rack of lamb. Menu goes beyond the typical.

Panzone's Pizza, 1100 North Bay Boulevard
Beach Haven
(609) 492–5103
Price Code: Inexpensive   Menu: Pizza
For pizza, Panzone's is the place. Tasty dough, spicy tomato sauce; one of the Jersey Shore's best pizzas.

Port O'Call, Engleside Avenue, (609) 492–0715
Price Code: Moderate   Menu: American
Seafood, prime ribs and veal dishes round out the menu. Early-bird specials; salad bar.

Romeo's Continental Cuisine, 100 North Pennsylvania Avenue
(609) 492–0025
Price Code: Moderate   Menu: Seafood and steaks
Good family restaurant with children's menu. Steak is good, seafood dishes are usually better.

6

 **The Pine Barrens**

They are a vast area; they cover nearly 25 percent of New Jersey. Much of it includes the last remaining true wilderness area on the Atlantic coast between New Hampshire and Virginia. They are an area of great green forests and swampy marshlands, of amber-tinted rivers and streams, of rich folklore and legends. People call the area the Pinelands or simply the Pines, although it's most commonly called the Pine Barrens. Unfortunately, it's also the most inappropriate name of the three.

How can an area that is the heart of New Jersey's agriculture industry, where the harvest of blueberries and cranberries is one of the largest in the nation, and where one can find 54 threatened plant species and 35 threatened wildlife species in thousands and thousands of acres of wilderness forest be called barren? There *is* a logical reason. The term *Pine Barrens* goes all the way back to the area's original settlers who found the sandy soil unsuitable for farming. The Pinelands were "barren" to them. And the name stuck.

But it certainly shouldn't be considered barren today—especially for the vacationer or visitor looking for the perfect alternative to the beach and boardwalk and the madness that grips the rest of the Jersey Shore each summer. It's here in the Pine Barrens where hikers can spend not hours, but *days* in the forest and not see another soul, where canoeists can paddle some of the East Coast's most scenic and mysterious rivers and where New Jersey campers can come to understand the meaning of "wilderness" without leaving their state. It's also here in the Pine Barrens where history comes alive in the form of a restored nineteenth-century bog iron community like Batsto and where bird-watchers and naturalists delight in the sights and sounds of waterfowl and migratory birds as they take refuge in the marshlands that lie between the ocean and the forest.

Far too many Shore visitors underestimate the excitement of exploring the Pine Barrens. From Toms River to Atlantic City and points farther south, the ride on the Parkway is, all too often, a swift, direct one. There are rest areas with picnic tables, toll booths, exit ramps—and little else. Or so they think. But beyond the guard rails on either side of the highway lies an unspoiled forest area practically the size of Yellowstone National Park that can make a man marvel at its beauty in this, the nation's most densely populated state.

A few interesting facts about the Pine Barrens. Underneath the thick forest is a 17-trillion-gallon lake called the Cohansey Aquifer, a vital drinking water supply for New Jersey residents. The sand that separates the aquifer from the surface is porous. There's been more than one threat to the water's purity due to pollution seepage on the outlying edges of the Pine Barrens.

Did you know that . . .

If the Cohansey Aquifer were drained, it would cover the entire state of New Jersey with 10 feet of water.

Legislators certainly had this in mind when they made the Pine Barrens America's first national reserve. The difference between a national park and a national reserve is that park land is federally owned, but reserve land is owned by local, state and federal agencies as well as private individuals. The land included in the Pinelands National Reserve is protected from indiscriminate development and unwise use of the land, the kind that would harm the delicate ecological balance there.

Interestingly enough, in the eighteenth and part of the nineteenth century, the Pine Barrens were the industrial center of New Jersey. Towns like Batsto, Weymouth, Atsion, Washington and Speedwell were bustling bog iron communities that supplied iron and iron products for the developing nation. Today, little of this era remains in the Pine Barrens except at Batsto in Wharton State Forest (see below), where one can step back in time and learn how this area played a critical role in the American Revolution.

Finally, the Pine Barrens are the birthplace and home of that infamous creature, the Jersey Devil. This horned half human and half animal, with batlike wings and a demon's tail, has been roaming the Pinelands for more than two centuries. It continues to terrorize residents, kill live-stock and perpetuate a legend that seems to grow a bit larger with each passing year. Actually, the Pine Barrens are filled with tales and stories that will make any night under the stars there a spooky one. Stories about Sam Giberson and his fiddle, the Rabbit Woman and Captain Kidd still float around the Pine Barrens. These and others are celebrated in song—Piney folk music—and by word of mouth. No other part of the Jersey Shore possesses more colorful legends and tales of days gone by.

If the Pine Barrens, because of their wilderness descriptions, seem in-accessible, they aren't. And that's what makes a visit even more appeal-ing. The Parkway will get you to the Pine Barrens; Route 70, 72, 539 and 563 crisscross the area, enabling the visitor to get to most points of in-terest, hiking trails and canoe launches with little problem. There are few places to stay in the Pine Barrens, however. Most visitors who plan to spend more than a day there, camp.

Not all of what is generally considered the Pine Barrens territory is wild and uninhabited. Tiny towns of fewer than 50 residents can still be found thick in the heart of the Pines. Toms River is a large, historically significant community that sits in the northeast corner of the area. The stretch along Barnegat Bay and the smaller bays to the south is dotted with old towns and villages that seemed to have been bypassed when tourism came of age on the Jersey Shore. Places like Forked River, Ware-town and Barnegat have retained much of their Pineland and bay her-itage, despite the presence of nudging residential developments and shopping malls. Farther down, you'll find wetlands and barrier islands that fill the void between forest and ocean and are frequented by bird-watchers year-round.

One could write an entire book on the Pine Barrens. Some, like John McPhee, already have. His book, *The Pine Barrens,* is an acknowledged classic, and anyone interested in Pine Barrens culture should read this absorbing work before exploring it. This chapter then, is meant as an in-troduction to the Pine Barrens, especially that area of it closest to the coast. The Pine Barrens extend beyond the Jersey Shore, so to keep within the boundaries of this book, I've concentrated on points of inter-est and things to do within an hour's drive of the Parkway.

Toms River

Set on the banks of the Toms River, the town of Toms River is the princi-pal community in Ocean County (also the county seat) and the site of an important revolutionary war skirmish. It was here in March 1782, that Capt. Joshua Huddy and his men were set upon by British regulars and Tory sympathizers. Huddy's militiamen were ordered to defend the

Toms River Block House and the nearby salt warehouses. (Salt was vital in munitions making and the preservation of meat and fish.) Huddy's men held out, despite being outnumbered more than four to one, until they ran out of gunpowder. Huddy fled, but was captured by the British. Later he was hanged in Highlands (see chapter 1).

The British forces destroyed the salt warehouses, something they had set out to do twice before but failed. Nevertheless, Toms River continued to play a part in the war effort until the war's conclusion a year later. Privateers continued to harass British shipping by attacking and plundering supply ships. In all, there were 77 recorded naval skirmishes off the Jersey Shore during the revolutionary war. Many of the privateer ships engaged in such skirmishes were out of port towns such as Toms River, Tuckerton and Little Egg Harbor.

Things to Do

Visit the Toms River Block House. Located at the intersection of Water Street and Route 166 in downtown Toms River is a replica of the Toms River Block House. The original block house was a crude log fort with no entrance way; one had to scale the wall using a ladder to gain entry. Inside the block house was a log barracks and an underground room where ammunition and gunpowder were stored. The original block house was built in 1776 to protect the port and the local saltworks. The British destroyed it in 1782.

Visit the Toms River Maritime Museum. Run by the Toms River Seaport Society, the Maritime Museum is housed in an old carriage house overlooking the Toms River. The museum is noted for its collection and restoration of old Barnegat Sneakbox boats, used by outdoorsmen on Barnegat Bay earlier this century. There are also photographs of other old boats indigenous to the area, boat models, sea chests and old sailing paraphernalia. The Maritime Museum, located at 78 Water Street is usually open only on weekends. Call (908) 349–9209 for more information.

Visit the Ocean County Historical Museum. To get a proper perspective on the history of Toms River and the rest of Ocean County, spend part of an afternoon at this fine museum. It's located at 26 Hadley Avenue in a house built sometime in the 1840s and is decorated with mostly Victorian furnishings. A guide will lead you on a tour of the house, which includes a Victorian parlor, dining room and kitchen, complete with mannequins dressed in original period clothes and with household items on display. All of this gives the visitor a good indication of what day-to-day living during the Victorian Era might have been like. Upstairs is a "one-room school," furnished with material used in various Ocean County schools some 80 years ago. Downstairs in the basement are numerous Indian artifacts, fossils found locally and memorabilia of the Lighter Than Air Era, namely the years between World Wars I and II when dirigibles dotted the sky. Remnants of the most famous dirigible, the *Hindenberg,* which exploded and burned at the Lakehurst Naval Air Station some 10 miles northwest of Toms River in 1937, are on display. (This is the only area museum where one can find exhibits pertaining to dirigibles, particularly the *Hindenberg.* Contrary to popular belief, the Lakehurst Naval Air Station does not have a dirigible museum, although Hangar No. 1, where the *Hindenberg* was serviced and stored, is a national historic landmark. Call (908) 341–1880 for museum hours and information on special exhibits.

Cattus Island County Park

Perhaps because it's a fairly new park (established in 1980), or perhaps because it's nearly surrounded by a sprawling residential area rarely frequented by tourists, Cattus Island is one of the Jersey Shore's best kept secrets. This 530-acre natural preserve of salt and tidal marshes, white cedar swamp, pitch pine forest and coastal lowlands is a nature lover's delight. The 10 miles of marked trails and views of both Silver and Barnegat bays make for fine hiking. But it's the Cooper Environmental Center and its numerous nature programs that make Cattus Island a "must" stop for Jersey Shore nature lovers, especially those with young children.

The Cooper Environmental Center, named after local environmentalists A. Morton Cooper and Elizabeth Cooper, is a nature learning resource center filled with hands-on displays, wildlife games and quizzes, and theme exhibits that pertain not only to the Cattus Island ecosystem but to all the ecosystems found in Ocean County. Much of this is aimed at young people. Naturalists, however, conduct all kinds of special programs designed to stimulate and educate young and old alike and do so in an area that is mere minutes from the southern half of the Barnegat Peninsula and downtown Toms River.

On a map, Cattus Island appears to be a peninsula; it separates Silver Bay from the much larger Barnegat Bay. Yet Cattus Island is referred to as an island because during high tide the saltmarsh floods and water surrounds Cattus on all sides. Cattus Island County Park is on Fischer Boulevard, which is off Route 37. The entrance to the park is two miles north of the Route 37-Fischer Boulevard intersection. No admission charge. (908) 270–6960.

Things to Do

Go on a Naturalist-Led Nature Walk. There is much to experience on the Cattus Island hiking trails. To walk with someone whose knowledge of the ecology is more thorough than yours makes for an interest-

Twelve Tips for Beginning Bird-watchers

1. Purchase a copy of Roger Tory Peterson's *A Field Guide to the Birds East of the Rockies*. Thumb through it before you go into the field. This way you'll become familiar enough with the way birds are described and the various sections of the guide to be able to use it effectively where it counts most—in the field.

2. Purchase a good pair of binoculars. Nikon and Bushnell are reputable names in binoculars and have midpriced models that are worth the $200 or so you can expect to spend on them.

3. Join a local bird-watchers' club and/or the New Jersey Audubon Society to meet and work with other "birders," as they're often called. It's also a great way to learn where the really good bird-watching spots are.

4. If you begin bird-watching on the Jersey Shore, start with shore birds. They're quite common and fairly easy to identify. Along with the Edwin B. Forsythe Wildlife Refuge, other sites such as Sandy Hook, Stone Harbor and Cape May are also excellent places to see birds.

5. Whenever possible, go bird-watching with an experienced bird-watcher. He or she will provide not only company but will teach you things about bird-watching that might take you months to learn.

6. Don't wear loud colors; browns and greens are best.

7. Move slowly. Don't talk and don't smoke. Whenever possible, stay in your car. Birds are afraid of people; they're not usually frightened by cars.

8. Never feel intimidated by other bird-watchers in the field who seem to be able to spot every bird in the vicinity and never have to open up their guidebooks. Bird-watching should be a pleasant, relaxing experience. As a novice, enjoy the sport within your capabilities.

9. Listen as well as look. You'll get just as much enjoyment out of identifying a bird by its whistle as by its coloring and markings.

10. If you plan to stay out in the field more than an hour or two, bring a snack and perhaps something to drink. Also, dress appropriately. A good pair of rubber shoes is a wise investment.

11. Keep track of your sightings by way of a "life list." If you become a serious bird-watcher, you'll be amazed at how many birds you spot each year.

12. Appreciate the joys that bird-watching brings, and support laws that seek to increase wildlife acreage in addition to protecting those already in existence.

ing learning experience. Two-hour nature walks usually begin at 2 P.M. and occur on weekends year-round. Rarely is there more than a handful of walkers, which allows better interaction among walkers and naturalists. Naturalists also conduct boat tours in the summer, but on a less frequent basis. Ask for details at the Cooper Environmental Center.

Go Seining off the Cattus Island Bay Beaches. Who knows what kind of marine life will be trapped in your net for inspection as you wade through the shallow bay waters? Because it juts out into the water, Cattus Island is one of the best places on the Barnegat to seine any time of the year, except, of course, the winter, when it's too cold to be in the water.

Bike the Cattus Island Fire Road. Trail bikes are better than 10-speeds, as the road is not paved. The fat trail-bike tires make for easier peddling and a smoother ride. The road is four miles long, which makes for a pleasant eight-mile round-trip. Bring your lunch or a snack and eat it as you admire the splendid view of Silver Bay and the Barnegat Peninsula at the end of the road. A good time to bicycle Cattus Island is during October when the weather is cool, the mosquitos are gone (hopefully), and the change in foliage is at its peak.

Island Heights

Island Heights, set snugly on the northern bank of the Toms River, has much in common with Ocean Grove (see chapter 2). Both began as Methodist camp meeting towns in the late nineteenth century, both are still dry towns today—meaning no liquor can be bought or served except in the privacy of one's own home—and both possess a number of beautiful Victorian homes, most of which have been meticulously restored. There are more than 100 Victorian structures in Island Heights. Unlike Ocean Grove or Cape May, however, Island Heights has not welcomed tourism in a grand way. There are no museums, no homes to visit (except during town-sponsored home tours) and no true Victorian selling points except the architecture of the homes. Be sure to drive along the Toms River on River Road—the homes that face the water are quite impressive.

Island Heights is located off Route 37, between Toms River and Barnegat Bay. Take the exit marked Island Heights and proceed down to the Toms River, where your auto tour of the town should begin.

Double Trouble State Park

Few people realize there's a state park called Double Trouble. That's because, though it's open to the public, it's not *officially* open. Located in Berkeley Township (Parkway, Exit 80) on Double Trouble Road West, the park's historic cranberry village is still very much in the restoration stages. State officials say they don't advertise Double Trouble the way they do other state parks in New Jersey because it has no parking or restroom facilities.

Don't let this stop you from visiting Double Trouble State Park, however. The caretaker will let you walk around the village homes, which once housed workers who worked the nearby cranberry bogs. Also, walk the 1½-mile hiking trail that begins at the packing house.

Did you know that . . .

New Jersey is the third highest cranberry-producing state, after Massachusetts and Wisconsin.

Double Trouble comprises 4,000 acres of prime Pine Barrens; a walk on the trail is especially recommended for those wishing to experience a bit of Pine Barrens forest without having to drive as far south as Wharton State Forest (see below).

The sawmill that is currently being restored is said to have been built in the mid-eighteenth century. According to local legend, the Double Trouble area got its name because of a beaver who first built one dam and then another, causing the water that ran the mill to trickle and the mill operator to run into "double trouble."

Once Double Trouble is fully restored, it's a sure bet it will become one of New Jersey's most interesting state parks, taking its place next to Allaire and Batsto as important historical sites in the Pine Barrens section of the Jersey Shore.

The Bay Towns

The best way to gain an appreciation of the small towns that sit on the western shore of Barnegat Bay is to drive along Route 9 rather than the Garden State Parkway. The Parkway is quicker and perhaps more direct if your destination is, say, the Edwin B. Forsythe Wildlife Refuge or the Historic Village of Batsto in Wharton State Forest. But you're certain to miss much of the Barnegat Bay tradition that seems to reveal itself in the oddest places. Case in point: You'll find no better example of Barnegat Bay and Pine Barrens culture than in the voices and guitar chords that echo each Saturday night from Albert Hall in Waretown. It's the home of the Pinelands Cultural Society (see below), a home, by the way that's located at the rear of a building that contains a Route 9 auto body shop.

As you ride up or down Route 9, you'll pass through such towns as Ocean Gate, Bayville, Lanoka Harbor, Forked River, Waretown and Barnegat. Individually, none of these old towns contains what one might call "must" places to visit, although some of them have interesting historical sections and local museums, and these are listed and described below. Rather, it's the Barnegat Bay ambiance, which is found in these communities, that makes a ride through them inviting.

As with so many places on the Jersey Shore, contrast is the rule of thumb. You'll see numerous residential developments and small shopping centers side by side with homes and churches that are 100 and 200 years old and cemeteries that contain the remains of the Barnegat Bay area's original settlers. Unfortunately, many of these old structures have not been restored, and there they sit, full of faded memories and little else.

Blocked by the Barnegat peninsula and Long Beach Island, these communities have no beaches, save those on the bay—which aren't nearly as nice or as spacious as those on the ocean. Because of this, activity revolves exclusively around the bay's excellent fishing, clamming, crabbing and boating. Marinas abound in this area.

But there are no amusement areas here, no boardwalks, little nightlife and few good restaurants. For most, these are more than enough reasons to continue south to Atlantic City or the opposite direction. Yet, a stop in Barnegat to browse through a few antique shops or a Saturday night visit to Albert Hall for an old-timey Piney hootenanny should certainly be considered.

Forked River

The **Forked River State Marina** is the second of three state-owned and operated boat basins on the Jersey Shore. (The northernmost state marina is located in Leonardo, see chapter 1. The southernmost is the Senator Frank S. Farley Marina in Atlantic City, see chapter 7.)

Unlike Leonardo, though, Forked River does not have a boat launch, which makes it less useful to the day visitor. But with so many other marinas in the area, the visiting boater will have little difficulty getting his boat in the bay. Forked River State Marina does possess 125 berths and reserves 2 of them for boaters wishing to moor their craft for one night only. Like Leonardo, there is a waiting list for the other 123 berths. The wait at Forked River is approximately six years, depending on the size of the boat. The marina is located at 311 South Main Street. For more information, call (609) 693–5044.

Going Clamming? Here's How.

When to Go: The summer and fall are the best times of the year to clam since you will be wading in water. However, ardent clammers clam year-round. Boots and warm clothing are obvious necessities, then. Bear in mind it is illegal to clam at night or on Sundays. The best tide to clam is low tide.

Where to Go: Barnegat Bay, Little Egg Harbor and Reed's Bay are good places, although certain areas in each of the three bays are off limits to clammers. To be certain you're not clamming in condemned areas, adhere to the "Condemned Areas Clamming Chart," which can be obtained at Marine Police stations or by writing to the New Jersey Department of Environmental Protection, Division of Water Resources, Bureau of Shellfish Control. Stoney Hill Road, Leed's Point, Star Route, Absecon 08021. Experienced clammers point to the waters around Waretown and Forked River as being fairly rich in clams.

What to Bring: You'll need a clamming license available from the New Jersey Division of Fish, Game and Wildlife or from a reputable sporting goods store on the Jersey Shore. You'll also need a clamming rake, gloves, a wooden peach basket in an inner tube with a piece of rope attached to it and to you to prevent it from floating away. Put the clams that you find in the basket. Clam tongs and clam forks are also good tools to have with you.

How to Do It: Scrape the clam rake along the sandy bottom of the bay as you move backwards. Move and scrape slowly until you feel the shell of a clam. Quickly dig under the clam and dislodge it from the bed. Rake in a recognizable pattern to avoid raking the same area twice. Clamming is hard, often backbreaking work. Be prepared to sweat a little. The rewards, though, are worth it, especially when you taste that first mouthful of homemade Jersey Shore clam chowder.

Each year regulations are posted concerning the size of clams you're allowed to keep as well as the number. Check these in advance. If you ignore such regulations or are ignorant of them, you'll pay a steep fine if you're found disobeying them.

Watertown

The music begins promptly at eight o'clock each Saturday night, and it doesn't wind down until near midnight. In the summer, when the air is thick with humidity, the picking and singing lasts much longer than that. Although the lights in **Albert Hall** are turned off and the doors locked, many of the musicians move outside to the parking lot where the "Sounds of the Jersey Pines" continue under the stars until the last singer is too tired to call out another tune.

The stage at Albert Hall is set to resemble the old lodge in the Pines where members of the Pinelands Cultural Society first gathered to pick and sing. The place was Joe and George Albert's secluded hunting cabin. When folks started bringing their friends to listen in, it was decided a bigger place was needed. Today, Albert Hall, named in honor of the Alberts, is located behind Monari Auto Body in Waretown Plaza on Route 9.

What you'll hear at Albert Hall are home-bred, self-taught groups of musicians and singers who blend interesting slices of traditional American folk, country and bluegrass with Pine Barrens and Barnegat Bay themes. It's a sound that's as indigenous to the Jersey Shore as Bruce Springsteen's and Southside Johnny's brand of rock 'n' roll farther north (see chapter 2).

The Saturday night lineup is filled with both regulars and newcomers. Each performer gets 20 minutes on the stage. No one gets paid. Everyone has a grand ol' time. A small admission charges goes into the fund currently being raised to build a new Albert Hall deeper in the Pine Barrens. Those interested in obtaining information about becoming a member of the Pinelands Cultural Society should write to the organization at P.O. Box 657, Waretown 08758.

Barnegat

Of all the towns on the bay, Barnegat is the one that has strived the hardest to preserve its past. The Barnegat Historical Society has a small museum on East Bay Street and a collection of old, semirestored buildings that have been spared destruction. The **Lippencott Falkinburg House** (circa 1800) is an excellent example of the types of homes built nearly 200 years ago on Barnegat Bay. Found next to the Lippencott Falkinburg House are buildings built in Barnegat more than a century ago and moved to this location for preservation. One of the most interesting is the old barbershop, a place where hair was cut and town politics discussed.

Much of Barnegat's historical preservation work began in 1976 during our nation's bicentennial. Since then, however, funds for local preservation projects have practically dried up, leaving much of the work unfinished. Because of limited funds, the Barnegat Historical Society Museum and related historical buildings are open only on weekends from June 1 to September 15. No admission charge.

Before visiting the museum, antique lovers might want to browse through the group of shops at the intersection of Bay Avenue and Route 9. **First National Antiques** (708 West Bay Avenue) and **Elegant Odds and Ends** (696 East Bay Avenue) have a wide selection of interesting pieces, many of which are local in nature. Also check **Yellow Bird An-**

tiques (Route 9 and Cedar Street), two blocks north of Bay Avenue on Route 9 and **Creative Clutter** (North Main Street). Good deals can be found in these shops.

After you've had your fill of antiques, one must stop at the **Hurricane House** on 688 East Bay Avenue, located smack in the middle of the Barnegat antique center for an old-fashioned ice-cream treat. The Hurricane House is Ocean County's oldest ice-cream parlor, initially established in 1920. Sip a malted at the shop's original ice-cream counter, or perhaps take a booth and feast on a scrumptious chocolate ice-cream sundae. You'll find few other ice-cream parlors like the Hurricane House on the Shore.

If one continues down East Bay Avenue, past the Barnegat Historical Society Museum and historic buildings, you'll come to Barnegat Bay. To your right (south) is the Barnegat Wildlife Sanctuary. East Bay Avenue eventually turns into Bayshore Drive, which loops around back to Route 9. It's on Bayshore where the town's marinas are found, along with its municipal dock, public swimming beach and a sweeping view of Barnegat Bay and Long Beach Island. A careful look on a clear day will provide the visitor with a view of Old Barney, the Barnegat Lighthouse at the northernmost tip of Long Beach Island. There is also a public boat launch here as well as fishing and crabbing facilities. Crabbing can be quite good in Barnegat, as can clamming, although a clamming license is needed (see above).

Oswego River Tour

The Oswego River, also known as the East Branch of the Wading River, is not recommended for first-time canoeists. There are simply too many difficult turns in the journey, which, combined with the narrowness of the river, can make canoeing a bit too challenging for some novices. The Oswego River tour, however, is the shortest of the four described here. One should get from Lake Oswego at the edge of Penn State Forest on the Route 563 Spur, your starting point, to Harrisville Pond, also on the Route 563 Spur, in approximately three hours.

This river tour is excellent for those wishing to see perhaps the biggest cedar trees in the Pine Barrens and also many of the wildflowers the area is noted for. Bring a wildflower field guide with you to help in identification.

The Wading River Tour

This is a better tour for novice paddlers because, except for the earliest part of the journey where the river is narrow, the Wading River is quite

Canoeing in the Pine Barrens

One of the most pleasant ways to explore and appreciate the natural, unspoiled beauty of the Pine Barrens is by canoe. So much of the best that the Pine Barrens have to offer is inaccessible by car. Therefore, traveling along an inland river with nothing but the calls of catbirds and warblers and the easy swoosh of the cedar-stained water to break the soft silence is the best way to go.

Some of the state's best canoeing can be found in the Pine Barrens, but that doesn't mean you'll find raging rapids and foaming white water. On the contrary. Most of the navigable rivers aren't really rivers at all, but quiet, lazy streams. Some are so quiet that it's possible to paddle upstream with little effort. That's good news for those unable to get someone to pick them up at the end of their journey.

Canoeing in the Pine Barrens is considered so good because of the magnificent scenery more than anything else. The Pines possesses a plethora of unusual plant life and vegetation on the banks of its streams and rivers. Some species can be found only in the Pine Barrens and nowhere else.

You'll see towering cedar and pine trees and sandy beaches, marshland, swamps and cranberry bogs. You might spot beavers busily working on dams and deer nibbling on the riverbank vegetation. You'll do lots of twisting and turning on some Pine Barrens rivers, which, at times, might require the skill of a seasoned canoeist. You'll also do lots of head-ducking as the vegetation gets quite thick in some areas.

Four excellent rivers for canoeing, the Oswego, Wading, Mullica and Batsto rivers, wind through Wharton State Forest and adjoining forest areas. These rivers provide canoeists with an unhurried, up-close look at the Pine Barrens, while at the same time allowing them to experience the serenity of the forest one only finds far from urban sprawl.

wide and thus easy to navigate. Launch your canoe at Speedwell on Route 563. Approximately five hours later, you'll come to Evans Bridge, your destination. For a longer version of the tour, continue past Evans Bridge and paddle on to Bodine Field, also on Route 563. Be advised, however, that the Wading River can get rather congested during the summer because it's the most popular Pine Barrens river on which to canoe.

The Mullica River Tour

The Mullica River is nearly as popular with canoeists as the Wading River. Good for beginners as well as for more experienced canoeists, the river winds through savannah marshes and clumps of cedar tree forest. It also provides the best possibility to see wildlife other than beaver, say veteran Pine Barrens river paddlers. Begin your journey on the shores of Atsion Lake and paddle to Pleasant Mills, just across from Batsto. It should take you approximately six hours to get there.

The Batsto River Tour

If you want wilderness canoeing, the Batsto River Tour is for you. The river is quite inaccessible, which discourages all but the most determined canoeists. It also can be difficult paddling across Batsto Lake if you're going against a headwind. You'll encounter a more varied riverbank than on any of the other tours. Virtually all of the ecosystems of the Pine Barrens can be experienced and seen on the Batsto River. Put in at Hampton Furnace and canoe to the end of Batsto Lake. It should take you about five hours.

For more detailed information on canoeing in the Pine Barrens, pick up a copy of Robert Parnes' superb book, *Canoeing the Jersey Pine Barrens.* No other book on the market gives so much material on the rivers, their history and vegetation, and the Pine Barrens' ecology that canoeists will paddle by than this one. Highly recommended.

Privately Owned Canoe Rentals

Adams Canoe Rental
Lake Drive, Atsion
R.D. #2, Vincetown 08088
(609) 268–0189

Art's Canoe Rentals
1052 Route 9
Bayville 08721
(908) 269–1413

Bel Haven Lake
Route 542, Green Bank
R.D. #2, Egg Harbor 08215
(609) 965–2031

Mick's Canoe Rental
Route 563, Jenkins
Chatsworth 08019
(609) 726–1380

Mullica River Boat Basin
Green Bank, R.D. #2
Egg Harbor 08215
(609) 965–2120

Paradise Lakes Campground
Route 206, P.O. Box 46
Hammonton 08037
(609) 561–7095

Pine Barrens Canoe Rental
Route 563, Box 27, Jenkins
Chatsworth 08019
(609) 726–1515

Pineland Canoes
Route 527
Jackson 08527
(908) 364–0389

Wading Pines Campground
Route 563, Jenkins
Chatsworth 08019
(609) 726–1313

Historic Towne of Smithville

Two hundred years ago James Baremore opened the Smithville Inn to weary South Jersey travelers. Because it was built on a stagecoach route, which connected Cooper's Landing in Camden to nearby Leed's Point, and because it served uncommonly good grub, the Inn's popularity grew until the advent of the railroad, which made the stagecoach in these parts diminish in importance. The Inn closed and fell into disrepair, until, in 1949, the Noyes family restored it and reopened it as a restaurant. To attract diners, old South Jersey buildings from the nineteenth century were moved to Smithville and also restored. At its peak, Smithville had more than 25 historic structures, which gave a good indication of what a South Jersey Pine Barrens town might have looked like in the nineteenth century. Craftspeople demonstrated the traditional skills of rug-braiding, soapmaking, and woodcarving, and brought to life a way of living that had been all but forgotten.

A second set of buildings was constructed in Smithville to capitalize on the influx of visitors. Replicas of old country stores were filled with crafts, clothes, candles, antiques and other merchandise. Today Smithville is worth a visit, as the shops and stores, which sell crafts and other goods, are great fun to browse through. Some of the shops are original historic structures brought to Smithville when those in the Old Village were brought there. The **Country Place,** for instance, which sells mostly country antiques, is located in an old gristmill. Built in the 1790s in Sharpstown, its workers ground such grains as wheat, buckwheat and rye for local consumption. The waterwheel on the side of the building still turns the water of Lake Meone.

Other shops that sit along the cobblestone streets of Smithville include **Barnacle Bob's,** which sells antique and oriental reproduction furniture; the **Gourmet Pantry,** where you'll find imported cheese, meat, tea and spices; the **Tomasello Winery,** where one can sample and purchase wines and champagnes made by one of South Jersey's leading wine families (see chapter 8); and the **Lil' Brass Duck Shoppe,** which offers brass lamps, weather vanes, bedposts and door knockers, among other items. Smithville has more than 30 shops in all.

Be sure to have lunch or dinner at the **Smithville Inn,** where the food is good and the atmosphere distinctively colonial.

Smithville is at its best during May and October, when the May Fest and October Fest occur, respectively. Arts and crafts shows, music, food sampling and other special activities make these annual events quite popular. For more information, call (609) 652–7775. Smithville is located on Route 9, 12 miles north of Atlantic City. Take Exit 48 for those coming via the Parkway.

Oceanville

Noyes Museum. The Noyes Museum is the Jersey Shore's largest fine arts museum, one of two found in the area. (The other is on the Atlantic City Boardwalk. It's called the Atlantic City Arts Center. See chapter 7.) Opened in 1983, the Noyes Museum sits in a rustic, serene setting amid tall pine trees on the shore of Lily Lake and adjacent to the Edwin B. Forsythe Wildlife Refuge (see below). Located just off Route 9 on Lily Lake Road, and less than 10 minutes south of Smithville, the museum regularly displays the work of some of New Jersey's most talented artists.

The museum, established by Fred W. Noyes and his wife, Ethel Noyes, has five galleries; one is devoted entirely to waterfowl and shore bird decoys. A resident woodcarver on the premises demonstrates the art of woodcarving to the public. Fred Noyes was once an avid decoy collector, and many of the finest pieces of his personal collection can be found here.

The remaining four galleries offer exhibits that change approximately every three months. At least two of the four galleries are usually dedicated to paintings; the other two often feature the work of sculpture and furniture makers.

The Noyes Museum is open year-round. Admission is charged. For information on current exhibits, call (609) 652–8848.

Edwin B. Forsythe National Wildlife Refuge. Formerly known as Brigantine National Wildlife Refuge, this 36,000-acre coastal salt marsh and wetlands preserve was initially established to protect a critical stopover for migrating waterfowl on their way south or north, depending on the season. The refuge is on the Atlantic Flyway, and more than 250 species of birds visit the marsh area each year. Needless to say, the Forsythe Refuge is a prime location for bird-watching. Nowhere on the Jersey Shore is it easier to spot birds in such large numbers or to photograph them.

It's possible to see loons, pelicans, cormorants, herons, swans, geese, ducks, vultures, falcons (including the peregrine falcon), grouse, quail, cranes, plovers, gulls, terns, finches, sandpipers, larks, swallows and woodpeckers among other birds. One can ask for a pamphlet entitled *Birds of Edwin B. Forsythe National Wildlife Refuge* at the Visitor Center; it contains a bird checklist, as well as information on what season you're most apt to see them and average number of yearly sightings.

Of course you don't need to be an avid bird-watcher to appreciate or enjoy the Forsythe Refuge. The mere sight of so many birds in their natural environment is interesting and quite special, even for those who can't tell a wren from a warbler. The best time to view birds is in the fall during their annual migration south. Spring is also a good time, although birds don't usually linger in the marshland there as much during this season as they do in the fall. Those bent on viewing the arrival of ducks and snow geese, which number close to 75,000 each year, should visit the refuge in November and early December. It's at this time that one is also apt to catch a glimpse of a bald eagle.

Visitors will find the self-guided Auto Tour on the elevated eight-mile loop road called Wildlife Drive an ideal and comfortable way to see the birds. The backdrop is the Atlantic City skyline and Great Bay, while just below you is the patchwork of tiny islands and marshland where birds rest and feed. Binoculars aren't a must, but they're highly recommended.

The Auto Tour has 14 stops and it takes about 90 minutes to complete, although one can easily spend the better part of a day observing and photographing the birds. Many do just that. You'll see automobile license plates from states all around the country, as the Forsythe Refuge is very well known among bird-watchers and naturalists everywhere.

Bird-watching, of course, is the overriding attraction at the Forsythe Refuge. Those who wish to get close to the birds and have more personal contact with the land they inhabit than what you get sitting in a car can walk Wildlife Drive or else hike along the Leeds Eco Trail and/or Akers Woodland Trail.

The former is just a half mile long, but it winds through a wonderfully scenic area of the refuge where the infamous Jersey Devil is said to roam. You'll walk by greenbriar and honeysuckle, red cedar and black cherry trees, salt marshes and shrubs and that seemingly ubiquitous plant, poison ivy. In addition to birds, you might catch a glimpse or two of white-tailed deer, a mink or a fox, snapping or box turtles, rabbits or fiddler crabs.

The Akers Woodland Trail is only a quarter mile long. It enables walkers to see nearly the same vegetation and possibilities of wildlife that the Leeds Trail offers, but in a shorter distance. Both hikes are made more enjoyable if you use the guide pamphlets available at the Visitor Center.

Speaking of the Visitor Center, take time to see the wildlife exhibits there and perhaps view one of the numerous nature slide shows shown in the auditorium. A ranger or volunteer is available to answer questions and pass out guides and brochures. Often asked of rangers is whether boating is permitted in the channels and waterways surrounding the marshland islands. The answer is no simply because such activity is apt to disturb the birds and the refuge's exceedingly delicate, yet complex ecosystem. One can, however, enjoy hours of boating on Great Bay as well as excellent fishing. Great Bay is the largest body of water in the area. It lies to the north of the refuge and contains the mouth of the Mullica River. On the south side of the Forsythe Refuge is Reed's Bay. Boaters venturing north or south on the Inland Waterway are permitted to pass through certain confines of the refuge.

As for hunting, it is permitted during hunting season in specially designated areas of the refuge, providing one possesses a valid New Jersey hunting license and follows the refuge's rules and regulations. The Edwin B. Forsythe Wildlife Refuge is open year-round, from dawn to dusk. It can be reached via Route 9 and Lily Road, where the Noyes Museum is located. The entrance to the refuge is just beyond the museum. There is an admission charge.

Chatsworth

Set at the crossroads of Routes 532 and 563, between Lebanon and Wharton state forests, Chatsworth is often called the capital of the Pine Barrens. It's here at Buzby's General Store, made famous by John McPhee's wonderful depiction of it in his book, *The Pine Barrens,* where you'll find Pineys sipping soda pop and trading local gossip. Chatsworth is also the home of the area's largest and most popular cranberry festival. Held each fall, usually on the third weekend in October, everything and anything relating to cranberries is on display. You can pick up all sorts of cranberry recipes, and the tastiest cranberry juice you've ever

The Jersey Devil

There are as many stories that seek to explain the origins of the Jersey Devil as there are descriptions of the notorious creature who has prowled the Pine Barrens since people can remember. Most accounts attribute the birth of the demon to a Mrs. Leeds of Estelville sometime in the early eighteenth century, perhaps 1735. Apparently Mother Leeds already had 12 children, and when she found out she was expecting yet one more time, she cried out in rage, "Not another child! I hope this one's a devil, then!"

Her wish was granted if you believe in the Jersey Devil. On the night of its birth, local midwives gathered at Mrs. Leeds' house and helped her along with her labor. At the point of delivery, they were horrified to learn that the child wasn't really a child at all, but a grotesque, horned, winged creature with the face of a horse and the tail of a devil. The demon either flew up the chimney or out the window and into the Pines. And from that time on, he became known by a number of names, but the Jersey Devil was the one passed from generation to generation.

Other stories differ significantly from the one mentioned above. According to one interpretation, Mrs. Leeds didn't curse her unborn child; a sorcerer did. Another interpretation has the Jersey Devil the product of a steamy extramarital affair Mrs. Leeds had with a young British army officer. There are also discrepancies as to where the Jersey Devil was born. Some people claim he was born in Estelville; others say he tasted, and watch local cranberry farmers determine who has the largest and the smallest cranberry in the Pine Barrens. There's also an arts-and-crafts sale, cranberry bog tours, a house-decorating contest and music by the Pinelands Cultural Society. For information on this year's Chatsworth Cranberry Festival, call (609) 859–9701.

Did you know that . . .

There is a South New Jersey cocktail called the Jersey Devil. The drink is made from cranberry juice, applejack and rum. Locals say that if you drink too much of it, you're bound to see one or two or three Jersey Devils as you stagger off.

Wharton State Forest

Wharton State Forest is New Jersey's largest state forest and the hub of virtually all Pine Barrens outdoors activity for the Shore visitor. Located off Route 542, less than 13 miles west of the Parkway (Exit 50 or 52),

was born in Leeds' Point, the small town in the middle of the Edwin B. Forsythe Wildlife Refuge, where many sightings of the Jersey Devil have supposedly occurred.

Descriptions of the Jersey Devil are just as diverse as the stories pertaining to his origins. Perhaps James F. McCloy and Ray Miller, Jr., in their fine book, *The Jersey Devil*, give the best description: "His size varies from eighteen inches to twenty feet. He has the body of a kangaroo, the head of a dog, the face of a horse, the wings of a bat, the feet of a pig, and a forked tail."

As for his dastardly deeds, the Jersey Devil has been accused of killing farm animals; causing forest fires, even wars; causing crops and good luck to fail; being the cause of unexplained events; and terrorizing Pineys and travelers alike. The Jersey Devil has also been linked in one way or another to the infamous pirate, Captain Kidd; the American naval hero, Commo. Stephen Decatur; and Joseph Bonaparte, the brother of Napoleon Bonaparte.

One thing about the Jersey Devil is absolutely certain. In Pine Barrens folklore, he lives! The area is brimming with all sorts of legends and tales, but none is so well-known or more believed than the Jersey Devil. It doesn't matter that people can't agree on what he is, where he came from, what he looks like and what he's responsible for. Ask any Piney about the Jersey Devil and he'll tell you he's indeed alive and well. Why, just the other day a neighbor of his . . .

Wharton sits in the heart of the Pine Barrens. It encompasses thousands of acres of tall pine trees, cedar swamps, yellow rivers and streams. It has some of the best camping areas, hiking trails and canoeing in the mid-Atlantic region, along with over 400 miles of sand roads, which provide fairly easy access to nearly all reaches of Wharton with a four-wheel drive vehicle.

Despite Wharton's vast natural wealth, its most popular attraction is the historic village of Batsto, once South Jersey's leading bog iron producer. Today, there are more than 25 restored iron workers' homes, barns and stables, and buildings such as the General Store, sawmill and iron master's mansion to visit, plus a visitor center, which also includes a small but excellent museum. Like Allaire Village in Allaire State Park (see chapter 3), Batsto is well preserved and provides visitors with a chance to step back to the days when bog iron furnaces burned bright and hot in the New Jersey heartland, furnaces that helped build America.

The Batsto Iron Works began operations in 1766. Its owner, Charles Read of Burlington, chose the site because of the availability of water power, the accessibility of the Atlantic Ocean via the Mullica River, which would enable ships to transport iron products made at Batsto to ports along the Eastern seaboard, and, finally, proximity of bogs and riverbeds rich in ore from which iron was extracted. (Ore is formed from decayed plant matter after it has blended with iron salts in rivers and swamps.)

In 1773, a Philadelphian named John Cox bought the Batsto Iron Works from Read. Cox was an ardent patriot, and once America claimed its independence from England he and those employed at Batsto began making cannonballs and other munitions for the Continental Army. So important was the military significance of Batsto that those who worked there were exempt from serving in the army.

Only once during the revolutionary war was Batsto threatened by the British. That was in the fall of 1778 when redcoats attacked Chestnut Neck on the Mullica River, the largest seaport in southern New Jersey during the Colonial Era and a haven for American privateers. The British destroyed Chestnut Neck and planned to proceed up the Mullica River to destroy Batsto. But news of the arrival of Gen. Casimir Pulaski's troops and a brief engagement with some of them prompted the British to turn back.

In addition to making cannonballs and munitions, Batsto also produced domestic iron products such as pots and kettles, stoves, even ducts in which fresh water was carried to citizens of some colonial cities. In 1812, Batsto was again called upon to make munitions for the American army, once more engaged in conflict with the British.

Like Allaire, Batsto thrived as a bog iron community until the 1830s, when coal was discovered in Pennsylvania as well as new iron ore deposits. The Richards family sought to revive Batsto by turning to the production of glass. The fine white sand of the Pine Barrens seemed perfect for the making of glassware; thus the Batsto Glassworks was created in 1846. But due to mismanagement and continuing financial woes, the Glassworks at Batsto survived only until 1867. Then in 1874, more than half the village was destroyed by fire, and Batsto was abandoned.

Two years later, Joseph Wharton bought the Batsto property along with other tracts of land in the Pine Barrens. Wharton, a shrewd investor and entrepreneur, realized the immense value of the Pine Barrens' underground aquifer and planned to sell the pure water to the city of Philadelphia. Things looked bright for Wharton and his water-selling scheme until New Jersey legislators passed a law that prohibited the export of water from the state. Batsto and the Wharton Tract, as it became known, sat idle until 1954, when New Jersey purchased it and made it into a state forest for use as a recreational area, natural preserve and historic site.

Wharton State Forest is open year-round. An admission fee is charged on weekends and holidays, from Memorial Day to Labor Day. For more information, call (609) 561–0024 or write Wharton State Forest, Batsto R.D. #4, Hammonton 08037.

Things to Do

Tour the Historic Village of Batsto. Your first stop in Wharton State Forest should be the Visitor Center, just outside the Batsto village. Here, you'll be able to pick up all the detailed information you need on current activities and special events in the park, as well as gain a good understanding of the historical significance of the Batsto Iron Works before touring the village that evolved from it. It is also a good idea to purchase a ticket for the iron master's mansion tour at this time, since only a limited number of tickets are sold each day and they go very quickly. You cannot enter the mansion unless you are part of one of the guided tours, which run a few times each day.

The Visitor Center is bright and modern and full of exhibits that pertain to the Pine Barrens, the bog iron industry in New Jersey in the eighteenth and nineteenth centuries, glassmaking, and, of course, Batsto. It also has remnants of items excavated by archaeologists who have conducted extensive digs in the Batsto area.

After the Visitor Center, a walk through the village is in order. Immediately outside it is an ore boat that was found at the bottom of Batsto Lake. It was used to haul raw iron ore to the Batsto furnace. An interesting display nearby explains the hows and whys of burning charcoal in the furnace. Continue walking toward the iron master's mansion. In its vicinity, you'll see the General Store and post office, various barns and worksheds, and the remains of the furnace. Many of the buildings are open to the public. In the craft houses, for instance, you'll find crafts-people demonstrating such things as the art of quiltmaking, weaving and candlemaking. A blacksmith is usually on the premises, too, and you might see a miller in the gristmill.

It is the iron master's mansion, however, that draws the most atten-tion. The largest building in the village, it is certainly the most interest-ing, architecturally speaking. The mansion has been remodeled several times, so it contains a variety of architectural styles. Inside are furnish-ings from various periods. Tastefully decorated and renovated, the Richards' Mansion, as it is also called in honor of Jesse Richards, the bog iron baron who owned Batsto during its last heyday, is the pride of Wharton State Forest.

Hike the Batona Trail. With the exception of the Appalachian Trail, there is no better hiking trail in New Jersey than the Pine Barrens' Batona Trail. The 52-mile trail cuts through some of the most scenic sections of the Pine Barrens and much of what is deemed "wilderness." It begins at Ongs Hat on Route 72 in Lebanon State Forest and ends in Bass River State Forest, if you're hiking north to south. Experienced hikers will want to walk the entire trail, taking a few days to do so. There are wilderness campsites at Lower Forge Camp and Batona Camp in Wharton, and one at the "300 Area" for summer hikers and at Butler Place for winter hikers in Lebanon State Forest. To camp in any of these areas, however, re-quires a camping permit.

The length of the Batona Trail should not discourage novices from en-joying a day's walk on the trail, or even for a couple of hours. The terrain is mostly flat and easy to traverse, and the trail is well defined with markers, which are simple to follow. Pick up a map of Batona Trail at Wharton's Visitor Center, and with the help of a ranger there, select a specific section within Wharton to walk.

A good choice for a day's worth of hiking might be to walk an end part of the trail, such as from Batsto to Evans Bridge, which is approxi-mately 10 miles long. A lesser distance walk might be from Batsto to Quaker Bridge, where two sand roads meet. The distance is approxi-mately six miles. Those wishing for anything less should settle for the short nature trails, which begin and end near Wharton's Annie Carter Na-ture Center (see below).

Along the Batona Trail, you'll walk through mostly pitch pine forest that's sprinkled with hardwood trees. You'll also pass cedar swamps, bogs and streams. All around you will be the remarkable sights and sounds of the Pine Barrens. You'll come across blueberry and huckle-berry patches, lush green carpets of forest ferns, and wildflowers. As for wildlife, there's a good chance you'll spot some white-tailed deer, and if you're particularly lucky, a fox, mink, otter or a beaver. Many kinds of birds and reptiles wander through here, including box and snapping turtles and the rare Pine Barrens tree frog, of which a glimpse would make the day for any hiker who has a special appreciation of endangered wildlife.

To guarantee solitude and minimum exposure to other hikers, a winter or late fall trek on Batona Trail is recommended. But winter hiking and camping should be done only by experienced woodsmen and walkers. This is a wilderness area, remember. Spring and fall are excellent times to hike Batona Trail, too. In the spring and early summer, you'll find the blueberries and huckleberries in season, which make for delicious trail treats. Summer is when Batona Trail is most crowded. But even then, the trail is long enough to accommodate large numbers of hikers. If you hike any time other than winter, don't forget insect repellent.

Did you know that . . .

The Pine Barrens are home to several species of carnivorous plants. Plants such as the northern pitcher and sundew eat insects. Pitcher plants bloom in early May; sundews bloom in early summer.

Go Camping. Wharton State Forest has nine camping areas, including the two that lie on Batona Trail. **Atsion Lake Camp** is on the north shore of Atsion Lake, just off Route 206. It's a good summer camping area because of swimming in Atsion Lake. **Batona Camp** is on the Batona Trail. **Bodine Field** is the largest of the Wharton camping areas; it holds some 300 people comfortably. You'll find many large groups camping here, which can make it quite noisy at night. It's located off the Route 563 Spur, behind the Harrisville ruins on the Wading River. **Buttonwood Hill Camp** is the smallest camping area in Wharton. It's located on Route 542 near the Mullica River. **Godfrey Bridge Camp** is on the west branch of the Wading River. Canoeists camp here often. It's located off Route 563. **Goshen Pond Camp,** off Route 206, is on the Mullica River but close enough to Atsion Lake, where swimming can be enjoyed. **Hawkin Bridge Camp** is another favorite camping area with canoeists; it's also located on the west branch of the Wading River. **Lower Forge Camp,** like Batona Camp, is on the Batona Trail. Here, you'll camp with many of the trail's hikers. The **Mullica Camp** on the Mullica River does not permit motor vehicles and, therefore, is a favorite camping area for those wishing to escape civilization for a few days.

No matter where you camp, you must have a camping permit. Permits are obtained at the Visitor Center. Because Wharton is so large and possesses so many camping areas, you'll almost always find a place to pitch a tent, even in the peak of the summer season. No other state park or state forest along the Jersey Shore offers as many areas or such a variety of sites as Wharton.

Visit the Annie Carter Nature Center and Auditorium. Set back behind the Batsto Village is the Annie Carter Nature Center and Auditorium, which contains numerous ecological exhibits and hands-on displays. You'll see, for instance, a 52-pound shell of a snapping turtle found in the Pine Barrens some years ago, as well as stuffed birds and other forms of wildlife whose natural habitat is the pine forests of Wharton. A naturalist is usually on the premises to answer your questions. Kids especially enjoy the nature center and auditorium, where slide shows depict the natural history of the area. The center and auditorium are open in the summer, from Memorial Day to Labor Day.

Near the center is the Batsto Lake Nature Trail, which in less than an hour's time gives one an interesting overview of Pine Barrens ecology. You'll walk through a portion of pine forest, see a cedar swamp and perhaps spot some wildlife. Take any of the trail spurs that lead down to the lake. Walk quietly and you might see a snapping turtle or box turtle on the shore. The ground is often wet and muddy. Wear rubber shoes.

Have a Picnic. Many people who visit Wharton State Forest, especially Batsto village, bring their lunch and picnic in the grove nearby. A concession stand is there, but its menu is quite limited. Also, there are few, if any, places to eat near the entrance to the village area.

Go Freshwater Fishing. Three lakes offer fishing in Wharton State Forest and vicinity. Harrisville, Oswego and Batsto lakes have pike, perch, pickerel and some largemouth bass. Spring is the best time to fish these bodies of water. During the summer fish stay in the deeper areas where the water is cooler. But during the spring you'll have good luck using light tackle and minnows for bait, especially if you're after pickerel. The Wharton State Forest rivers provide fishing, too, and some regular anglers insist the fishing is much better in them than in the lakes. All anglers must have a valid New Jersey fishing license.

Go Deer Hunting. Deer hunting is very good during the season in the specified hunting areas of Wharton State Forest. One hunting area is west of Quaker Bridge and the Mullica River. The other area is near the Pine Barrens town of Friendship in the thick of the forest. A New Jersey hunting license is mandatory. Check with a park ranger for rules and regulations regarding hunting areas.

Go Horseback Riding. In addition to hiking, another excellent way to enjoy Wharton State Forest and the Pine Barrens is on a horse. Although Wharton does not have horses for hire, visitors can bring their own or else rent them from nearby stables. The southeast and north-west sections of the park offer particularly good riding, and horses are permitted in all but three camping areas (Atsion Lake, Buttonwood Hill and Godfrey Bridge). A ranger at the Visitor Center will tell you where to park your car and trailer.

Wharton State Forest Special Events. Each year Wharton sponsors at least five annual events that attract thousands of visitors. In June and July, woodcarvers bring their duck decoys to display and sell at Batsto. Then in September, there's an art show, an antique show and a glass and bottle show; and in October, there's the Country Living Fair, which cele-brates what else but the art of country living. You'll see basket-making, spinning and weaving exhibits, needlework, stained-glass and quilt-making displays; you'll pick up cranberry recipes, learn how to repair a canoe, and watch a woodcarver in action. For information on these events, including this year's dates, call (609) 561-3262.

Where to Eat in the Pine Barrens/ Barnegat Bay Area

Allen's Clam Bar, Route 9 (New York Road), New Gretna
(609) 296-4106
Price Code: Inexpensive   Menu: Seafood
The Shore's best clam bar. Oyster stew and clam fritters are a must. Ca-sual atmosphere. Everything fresh and wonderfully tasty.

Carla and Ezio's, 1450 Route 88 West, Brick Township
(908) 458-5411
Price Code: Expensive   Menu: Italian
Brick Township isn't exactly the Pine Barrens, yet Carla and Ezio's must be mentioned somewhere. Mouth-watering North Italian specialties and delicious salads. Go once and you'll go again.

Clayton's Log Cabin, Route 72, Barnegat, (609) 698-4407
Price Code: Moderate   Menu: German-American
Set in a real log cabin, the German dishes are a delight. Lunch menu is as tempting as the dinner menu.

Joe's Place, Route 9, Smithville, (609) 652-8819
Price Code: Moderate   Menu: International
Good food, chic setting, interesting menu. A good alternative if the Smithville Inn has a wait.

Ram's Head Inn, 9 White Horse Pike, Absecon (Galloway Township)
(609) 652–1700
Price Code: Expensive   Menu: Continental
Classy setting (jackets required). Go for the glazed roasted duckling with
wild rice and amaretto sauce.

Smithville Inn, Route 9, Smithville, (609) 652–7777
Price Code: Moderate   Menu: Traditional American
Most popular of the Smithville restaurants. Varied menu; warm, colonial
setting. Expect a wait if you go on a weekend or holiday.

7

Atlantic City

Atlantic City is the crown jewel of the Jersey Shore. Within a few short years after New Jersey legalized gambling there in 1976 and the first casino, Resorts International, opened in 1978, Atlantic City has come to rival America's other glitzy and glamorous gambling resort, Las Vegas. Today, Atlantic City has even gone a step further. It's now one of the top vacation cities in the entire country and an internationally known, year-round playground for the world's rich and famous.

They call it the Queen of Resorts, the City-by-the-Sea, Casino City, the Gay Dowager. Whatever, it is indeed a city of endless activity. Enter into any one of Atlantic City's 12 casinos and you're instantly transformed into a world seemingly oblivious to everything but excitement, pleasure and pampering. Such things come in many forms and cater to all five senses. There are blinking bright lights, the perpetual patter of the slot machines and cocktail waitresses clad in seductive outfits at your service. Down the corridor, away from the betting action, are elevators that take you to plush hotel suites, spas, convention rooms, exquisite restaurants and expensive shops for those wishing to spend what they've won.

Men in tuxedos, women in evening gowns. High rollers and Slot Machine Sallys. World-class entertainment: Performers like Frank Sinatra, Dionne Warwick, Bob Hope, Eddie Murphy and Raquel Welch grace Atlantic City stages nightly. World-class sporting events such as championship boxing matches and top-notch tennis tournaments are held there regularly. Atlantic City offers, as one writer put it, "the feeling of having *been* somewhere."

And where, exactly, is that? On Absecon Island, an eight-mile long barrier island, seven miles off the mainland, which also includes the Atlantic City suburbs of Ventnor, Margate and Longport. The city sits just south of the Edwin B. Forsythe National Wildlife Refuge and just north of Ocean City and the rest of the South Jersey Shore. Surrounded by marshland and twisting, shallow waterways, it would seem to be the last place a city of such fame, fortune and fabulous entertainment would be located.

You can get to Atlantic City by bus; literally hundreds pull into and out of the city each day and night. It's the cheapest way to go, because on your arrival, you'll receive as much as $20 in quarters to get you started in slot machine mania. You'll also get meal tickets and drink discounts. Call the casino of your choice for information on bus lines that leave from your area. (See "The Casinos" section (pages 146–159) for toll-free casino telephone numbers and other information pertaining to the casinos, hotel reservations and such.)

You can arrive by car. There are three ways to drive into Atlantic City: the Atlantic City Expressway, which goes from Philadelphia and cuts right across the state, leaving you in downtown Atlantic City; the White Horse Pike, which is actually Route 30 and, in the city, Absecon Boulevard, which connects with Route 9 and points north; and the Black Horse Pike, which, in the city, is Albany Avenue, which connects with Routes 40 and 322 as well as Route 9 and points south. All three eventually link up with the Garden State Parkway. By car, Atlantic City is an hour from Philadelphia and 2½ hours from New York City.

You can travel to Atlantic City by plane. Bader Field Airport has shuttle and charter services from Philadelphia, Washington and other cities. You can even take a helicopter; consult your travel agent for flight times and airfare, or call the casinos and request information on package deals.

You can also arrive by boat. Beach Haven, on Long Beach Island, for instance, has daily boat excursions to and from **Harrah's Marina Casino** and **Trump Castle.** Other resorts and beach towns near Atlantic City are doing the same.

You can even arrive by train. Both New York and Philadelphia offer daily rail service to Atlantic City's new rail terminal.

When should you come to Atlantic City? Because it is truly a year-round resort, unlike many of the other resorts on the Jersey Shore, anytime is the right time. However, as might be expected, summer is peak season and hotel rooms are at a premium. The more budget-minded visitor might consider coming in midwinter—January through March—when almost all of the hotel-casino complexes offer outstanding deals and discounts and the facilities in town are much less crowded. It might be a bit too cold for some (but not all) to stroll Atlantic City's famous boardwalk, but much of the city's excitement is indoors, no matter what season it is.

And what if you're not a gambler? Are there things for you to do in Atlantic City? Absolutely. For starters, there's the beach and the Boardwalk. Both are free and both can mean hours of fun and entertainment. Atlantic City also boasts, and rightfully so, the best collection of first-class, four-star restaurants on the Jersey Shore. Many are located in the casino complexes, but more and more are popping up away from the Boardwalk. As already noted, Atlantic City's stage entertainment has few rivals; a night of Sinatra or Pavarotti is what some people consider the ultimate in evening entertainment. Also, small clubs in the city have nightly jazz, pop, piano bar and disco entertainment. It's here where you'll find many of the casino workers as they unwind after their shift on the casino floor.

Did you know that . . .

The great American parlor game, *Monopoly*, devised by Philadel-phian Charles Darrow and presented to the American public by Parker Brothers in 1935, is a game about buying and selling real estate in Atlantic City.

Did you also know that . . .

Marvin Gardens is the only non-Atlantic City property on the *Monopoly* game board. It's located in nearby Margate and, in the game, is misspelled. It's really Marven Gardens.

There are also such things as shopping and sightseeing to enjoy, too. Ocean One, the huge mall on the boardwalk, has many shops and eateries; Gardner's Basin, Absecon Lighthouse, Lucy the Elephant (in Margate) and the Atlantic City Art Center are all worthy of a visit. Finally, *you* don't have to bet, but you can watch others do so. Walking around the casinos, especially in the evening when the action is hot, is also entertainment. Thousand-dollar bets go on a roll of the dice. Tension, excitement, jubilation or devastation are the highs and lows felt every minute where millions change hands each day. It's all enough to dazzle participants and observers alike.

Unfortunately, not all of Atlantic City glitters. As you enter the city and approach the Boardwalk and casino area, you'll be surprised, even shocked, at the poverty and blight that encompasses most of Atlantic

City. It's a sad, sorry sight. Here live welfare families in ghettolike conditions, while a mere quarter mile or less away, on the very same street, millions are being wagered in the name of entertainment.

Government officials and proponents of further casino expansion in Atlantic City say eventually all of the city's residents will profit from the incredible inundation of money, big money, here. Perhaps *someday* they will. Already derelict buildings on Absecon Inlet are being torn down and condominiums constructed. But any overnight transition of the "other" Atlantic City is simply, er, not in the cards. Visitors should therefore be prepared, for the gap between rich and poor is indeed a big one.

The Boardwalk

Long before the casinos changed the skyline of Atlantic City, it was the Boardwalk that attracted tourists. Boardwalk is spelled with a capital "B" in Atlantic City because it's a legitimate "street" on the city map and per-haps also, as some insist, out of honor. The very first boardwalk in the world, you see, was constructed in Atlantic City in 1870.

The story behind its creation is a story of practicality. A conductor on the Camden & Atlantic Railroad named Alexander Boardman was fed up with passengers tracking sand into his rail car after a visit to the Atlantic City beach. He thought hard about how people might enjoy the sand without bringing it onto the train and came up with the idea of a collapsible footpath made of wooden planks, or boards.

Boardman took his idea to local hotel owners who were also tired of sand in their lobbies. With the city's support, a boardwalk 10 feet wide was built 1½ feet above the sand. The 12-foot sections would simply be picked up whenever there were unusually high tides or storms and then permanently packed away for the winter. The Boardwalk was such a success that people came from all over to walk on it. The original Boardwalk gave way to a second Boardwalk, this one built on pilings; it extended some two miles along the beach. Also, it was 20 feet wide instead of 10.

After an 1889 hurricane did much damage to the Boardwalk's structural support, it was agreed by city officials to reconstruct it on steel pilings rather than wood, make it 24 feet wide, and increase it to four miles in length. Today's version of the Boardwalk is 60 feet wide and six miles long, and although it has seen better days, the Boardwalk is still a major Atlantic City attraction. It also remains the longest and most popular boardwalk in the world.

Prior to World War II, when Atlantic City experienced its first Golden Age, the Boardwalk had a number of piers attached to it that contained amusement rides, side shows, dance halls and restaurants. The Steel Pier grew to be Atlantic City's most famous pier. But due to storms, fires and general neglect, the piers lost their charm; some became eyesores. Today renovation is under way to restore the piers. The Garden Pier, for instance, is now the home of the Atlantic City Art Center (see below). Formerly the Million Dollar Pier, Ocean One juts out into the ocean in the form of a huge luxury liner. Located on the Boardwalk at Arkansas Avenue, it has over 150 shops and boutiques, fast-food parlors and ocean-view dining on its upper decks. Resembling more a large, sprawling suburban mall than a classic Atlantic City pier, it contains stores that are pretty standard. But some shops carry quality clothing and women's accessories, including jewelry, while the others are simply places to spend money won at the blackjack table or slot machine.

Another part of Atlantic City's past is coming back into vogue. Hand-pushed "Rolling Chairs," a leisurely and nostalgic form of Boardwalk transportation, first appeared on the Boardwalk in 1887. Today, these canopied wicker chairs on wheels can be hired to get from one point on the Boardwalk to another. There are also "Boardwalk Rolling Chair Tours" during the summer. For information and reservations, call (609) 347–7148. Finally, motorized trams ride up and down the Boardwalk, a fine alternative to walking. Trams run from Albany Avenue to the Garden Pier; they're in service 10 A.M.—9 P.M. on weekdays and to midnight on weekends and throughout the summer.

The Atlantic City Boardwalk differs from all other major boardwalks on the Jersey Shore not only because of its long tradition, but because it's all but void of amusement rides and wheels of chance. There are plenty of fast-food outlets and tacky T-shirt stands, but generally what you'll find on the Boardwalk here is a slightly higher standard shop, even stores that sell clothes, fashionable beach apparel, hats, and ladies' handbags and footwear.

An excellent selection of fudge and taffy awaits you at **Fralinger's** (1325 Boardwalk), where in 1885 Joseph Fralinger made his first tasty batch of Atlantic City saltwater taffy (see below). You can purchase 16 different flavors of the chewy stuff, including chocolate-dipped taffy, as well as peanut butter chews, almond macaroons and sea foam fudge. It's virtually impossible to pass Fralinger's without stopping. The same holds true for **James' Candy** (1101 and 1519 Boardwalk), **Steel's Fudge** (1112, 1633 and 2719 Boardwalk) and the **Peanut Shoppe** (2633 Boardwalk).

Irene's Souvenirs & Gifts (1239 Boardwalk) is Atlantic City's oldest gift shop; if you're looking for that Atlantic City novelty item to take home with you (T-shirt, sweatshirt, ashtray, mug), you'll probably find it here. For more unusual Atlantic City novelties, try **Rainbow's End Gift Shop** (1409 and 2215 Boardwalk). And at **Ol' Times** (1639 Boardwalk) you can buy custom-blended tobacco, snuff and imported cigars.

Undoubtedly the most noted Boardwalk landmark is Atlantic City's

Convention Hall. This 532,800-square-foot arena is the largest convention and exposition hall in the Northeast and the home of Atlantic City's most famous event, the Miss America Pageant. Located on the Boardwalk between Mississippi and Florida avenues, Convention Hall recently received a $23 million facelift. The extensive renovations have led to an increase in conventions that city officials say will become even more pronounced in the next three years. There are also plans to stage more sporting events there, such as championship boxing and tennis matches, as well as concerts.

In addition to Convention Hall, there are plans for a brand-new convention center in Atlantic City. To be built on the site of the former rail terminal at the entrance to the Atlantic City Expressway, this new convention center will stand beside the new rail terminal and share the convention and sporting event business with Convention Hall.

THE CASINOS

Merv Griffin's Resorts
(North Carolina Avenue and the Boardwalk)

Under popular TV-talk-show host Merv Griffin's ownership, Resorts (originally called Resort's International, the very first casino to open in Atlantic City in 1978) has received an extensive $400 million face-lift designed to make it competitive with the other Atlantic City casinos in the 1990s. Resorts now sport an attractive Art Deco theme that blends smartly with the existing design of the casino-hotel, once the Chalfonte-Haddon Hall.

In addition to the theme change, Resorts redecorated many of its hotel rooms and refurbished the lobby and Superstar Theatre; replaced all the carpet and wall coverings; renovated the Rendezvous Lounge, which features daily, live entertainment; remodeled the Capriccio, considered one of the best Italian restaurants in Atlantic City; and opened a new restaurant, the Beverly Hills Buffet, that's capable of serving up to 4,000 guests per day.

As with all the casino complexes in Atlantic City, the best dining and shopping can be found mere steps away from the betting tables. Resorts has seven quality restaurants under its roof. The most noted are **Capriccio,** with its sumptuous Italian specialties; **Le Palais,** which offers a Continental cuisine in a room reminiscent of Grand Old Europe; **Camelot,** which is distinctively English; and the **House of Kyoto,** where guests enjoy tempura, sushi and other Japanese culinary delights. Some of the more exclusive shops found in the Resorts complex include **Pierre Ger-**

The Short and Long of Saltwater Taffy

Saltwater taffy is made with salt water, true or false. If you answered false, you're correct. The only salt that is found in saltwater taffy recipes is salt used in *any* candy recipe. It seems that the idea of calling the first taffy made and sold in Atlantic City "saltwater" taffy was more gimmick than anything else. One legend has it that the taffy became "Saltwater" taffy after seawater soaked the supply of a taffy vendor named David Bradley in an 1883 summer storm. He jokingly referred to the candy as "saltwater" taffy, and the name stuck.

But it wasn't Bradley who *invented* taffy, as some people believe. No one knows for certain who was responsible for the sweet, sticky stuff that tastes delicious. Once again legend has it that it was created by the Ritchie Brothers and Windle Hollis in 1880. But taffy historians (there are such people) claim that taffy was being sold at Midwest county fairs that same year. So, although the Ritchie Brothers and Mr. Hollis were the first to make the candy in Atlantic City, they may or may not have been the candy's true creators.

One thing is certain, though. It was Joseph Fralinger who popularized saltwater taffy and became Atlantic City's first Saltwater Taffy King. Fralinger not only realized the poten-tial of selling candy to bathers and boardwalkers, but he also figured there was a market for taking home taffy as an Atlantic City souvenir. He boxed some of the candy as an experiment and quickly sold out.

As with all good marketing ideas, competition sprouted quickly. Fralinger's biggest rival was confectioner Enoch James and his sons; they had heard about the taffy hoopla going on in Atlantic City out in the Midwest and moved to the Jersey Shore to set up shop just down the Boardwalk from Fralinger's. Supposedly, James added vegetable oil to his brand of taffy in order to lessen the chances of its pulling out dentures, and he cut his candy "to fit the mouth." Fralinger's, on the other hand, had taffy that was long and slender rather than rectangular, and Atlantic City's first taffy war was on. To this day, Fralinger's and James' taffy stores are in keen competition with each other.

Others joined in the fray, so by the mid-1920s, when saltwater taffy was at the height of its popularity, more than 450 companies were making and selling saltwater taffy. Despite the fact that it was sold all over, Atlantic City remained the saltwater taffy capital of the world, and the candy is still synonymous with the Boardwalk here.

ard Men's Fashions, Brittany Jewels, Andrew Geller Fashion Footwear, and the Antiquarium.

A number of excellent package deals are offered by the hotel during the winter, which include reduced room rates and discounts or free admission to floor shows, the Resorts Health Spa and some of the eateries on the premises. There are nearly 700 guest rooms; 511 of them are located in the East Tower, while the remaining 160 are located in the Terraces (formerly the North Tower). For reservations, call (800) 438–7424.

Caesars's Atlantic City
(Arkansas Avenue and the Boardwalk)

The theme at Caesar's Atlantic City is decidedly Roman, as you might expect. The bold, lusty motif of red, purple and gold coupled with marble columns and staircases is enhanced by reproductions of famous works of Italian art, including a 17-foot-tall replica of Michelangelo's statue of David, carved from the same quarry used by the Renaissance master.

In the main lobby, you'll find other classic statues like **Farnese Hercules** and **Victory of Samothrace.** An 18-foot replica of **Caesar Augustus of Prima Porta** stands tall and stately at the corner of the Boardwalk and Arkansas Avenue. You'll also see toga-clad waiters and wine servers and experience a festive, frequently bacchanalian spirit, which permeates much of the complex. Formerly the Howard Johnson's Regency, Caesar's was first called Caesar's Boardwalk Regency. It was the second casino to open in Atlantic City, taking its first bet in June 1979.

Aside from its lavish casino, Caesar's is also noted for its 1,100-seat luxury **Circus Maximus Theater,** which is ideally suited for boxing matches, floor shows and performances by internationally known singers and entertainers.

For added entertainment, try **Grayhound's Electric Company,** a fun, coin-operated amusement arcade, or rooftop tennis. **Caesar's Health Spa** includes a coed Universal weight room, plus steam baths, saunas, sun booths, Jacuzzis and dressing rooms. Massages are available by appointment. As for shopping, Caesar's offers such elegant shops as **Gucci, Brittany Jewelers,** and **Les Enfants Children's Boutique.**

There are 12 restaurants in the Caesar's complex, including the sinfully satisfying **Le Posh,** which serves gourmet Continental dishes; **Primavera,** which specializes in dishes from both northern and southern Italy (do try the Fettucine Primavera); the **Imperial Steakhouse,** which features not only juicy, perfectly prepared steaks, but also veal, lamb, and New England lobster; and the **Hyakumi Japanese Restaurant,** where **teppan-yaki** chefs cater to your tastebuds and serve a seven-course dinner at your table.

Caesar's Hotel contains 636 units; 427 rooms and 24 suites are located in the 12-story Regency Tower, and another 140 suites and the remaining rooms are in the 19-story Boardwalk Tower. For reservations, call (800) 582–7600.

Bally's Park Place
(Park Place and the Boardwalk)

Unlike other Atlantic City casino-hotels that are thick with glitz and gaudy facades, Bally's Park Place is a study of subtlety—if there is such a thing in this town. The Bally's "tree" logo can be found throughout the complex as can flowers, plants and beautiful greenery, which, against a backdrop of perpetual purple, provides an interesting juxtaposition of nature and neon.

Bally's opened in December 1979 as Atlantic City's third casino/resort. To make way for it, the Marlborough and Blenheim hotels were demolished. However, many of the gargoyles and ornaments from these old structures were preserved and can be seen throughout the complex. A third old hotel, the Dennis, was renovated and became part of the resort. Bally's Park Place Casino Hotel has 1,300 guest rooms. The Tower contains more than 800 of these rooms; most of them have a panoramic ocean or bay view.

Bally's offers a selection of fine restaurants that rank with Atlantic City's best. **By the Sea** recalls the ambiance of luxury-cruise liners and features gourmet Continental cuisine. Specialties frequently include Stuffed Veal Chop Valdostana, Flounder Florentine, and Risotto with Shrimp and Asparagus. **Prime Place** features classic American steaks cooked to order. **Ferrara of New York** is a great place to feast on pastries, cakes, gelati and imported Italian soft drinks. You can get fresh clams, mussels or shrimp at **Jib's Oyster Bar.**

For entertainment other than gambling, **Bally's Park Cabaret,** although small in comparison to, say, Caesar's Circus Maximus, nevertheless features first-class entertainment. The more intimate setting (400 seats as opposed to 1100 in Circus Maximus) is perfect for Bally's rave revues. Call (800) 772–7777 for ticket information. **Billy's Pub,** the former jazz lounge that once featured the sounds of Dizzy Gillespie, Charlie Byrd and Hugh Masakela, now features Top 40 pop bands. Finally, shops such as the **Park Place Boutique,** the **Circle Gallery of Atlantic City** and the **Avant Garde at Bally's** carry quality merchandise and are fun whether you browse or buy.

The Sands
(Indiana Avenue at Brighton Park)

The Sands is located on the Brighton Park Mall, which also includes the Claridge and Bally's Park Place, and is the hub of casino activity in Atlantic City. Formerly the Brighton, the Sands was Atlantic City's fourth casino. It was renamed the Sands in 1981, two years after the Brighton Hotel and Casino began taking bets. Since then, business has improved dramatically, thanks to better management and more than $50 million spent in refurbishment and expansion.

The Sands offers much in the way of special concepts and amenities. The **Sands Country Club,** located in nearby Somers Point, is part of the Sands' facilities. There, guests can play golf on a par-70 championship course and can enjoy a fully equipped clubhouse, pro shops, driving range, outdoor swimming pool and restaurant overlooking the 18th green. The Sands Country Club is also home to the annual LPGA Atlantic City Classic Golf Tournament. The course is rated as the toughest on the LPGA tour.

For budget-minded guests, there is the Food Court at the Sands, an atrium plaza that offers the widest selection of fast-food eateries in any Atlantic City casino complex. **Boston Pizza, Boston Subs and Salads, Dipstix, Jack's Corn Crib, Nathan's, Pat's Steaks,** and **Sly's Hamburgers** offer quick lunches and suppers and are cheap enough so that day-trippers with only a limited amount of money to spend in the casino can eat without seriously denting their cash stash.

The Sands doesn't offer guests just fast food. At **Mes Amis** you can dine on delicious Continental dishes. Italian specialties presented in a gourmet buffet setting are what you'll find at **Rossi's,** while at the **Brighton Steakhouse** you can choose between steaks and seafood.

For live entertainment, it's the Sands **Copa Room,** complete with deep red banquettes, elegant carpeting, high ceilings and a superb sound system. The Copa Room seats 850 and has featured such headliners as Eddie Murphy, Linda Ronstadt and Robin Williams. For ticket reservations, call the Copa Room box office at (609) 441-4591.

The Sands Hotel has 501 guest rooms, 43 suites, 9 cabana suites, and 7 palatial super suites. For reservations, call (800) 257-8580.

Harrah's Marina
(Brigantine Boulevard)

Not all of Atlantic City's casinos are situated on or just off the Boardwalk. Harrah's Marina (along with Trump Castle, see below) is located on Absecon Inlet across from the Frank S. Farley State Marina. At first, this might seem a bit inconvenient, especially for those who wish to gamble and visit more than one casino. But Harrah's is just two miles away from the Boardwalk and is easily connected to the other casinos at Brighton Park by jitneys that transport people back and forth for a small fee.

Being on the water, Harrah's pays special attention to boaters. More than 100 slips are available for customers' use from May through October. Docking fees vary according to the size of the boat. Harrah's also runs daily boat trips on the *Harrah's Belle.* These hour-long cruises depart six times daily, seven days a week from the Harbour at Harrah's and tour a part of the Intracoastal Waterway. *Harrah's Star,* a 46-foot sport-fishing yacht, can be chartered for offshore angling excursions as well as for sightseeing and private parties. Harrah's even has its own boardwalk. It's called the Baywalk and wraps around the bay side of the complex.

It was in Harrah's casino where one of the most incredible slot machine payoffs took place. Here's how Harrah's explains it: "A man won $1.25 million on a progressive slot machine. During a press conference the next day, the man returned to the exact machine for publicity photos. Asking a woman who was playing to step aside for a moment, the lucky winner deposited his coins, pulled the handle and hit for another $11,000. Harrah's also paid the woman who had so graciously given up her spot."

Those who wish to dine in elegance before or after gambling or after attending a show at the **Broadway by the Bay Theatre** need not leave the Harrah's complex. **The Meadows** is Harrah's most raved-about restaurant; gourmet French specialties, including Rainbow Brook Trout and Veal Pignola, have made the restaurant a frequent award winner in culinary competitions. **The Steakhouse** features prime beef and lamb and has an impressive wine list. **Andreotti's Ristorante** features homemade pasta and dishes from both northern and southern Italy.

As for accommodations, Harrah's offers more than 750 rooms, including 244 suites. If you choose a suite, you'll stay in the 16-story Atrium Tower where every bedroom has a view of the Atlantic City skyline or the adjoining wetlands and bay area. Call (800) 242–7724 for reservations.

Did you know that . . .

Harrah's is the only gaming corporation with properties in all major United States gaming locations: Reno, Las Vegas, Lake Tahoe and Atlantic City.

Bally's Grand
(Boston Avenue and the Boardwalk)

Formerly the Golden Nugget, Bally's Grand sits at the southern end of the Boardwalk. Although it's not one of the largest casino-hotel complexes in Atlantic City—its gaming area is only 45,000 square feet—

Bally's Grand is one of the most elegant, and its relatively small size usually ensures first-class treatment for regular and first-time patrons alike.

Bally's Grand is dressed in plenty of glass, chandeliers and hand-painted murals (there's a huge mural depicting the 1890 Atlantic City Easter Parade at the entrance to the building on Pacific Avenue). The extensive Italian marble and luxurious floor coverings accent Bally's elegant environment and provide visitors with a certain sense of sophistication.

In addition to its 510 guest rooms and suites, which all have an ocean view, Bally's also offers first-class restaurants in its complex. **Mr. Ming's** features exotic Oriental dishes. **The Oaks** specializes in beef and fresh fish. And **Caruso's** is an excellent place for pasta and veal dishes. Less formal dining and tasty desserts can be had at the **Cornucopia Cafe,** the **Sweetheart Cafe** and the **Creamery.**

There is more than gambling going on at Bally's Grand. The 540-seat **Opera House** is an excellent venue to see and hear the likes of Frank Sinatra, Jerry Lewis, Julie Andrews and Lou Rawls, among many others. It was Sinatra, Lewis and the late Sammy Davis, Jr., who headlined the star-studded celebration in 1987 when the Golden Nugget became Bally's Grand. There is also good music at **Gatsby's,** a popular cocktail lounge; electronic and traditional pinball games (after all, the Bally's Corp. invented the pinball machine) in **The Arcade,** and a 9,000-square-foot swimming pool in a tropical garden setting. Shopping opportunities include **The Emporium,** which specializes in men's and women's contemporary wear, and **Le Salon,** a boutique with an emphasis on designer sportswear.

For reservations, room rates and information on Bally's Grand package deals, call (800) 257–8677.

The Claridge
(Indiana Avenue and the Boardwalk)

Despite being the smallest casino in Atlantic City (43,030 square feet of casino space as opposed to 120,000 square feet at the largest casino, the Taj Mahal), the Claridge still has something to offer to the Atlantic City gambler. The Claridge's refined, even chivalrous ambiance, a product of the complex's European and English decor, is a welcome alternative to the more brightly lit, glitzy casinos. There is, in fact, a deliberate downplay of loud ornaments and designs in the Claridge. Some gamblers enjoy the relaxed, subdued decor; other opt for more spectacle and eventually wind up betting at Caesar's or the Taj Mahal.

Intimacy and refinement are what the Claridge's **Palace Theater** and **Celebrity Cabaret** also strive for. The former features Broadway-style musicals Saturday through Thursday evenings, while the latter features three comedians six nights per week. (Tuesday is "Open Mike Night" at the Celebrity Cabaret, with four amateur comedians performing with three tried-and-true professionals.) For Palace Theater ticket information, call (800) 752–7469.

Before or after the show, visit the **Twenties Supper Club and Lounge** for a drink and a bite to eat, or the **Great American Buffet,** which offers a constantly changing though complete menu of American hot and cold entrees and tempting desserts. For a bit more formal dining experience, try **Martino's** for good Italian food.

The Claridge Hotel has 504 rooms, many of which have ocean or bay views. This wonderfully restored two-story brick-and-limestone building has been a part of the Atlantic City skyline for many years. A half century ago, the Claridge's clientele included many wealthy vacationers who viewed Atlantic City as one of the East Coast's most favored summer resorts.

The Claridge offers a fine selection of package deals. Potential guests should inquire about them if they plan to visit during the winter season, because during the cold months of January and February the Claridge's packages are real bargains. For reservations and package-deal information, call (800) 582–7676.

Did you know that . . .

The average daily total win in Atlantic City's casinos is more than $5 million.

Trop World
(Iowa Avenue and the Boardwalk)

It seems Trop World (formerly called the Tropicana) goes out of its way for the mid-range gambler more than any other casino in Atlantic City. For slot machine players, that part of the Trop World casino called **Slot City,** which includes 2,400 slots in an astounding variety of shapes, colors and sizes, can best be described as a slot machine paradise. The rows of machines have names like Big Bertha Boulevard, Easy Street, Wall Street and Million Dollar Drive—it was on a slot machine on Million Dollar Drive that a patron won $2.2 million, the largest jackpot ever paid at the Trop World casino.

Trop World also features a terrific variety of slots to serve every customer. You can bet a nickel or $100, and you can do it on everything from standard slots to video-poker machines. There is also a new "Slot

City by the Sea" section that contains four big aquariums filled with tropical fish.

When you tire of gambling, Trop World offers the best variety of alternative entertainment. Whether you choose the **Comedy Stop,** the Trop's popular comedy club; **Sizzles,** a lounge that features live music and dancing; the Trop's 1,700 seat showroom that regularly features world-class entertainers; or the **Sandbar,** another popular club that's dècorated with a rolling ceiling and the four large aquariums that separate it from Slot City, you won't be bored. And when you add the Trop's main alternative to gambling, **Tivoli Pier,** it's no wonder Trop World considers itself a casino-hotel *and* entertainment resort.

Tivoli Pier, a two-acre indoor theme park, is a throwback to the old piers that jutted out from the Atlantic City Boardwalk and were filled with thrilling rides and attractions. At Tivoli Pier, you can ride a four-story indoor Ferris wheel and a simulated space capsule, romp through a fun house that will get everyone laughing, get bumped by bumper cars, take a ride through Atlantic City's history on a simulated holography tour of the resort and enjoy a number of other amusement rides and attractions.

The Trop also has a wide selection of five-star restaurants and less formal eateries. The **Phoenix** offers fresh seafood, steaks and pasta dishes. **Il Verdi** is the place to dine if you enjoy northern Italian seafood and veal dishes. The **Regent Court** is known for its steaks, while **Pier 7** serves up lobster and the catch-of-the-day.

The Trop World Hotel has 1,000 rooms, including 300 luxury suites. Before you make reservations, look into Trop World's assortment of package deals. Most include free gifts, food credits, welcome cocktails and room rates that are surprisingly economical. For more information, call (800) 257–6227.

Trump Plaza
(Mississippi Avenue and the Boardwalk)

Trump Plaza used to be called the Trump Casino Hotel. Owned by internationally famous tycoon Donald Trump (he also owns the Trump Castle and Atlantic City's biggest, most luxurious casino complex, the Taj Mahal), you can rest assured that classy accommodations, glitz and glamour, and that certain touch of Trumpian opulence fill this casino, as well as his other two.

Located next to Atlantic City's Convention Hall, the Plaza is connected to the huge arena by an enclosed overhead skywalk. Such proximity and accessibility make rooms at the Trump Plaza much in demand when special events like the Miss America Pageant and business conventions are held in the Hall.

Trump Plaza's 556 rooms include a number of suites and super suites that bear "the Trump signature of excellence," say the Plaza brochures. Although less luxurious, most of the other rooms have benefited from a $100 million expansion and facelift. In fact, as of 1990, the Trump Plaza Hotel was the only hotel in Atlantic City to be given four stars by Mobil and four diamonds by AAA—two of the most respected hotel rating groups in the country. The Trump Plaza is routinely named as one of the top ten hotels in America.

With the first-class service you get in the Plaza hotel, you might be lured into spending too much time there. Don't let that happen. The **Trump Plaza Theater** regularly features such superstars as Paul Anka, Anita Baker, Ben Vereen, the Temptations and Gladys Knight. The Plaza's dazzling selection of restaurants where you can feast on everything from award-winning French specialties (**Ivana's**) to succulent steaks (**Max's Steak House**), to homemade pasta (**Roberto's Ristorante**), to Cantonese lobster in shrimp sauce (**Fortune's**) to a giant, overstuffed pastrami sandwich on rye with the tastiest pickles this side of the Hudson River (**Harvey's Deli**)—is second to none. You can also treat yourself to Ben & Jerry's gourmet ice cream at **Scoops,** sip a cool drink at **Jezebel's** or **Trump's,** or crack open oysters at **Oyster Trump.**

You can unwind from all the gambling excitement at the **Plaza Spa.** In addition to state-of-the-art exercise equipment, you can also treat yourself to a massage, an herbal and a soft-glo loofah cleansing. Amenities like fruit and fruit juices and wide-screen television supplement your wind-down.

The Taj Mahal and Trop World get a lot of attention because of their size, but Atlantic City regulars say the Trump Plaza might well be the best casino-hotel complex in Atlantic City when it comes to service and class. For more information and room rates, call (800) 677–7378.

Trump Castle
(Huron Avenue and Brigantine Boulevard)

Formerly the Atlantic Hilton, the Trump Castle is the second of two casinos on Absecon Inlet located directly across from the Frank S. Farley State Marina (the other is Harrah's Marina). Since the complex is so close to one of southern New Jersey's best marinas, it's not surprising that Trump Castle takes full advantage of its nautical connection. Stay at the Castle and you can enjoy dockside dining at the **Harbor View** and pleasure cruises along the Atlantic City shoreline. If you arrive by boat,

Some Things to Remember When Gambling

1. The axiom, "Bet with your head, not over it," is a good one and worth keeping in mind whenever you walk into an Atlantic City casino.

2. Betting schemes don't work. No matter how elaborate yours is, your fortune (or misfortune) rides on your luck.

3. You must be 21 years old to gamble in Atlantic City.

4. Before you enter a casino, set a limit on how much you can lose *before* it starts to hurt—and stick to it.

5. Gambling should be fun, not a make-or-break situation.

6. Atlantic City casinos open at 10 A.M. and close at 4 A.M. on weekdays and 6 A.M. on weekends and holidays.

7. Know the rules of the games you play. You can pick up a pamphlet called *Rules of the Game* at most casino security booths.

8. Taking photographs in the casinos is not allowed.

9. The Casino Control Commission of New Jersey states that all slot machines must be designed to return a minimum of 83 percent to bettors.

10. Cheating in the form of marked cards, weighted dice and diversionary tactics doesn't work. Undercover security men, pit bosses and state police detectives are always on the floor.

11. The smartest bettor stops betting while he or she is ahead.

you'll dock next to luxurious yachts and sailboats. And always there is the beautiful view of the nearby Brigantine section of the Edwin B. Forsythe National Refuge, with its thousands of visiting birds and ducks.

When not cruising on the ocean or bay or gambling, guests at Trump Castle can take in a show at the **Crystal Room,** which plays host to big-name entertainers such as Billy Crystal, Dolly Parton and Rodney Dangerfield; enjoy the variety show at the **King's Court Showroom;** dance the night away at **Viva's Nightclub;** ease tension on the **Trump Castle's recreation deck,** which includes a jogging track, tennis courts, weights, steam rooms, saunas and whirlpool baths; or browse through such in-complex shops as **With Love, LaClotique II, Ginanni Men's Wear** and **Kron Chocolatier.** If all this isn't enough, you can catch a jitney to the Atlantic City Boardwalk, located just minutes away, and casino-hop or simply stroll the boards.

In addition to the **Harbor View,** Trump Castle also features three other top restaurants. The one that has garnered its share of rave reviews is **Delfino's,** thanks to its Continental specialties and excellent wine list. However, **Portofino,** with its northern Italian dishes, and the **Castle Steak House,** with its Old West decor and thick, meticulously cooked steaks, should not be missed, either.

Your room at the Trump Castle will be in either the Bay Tower, with its 607 rooms decorated with smart Art Deco flair, or the Crystal Tower, where there are 100 suites, complete with marble floors, custom-woven carpets and individual butler service. No matter which tower you choose, your room is bound to have a great view of the nearby bay and wetlands or the Atlantic City skyline.

For room rates, information on package deals and slip reservations for those guests arriving by boat, call (800) 365–8786.

Showboat
(Delaware Avenue and the Boardwalk)

Situated next to Trump's Taj Mahal on the northern end of the Atlantic City Boardwalk, the Showboat has some stiff competition. But despite what some might say to be its unfortunate location, the Showboat shows a yearly profit margin that's higher than more than half of the other Atlantic City casino-hotel complexes. And Showboat officials believe the casino-hotel's proximity to the Taj will only increase the Showboat's profits. They point to the isolation of the Showboat at the end of the Boardwalk before the opening of the Taj in 1990.

The key to the Showboat's success, aside from shrewd management policies and clever marketing strategies, has been the warm, Southern-style hospitality it offers to guests. The entire first floor resembles turn-of-the-century New Orleans, with wrought-iron and brass and Bourbon Street facades in every view. Strolling musicians wander through the crowd, and the sound of Dixieland jazz bands fills the air. The enclosed, climate-controlled bridge that connects the Showboat with the Taj Mahal is decorated so that guests can imagine they're walking on the deck of a Mississippi Riverboat. A taped soundtrack of passing ships and churning water and a robot dressed as a captain that welcomes everyone aboard add to your sensory voyage up the Mississippi. And, in case you've forgotten, the most exciting activity on these old paddle-wheeled riverboats was gambling.

When it comes time for evening entertainment and dinner, the Showboat scores high marks. The **Mississippi Pavilion** is where talents like Bob Hope and Willie Nelson perform, while the **Mardi Gras Showroom** offers lesser name entertainers nightly. For dinner, you have your choice of **Lafayette's,** the Showboat's most elegant restaurant, which features sumptuous Continental cuisine; the **Mississippi Steak &**

Seafood Co., where you'll enjoy the best in steaks and fish dishes; or **Casa Di Napoli,** where the menu is stocked with southern Italian entrees. You can also eat and run at **Deli on the Square,** or stuff yourself silly at the **Captain's Buffet,** an all-you-can-eat restaurant that offers a delicious seafood buffet one night a week.

Most of the Showboat's 516 rooms in its 25-story hotel tower have been decorated with an eye toward Victoriana. All rooms come with color cable TV, and there's a telephone in every bathroom. For more information, call (800) 677–7378.

The Taj Mahal
(Virginia Avenue and the Boardwalk)

The Taj Mahal is the largest casino-complex in the world, taking up more than 17 acres of prime Atlantic City real estate. It has the largest casino in the world, covering 120,000 square feet and including more than 3,000 slot machines. More than $14 million worth of Austrian crystal chandeliers hang from the Taj's ceilings. Standing on the 51st floor of the Taj hotel, you're 429 feet above sea level and have one of the finest views of the south Jersey Shore. The Taj Mahal is, in a phrase, the ultimate Trump turn-on.

Partly because of the Trump mystique, and partly because of its massive size and shine-in-your-face opulence, the Taj Mahal has become the flagship casino and hotel in Atlantic City. Although it's located at the northern end of the Boardwalk, away from the hustle and bustle around Brighton Park, the Taj is still the most frequented casino in town. More bettors spend more money there than at any other casino. And it's a good thing, because the Taj must take in $1 million a day just to break even.

How does it lure such big bucks day after day? The Taj's casino has more than 160 gaming tables and a decor that includes jeweled ceilings, beveled mirrors and twenty-four 5,000-piece chandeliers (that cost a quarter of a million dollars each), not to mention other glittering amenities too numerous to mention. Its exterior, which, of course, resembles the Taj Mahal of India, features minarets and onion domes, beautifully landscaped grounds, large fountains, and nine two-ton stone Indian elephants that greet visitors to the complex.

Concerts, stage shows, tennis and boxing matches and special events such as the Moscow Circus are held at the Taj's **Mark Grossinger Etess Arena,** a huge all-purpose hall that ranks second only to Atlantic City Convention Hall in sheer space. It has enough seats for more than 5,500 people.

The 12 restaurants on the premises can accommodate 3,000 diners at one time. You can get deli-style sandwiches at the **New Delhi Deli;** '50s-style hamburgers, hot dogs and milk shakes at **Rock and Rolls;** Oriental cuisine at **Dynasty;** a buffet "fit for a sultan" at **Sultan's Feast;** seafood at **Sinbad's;** Italian pasta at **Marco Polo;** steaks at the **Safari Steak House;** and international dishes at **Scheherazade,** where diners can watch a baccarat pit.

There are also four popular bars and lounges. The **Casbah** and the **Oasis** have live music. **Paddy's Saloon** and the **Rain Forest** have more intimate settings.

For accommodations there are more than 1,250 rooms and lavish suites—all with great views of the Atlantic Ocean or the Atlantic City skyline. The top 12 floors of the hotel have a private club and house 237 ultraluxurious suites each beautifully decorated and complete with private saunas, powder room, dining room, and bar.

No trip to Atlantic City would be complete without at least a stroll through this magnificent structure. The Taj Mahal is surely Atlantic City's centerpiece. But while it redefines opulence and bigness in the casino industry, it begs the question: How much is enough?

For information on room rates and package deals at the Taj Mahal, call (800) 255–7777.

Around Atlantic City

Things to Do

Visit the Atlantic City Art Center. Located on Garden Pier (Boardwalk and New Jersey Avenue). Paintings, photographs and sculpture exhibited here feature the talents of Art Center members, as well as those artists from outside the fold whose work is on special display. Along with the Noyes Museum in nearby Oceanville (see chapter 6), the Atlantic City Art Center provides visitors with the opportunity to view the work of some of South Jersey's best artists. Call (609) 347–5844 for information on the latest exhibits. Admission is free.

Visit the Atlantic City Historical Museum. Also located on Garden Pier adjacent to the Atlantic City Art Center is the Atlantic City Historical Museum. It should be considered a must for those fond of nostalgia. Few American cities have undergone such a rapid and profound change in their overall makeup as Atlantic City. Here at the museum you will get a good idea of what Atlantic City B.C. (Before Casinos) was like. See the displays and exhibits on the city's old theaters and cabarets, memorabilia pertaining to the Boardwalk's Golden Age as well as photographs of the beach and piers and the slew of special events and promotional stunts that seemed to keep Atlantic City in the news during the 1930s and 1940s. For those interested in immersing themselves further into Atlantic City history and culture, pick up a copy of *Atlantic City: 125 Years of Ocean Madness* by Vicki Gold Levi and Lee Eisenberg. Much of Levi's memorabilia is on display in the museum. Admission is free. Call (609) 927–5218 for more information.

Visit the Absecon Lighthouse. Like Old Barney on Long Beach Island, Old Ab was designed and built by Gen. George Gordon Meade in 1857 and for a long time was an Atlantic City symbol and trademark. Today, Absecon Lighthouse is a symbol of yesteryear as it stands on a barren lot surrounded by urban renewal and urban blight. Located on Pacific and Rhode Island avenues, the lighthouse is, unfortunately, no longer open to the public.

Visit Gardner's Basin. It was to this cove off Absecon Inlet where pirates and privateers retreated when they weren't confronting merchant vessels off the Jersey coast in the eighteenth century. It was also here, later on, that whalers and whaling boats created much activity on the docks during the height of the hunting season. Today the basin is home to a historic maritime village that contains old, restored buildings moved from various parts of South Jersey and brought here for preservation. On display nearby is a two-man research submarine that was designed to assist in the underwater efforts of salvaging sunken ships. Gardner's Basin is located at North New Hampshire Avenue and the Inlet. Admission is free.

Boat Watch at Senator Frank S. Farley State Marina. Located on Clam Creek just across from Trump Castle and near Harrah's Marina, the Frank S. Farley State Marina has berths for 432 craft and is the center of boat activity in Atlantic City. Looking to crew on a sailboat? Dockside here at the Farley Marina is a good place to start inquiring which boat is in need of an extra mate. There are big yachts here, small fishing skiffs and annual fishing tournaments; it's the best place in the area to boat-watch and mingle with sailors. For information on mooring privileges and berths, call (609) 348–2292 or write Senator Frank S. Farley State Marina, 600 Huron Avenue, Atlantic City 08401.

Take a Peek Inside Lucy the Elephant. Lucy is a 65-foot-high, 90-ton pachyderm that was built in 1881 by a Philadelphia real estate developer to lure prospective land buyers to South Atlantic City or what is today the Atlantic City suburb of Margate. Blessed with a tin skin and the loving care of the Save Lucy Committee, which raised thousands of dollars to restore the elephant, the architectural oddity is a favorite with both kids and adults. Now listed as a National Historic Landmark, Lucy stands at the intersection of Atlantic and Decatur avenues. Guides take tourists inside the giant elephant's belly by ascending a flight of stairs inside its hind legs. A small museum houses exhibits pertaining to

Lucy's 100-year history. Visitors are also able to peer out Lucy's eyes and check the view from the observation deck atop the elephant, which is in the form of a howdah, or Indian-styled traveling basket designed to carry prominent citizens.

During the summer, free weekly concerts are held at Lucy Park next to the elephant; big band, Dixie and country music usually constitute the schedule of musical entertainment. Nearby is a Lucy gift shop where you can buy Lucy T-shirts, stuffed elephants and knickknacks. All proceeds go toward the continued upkeep and restoration of the elephant. There is an admission charge to tour Lucy.

Visit the Atlantic City Race Course. If there's not enough betting action for you in the casinos, or if blackjack, craps or slot machines just aren't your style, what about thoroughbred racing? Take the Atlantic City Expressway to Exit 12, or head west on the Black Horse Pike to McKee City, 15 miles outside of town, for yet another form of gambling and entertainment. The racing season runs from June to September. Post time is 7:30 P.M. Call (609) 641–2190 for the latest racing information.

Where to Eat in Atlantic City

Abe's Oyster House, 2031 Atlantic Avenue, (609) 344–7701
Price Code: Moderate   Menu: Seafood
Steamed clams are the house specialty. Open from Memorial Day to Labor Day.

Angelo's Fairmount Tavern, 2300 Fairmount Avenue,
(609) 344–2439
Price Code: Moderate   Menu: Italian
No restaurant serves better meatballs. Many other homemade specialties. A big favorite with locals, and with good reason.

Dock's Oyster House, 2405 Atlantic Avenue, (609) 345–0092
Price Code: Expensive   Menu: Seafood
A noted Atlantic City restaurant for years. Oyster dishes are popular, but the poached Norwegian salmon is tops.

Johan's, 3209 Fairmount Avenue, (609) 344–5733
Price Code: Expensive   Menu: Continental
Gourmet dining all the way; expensive, but well worth it. Excellent wine list.

Knife and Fork Inn, Atlantic and Pacific avenues, (609) 344–1133
Price Code: Expensive   Menu: Seafood
If Doris and Ed's (see chapter 1) is the best seafood restaurant north of Atlantic City, the Knife and Fork Inn is the best in and south of Atlantic City. An exquisite dining experience.

Los Amigos, 1926 Atlantic Avenue, (609) 344–2293
Price Code: Inexpensive   Menu: Mexican
Burritos and Mexican pizza are best bets. The margaritas are the tastiest in town.

Peking Duck House, Iowa and Atlantic avenues, (609) 344–9090
Price Code: Moderate/Expensive   Menu: Chinese
Specialty of the house? Why, duck, of course. Szechuan, Mandarin and Cantonese cuisine.

White House Sub Shop, 2301 Arctic Avenue, (609) 345–1564
Price Code: Inexpensive   Menu: Submarine sandwiches
No question about it—the Jersey Shore's best subs are made here. The right place for lunch when you're absolutely famished.

8

The South Jersey Shore

The South Jersey Shore sits comfortably between New Jersey's largest and most popular resorts: Atlantic City to the north and Cape May to the south. It is an area of striking beauty in the form of more than 150 tiny islands; wide, sandy beaches; bays, both big and small; marshlands; nature preserves; bird sanctuaries; and summer resort towns. It is a place that, for years, resisted the often uncontrolled development and the hurried, hectic pace found farther north along the coast.

Strangely enough, the charm of the South Jersey Shore was first discovered by wealthy Philadelphians and southerners from cities such as Baltimore and Washington, D.C. Before they arrived, the area was inhabited by fishermen, whalers and shipbuilders. They came from New England to exploit the area's excellent fishing grounds, its proximity to migratory whale routes, and its cedar swamps, which provided the wood to build some of the finest ocean vessels of the nineteenth century.

Philadelphians came to the South Jersey Shore to escape the city summer heat and humidity. They arrived by coach, train and steamboat. The word spread south that New Jersey's beaches were the best in the mid-Atlantic and Upper South regions, and eventually wealthy southerners were making the trek north to bathe in the South Jersey Shore's warm ocean waters and to sail in its back bays. Few realize it, but much of the South Jersey Shore lies below the Mason-Dixon Line, including Atlantic City. And although New Jersey was most definitely a Yankee state during the Civil War, there were some southern sympathies on the South Jersey Shore.

Today, the area is still dominated by vacationers from Pennsylvania, Delaware, Maryland and, believe it or not, Canada. In Quebec, for instance, the Jersey Shore is regarded as an ideal summer retreat. Walk along the streets of Ocean City or Stone Harbor—two popular South Jersey beach resort towns—and you'll probably find as many out-of-state license plates on cars parked there as you will cars with New Jersey plates. It's a fact that Baltimore is closer to the South Jersey Shore than New York or even parts of North Jersey. And, of course, Philadelphia is closest of all. With the Cape May-Lewes, Delaware Ferry bringing visitors from the Upper South to the South Jersey Shore (see chapter 9), and with the Atlantic City Expressway providing an excellent link to Philadelphia, it's no wonder that the area is as popular as it is with out-of-staters. Add to that the lure of Atlantic City with its casinos and legalized gambling, and the thousands of visitors from New York and northern New Jersey who are exploring the South Jersey Shore for the first time, and you have an area along the Jersey coast whose popularity is growing in leaps and bounds.

In addition to its superb beaches, most of which are wider, cleaner and prettier than what you'll find anywhere else in New Jersey, the South Jersey Shore provides visitors with the opportunity to make day or evening runs into Atlantic City and Cape May. And for those wanting to enjoy the beaches, yet who are not fond of hotels or motels, South Jersey is the state's major camping area. There are many campgrounds to choose from: Some sites are primitive and situated deep in a state forest; others have almost all the conveniences of home. Most of the campgrounds are within fairly easy access of the beaches and resort towns.

Once you arrive at the South Jersey Shore and wish to get around, there are three different routes to consider. The Parkway is the main artery and is usually the quickest route to get from one point to another. But those wishing to experience a sample of the small towns and lowland countryside situated in the vicinity of the beach area should opt for Route 9. It is a two-lane road and local traffic often meanders along. But you'll come across farms, picturesque towns, roadside vegetable stands, antique dealers, old homes that date back as far as two centuries, quiet rivers, wetlands and places to camp and go horseback riding.

The most popular route, however, and one that is also highly recommended, is Scenic Ocean Drive, which extends from Absecon Inlet at the northern tip of Atlantic City to the edge of Cape May Point. Going from north to south, the route is approximately 40 miles long and weaves through the marshland and beach towns of the South Jersey Shore. As you follow the "Flight of the Gull" signs, you'll drive through Atlantic City and the suburban towns of Ventnor, Margate and Longport, pass over the Ocean City-Longport Bridge, into and through Ocean City, down through Corson's Inlet State Park, where the Corson's Inlet Bridge connects it to Strathmere and Sea Isle City. From there, you'll pass over Townsend's Inlet Bridge and onto Seven Mile Beach, where Avalon and Stone Harbor are located. Grassy South Bridge takes you over Hereford Inlet and onto Five Mile Beach. Here, you'll drive through the Wildwoods—North Wildwood, Wildwood and Wildwood Crest. Finally, you'll come to the Middle Thorofare Bridge, bypass the U.S. Coast Guard Receiving Station and head into historic Cape May.

Along the way, you'll see some of the East Coast's most valued marsh and wetlands and get an excellent idea of what the South Jersey Shore has to offer. Be advised, though, that on weekends and holidays during the summer, traffic can be rather heavy along Ocean Drive, as all the bridges are toll bridges.

Ocean City

Ocean City proudly proclaims itself "America's Greatest Family Resort." You see the slogan all over the South Jersey beach city: on billboards and welcoming signs, on postcards and tourist booklets, on the boardwalk and even on the beach. Ocean City doesn't want visitors to forget where they are or why they came.

Such a bold claim would be considered little more than hot air or perhaps a clever publicity gimmick if Ocean City did not actively work to make such a statement as valid as possible. Few people on vacation in Ocean City can cry boredom during the summer. Literally dozens of activities are sponsored each month by the city—most of them free— that encourage participation from all age groups. Everything from sand-sculpture contests to free concerts, from a baby parade to a Miss Crustacean Contest, from a hermit crab race to a half marathon, from a Bike-A-Thon to a Big Band Dance and Banjo Bash, from an art show to a sun tanning tournament, from a crafts show to a variety show. And the list goes on.

Then there's the calendar of events sponsored by the Ocean City Recreation Department. Ocean City's playgrounds and ball fields are manned by counselors every day during the summer. There's basketball, tennis, volleyball, softball, gymnastics, shuffleboard and much more.

Next, there's the boardwalk and the beach, the amusement rides and the fine restaurants, the marinas and the sailing, the bay and the ocean, the warm weather and the sun. Is there anything, one might ask, that Ocean City doesn't offer vacationers?

Yes, there is. Ocean City does not have, nor does it care to have, a nightlife, other than what's found on the boardwalk. It is, always was, and if some people have their way, always will be a dry town. That means no public drinking, no bars, no nightclubs. Ocean City is a family resort with an accent on family. You can be sure that anything that might tarnish Ocean City's rather polished image will be frowned on at the very least.

The reason why Ocean City is a dry town, much like Ocean Grove and Island Heights to the north, is that it was settled more than a hundred years ago by three Methodist minister brothers: Samuel, James and Ezra Lake. Their aim was to establish a summer community where families could not only come and pray, but do so in an environment free from vices such as liquor and gambling. And they did just that. The three signed a covenant in 1879 under a large cedar tree near what is now North Street that provided the framework for Ocean City's growth as a religious retreat.

Yet, it is rather amazing that Ocean City's blue laws have remained in effect all these years. Unlike Ocean Grove (which is a sealed community, actually enclosed with natural and man-made impediments, and which has kept its religious commitment far above any commitment to tourism), Ocean City covets summer visitors and tourists—just as long as they remain within the confines of propriety and decency.

Given all this, it's not surprising, then, that Ocean City calls itself America's Greatest Family Resort. Certainly enough people believe it, for the beach city continues to attract hordes of visitors and vacationers during the summer. Ocean City's year-round population is somewhere in the neighborhood of 18,000. In the summer, some city officials say the population balloons to 150,000. Without a doubt, Ocean City is an extremely popular South Jersey resort, ranking behind only Atlantic City in sheer numbers, and regularly entertaining visitors from as far west as Ohio, as far south as Virginia and as far north as Canada.

Ocean City is less than 10 miles south of Atlantic City on a barrier island that lies between Great Egg Harbor and the ocean. The best way to get to Ocean City is to take the Garden State Parkway to Exit 30; you'll then approach Ocean City via Route 52 East and thus will be able to stop at the Information Center just before entering town.

It is not advisable to come to Ocean City in the summer without lodging reservations. But if you do, the Information Center, which is open year-round, has a computerized telephone-access board sponsored by the Ocean City Guest and Apartment House Association that will give you free, up-to-the-minute information on the guesthouse or apartment of your choice. The center is also staffed by very knowledgeable and helpful guides who will give you all the information you need to make your stay in Ocean City an enjoyable one. There are information centers at the old municipal building on 46th Street and West Avenue and at the Music Pier on the boardwalk, too. The latter is open only during the summer. Ocean City also has a toll-free telephone number to call for accommodations and general information: (800) BEACH NJ. It's a good idea to call and request a copy of the Ocean City Vacation Guide; it will help you select the best place to stay, given your budget.

Ocean City's main attraction is its eight-mile-long beach. Beach badges are mandatory. Seasonal, weekly and daily badges are available; if you purchase yours prior to the start of the summer season, you'll receive a discount. Call the Information Center (the above number) for current rate and information on when badges go on sale. Badges can be obtained at the Music Pier Information Center, the City Clerk's office (Municipal Hall), the Information Center on 46th Street and West Avenue, the Information Center on Route 52, or any of the small booths on the boardwalk located at the entrances to the beach.

You'll find Ocean City much more than a standard summer resort. It has a fine year-round downtown shopping section, which boasts a number of fine stores and restaurants. For world renowned entertainment, Atlantic City is only minutes away. Corson's Inlet, where fishing, boardsailing, bicycling and bird-watching are favorites, lies just south of Ocean City. It too is mere minutes away.

In many ways, Ocean City resembles Long Beach Island. People who summer at Ocean City usually do so year after year. Many eventually buy summer homes there. There's much interaction between neighbors and there's a strong sense of civic pride even though many will leave Ocean City on Labor Day Weekend. You'll find more than one regular summer visitor who will heartily agree that if Ocean City isn't America's greatest family resort, then it's got to be a mighty close second.

Things to Do

Stroll the Boardwalk. There are three classic boardwalks on the South Jersey Shore: Atlantic City, Wildwood and Ocean City. The Atlantic City Boardwalk is, of course, the granddaddy of all boardwalks, and a stroll on it is something every visitor to the South Jersey Shore ought to do at least once. Wildwood is the thrills-and-chills boardwalk; no boardwalk in New Jersey, or anywhere else for that matter, has the sheer number of rides that Wildwood does. Geared especially towards the 14–24-year-old age group, the pace on the boards there is fast and lively. Ocean City is the family boardwalk. There are amusement rides, but not an impossible number of them. There are specialty shops and a shopping area known as **The Flanders** (11th Street and Boardwalk) that has wonderful men's and women's apparel shops. You won't find a plethora of shops selling T-shirts with bawdy slogans on them ("Party Naked," "I'm Hot for U," "Party Animal," and "Sex is my Mission"), the kind that seem to overwhelm Wildwood and Seaside Heights up north.

Common Sense in the Sun

1. Respect the sun. Its rays are stronger than you think.

2. Respect your skin. It's more delicate than you think.

3. Don't attempt a summer's worth of sun the first day on the beach. Limit your first couple of outings to approximately 30 minutes and gradually build up your exposure time.

4. If you burn easily, use a sunscreen or sunblock. Sunscreen diminishes the amount of ultraviolet rays, which not only cause sunburn but can also wrinkle your skin prematurely and, worse, cause skin cancer. Note the initials SPF on sunscreens. The letters stand for sun protection factor. The greater the SPF, the greater the protection from the sun.

5. Sunblocks are stronger than sunscreens. Sunblocks literally block out the sun's ultraviolet rays, whereas sunscreens simply screen out some of the rays.

6. Use a suntan oil if you tan easily. You'll acquire a deeper, darker tan if you do. Be careful, however, not to overdo it. Too much sunning with oil or lotion is apt to leave your skin leathery in appearance.

7. Always use a moisturizer after a day at the beach. Regular use will cut down on peeling and drying.

8. If you get a sunburn, treat it with Aloe Vera, a natural moisturizer.

9. Drink plenty of liquids. Gator-ade is a good choice. Take Tylenol or aspirin for pain. Cool, wet dressings will take the sting out of the sunburned area.

10. If your body temperature reaches 101 degrees and you become nauseated, see a doctor.

11. If someone you're with vomits and seems confused or dopey due to too much sun, call a doctor immediately. The person could very well be suffering from heat stroke, a life-threatening situation.

12. On the beach, wear sunglasses that filter out ultraviolet rays. If you plan to be out in the sun all day, wear white, cotton clothing.

Gillian's Wonderland Pier and Playland are where the amusement rides are located. If you plan to eat on the boardwalk, try **T.R. Fenwick's Breakfast and Dinner Buffet,** especially if you've worked up a sizable appetite. Reasonably priced, it's all you can eat. A steak sandwich at **Del's** is also a good bet. To quench a sunbaked thirst, try a delicious orange drink at **Titter's** or **Kohr's.** And for snacking, **Shriver's** is the best place on the boardwalk to get saltwater taffy and fudge; it's the oldest candy shop in Ocean City.

Enjoy the Beach. You'll find less crowded beaches farther south in towns such as Avalon and Stone Harbor. But Ocean City's beaches are nonetheless nice; they're also guarded by some of the best lifeguard crews on the South Jersey Shore. Due to offshore sandbars, the waves gently approach the shore, which makes swimming and frolicking in the water a delight for youngsters.

Attend a Concert on Music Pier. Throughout the summer, there are a number of concerts and musical programs on the Music Pier at the north end of the boardwalk. The Ocean City Pops Orchestra is a regular attraction, although most kinds of music, including soft rock, traditional jazz and gospel are well represented. You can pick up a calendar of events for the entire summer at any of Ocean City's information centers.

Visit the Ocean City Arts Center. The Ocean City Arts Center, on 36th Street and Bay Avenue, features the paintings, drawings and sculpture of area artists. The Ocean City Historical Museum contains artifacts, cargo, photographs and sailing papers of the ship *Sindia,* a four-masted barque that sank during a storm off Ocean City in 1901. As you'll find out, the *Sindia* was carrying approximately 3,000 cases of fine china on board. One thousand cases were removed; the rest remain trapped inside the ship's hull.

There's also a Fashion Room where visitors will find Victorian costumes and period furniture, all nicely presented; a wonderful doll collection; and memorabilia pertaining to Ocean City's history. Admission is free, although donations are encouraged. Open all year. For more information, call (609) 399–1801.

See the Remains of the *Sindia*. There isn't really much left to see of the *Sindia,* save the rudder post and tiller. But Ocean City has adopted the sunken ship as you'll see "Sindia this" and "Sindia that" throughout the resort. Make the pilgrimage to 16th Street and the boardwalk, as most who visit Ocean City eventually do.

Visit the Discovery Seashell Museum. The family that runs the Seashell Museum has amassed a large and interesting collection of seashells from around the world. The museum, for instance, claims to have the only Siamese-twin helmet shell ever found. About 10,000 varieties of seashells are on exhibit. In addition, crates of shells are for sale as well as hermit crabs, carved shells and beachy bric-a-brac. A must for beachcombers and shell collectors. Free admission. Located at 2717 Asbury Avenue, the telephone number is (609) 398–2316.

Visit the Ocean City Tabernacle. The current structure was built in 1957, but it stands on the site of Ocean City's first church, which was constructed in 1881. Located between 5th and 6th streets and Wesley and Asbury avenues.

View the Birds on Cowpens Island. Located west of Ocean City, south of the 9th Street Bridge, and quite near the Information Center on Route 52 is the Cowpens Island Bird Sanctuary. Go there with your binoculars at dusk and you'll probably get to see your share of egrets, heron and perhaps a glossy ibis or two.

Play Golf. Ocean City even boasts its own golf course. Located at 26th Street and Bay Avenue, the Ocean City Golf Course is a 12-hole course. Not for the seasoned pro, but a good alternative to sunbathing on the beach. And what good would a golf course be in Ocean City without golf tournaments? Yes, there are city-sponsored tournaments throughout the summer. Call (609) 399–6111 for further information. The golf course is open seven days a week during the summer; discounts are available.

Ride the Ocean City Trolley. A good way to get a feel for Ocean City is to take a ride on one of the trolleys that run every 25 minutes from 8:30 A.M. to midnight. The most popular route extends from 59th Street up to 15th Street, Ocean Avenue to 9th Street, then Atlantic Avenue along Battersea to the Longport Bridge. It returns via the same route. Pick up a free map of Ocean City and further information on the trolleys at any of the information centers. Discounts for senior citizens and children.

See a Parade. Mark your calendar for two of Ocean City's biggest and most popular summer events. The **Annual Baby Parade,** which takes place on the boardwalk, draws thousands of spectators. You'll see dressed-up, made-up, spruced-up tots and kids up to the age of 12 strutting their stuff. Decorated carriages, strollers, wagons and bicycles, and bands and floats add to the fun. The Baby Parade goes back to the turn of the century and has been a summer tradition in Ocean City ever since. It's the oldest baby parade on the Jersey Shore and undoubtedly the best. The parade is usually held in August; check with the information center for a specific date.

Night in Venice is a carnival of seacraft and just as popular as the Baby Parade. Held in July, nearly everyone turns out for the annual dazzling display of Ocean City's pleasure boats, most of which are lavishly decorated with the hope of landing the grand prize for best-looking boat. The Night in Venice festivities take place on the bay side of Ocean

City. Bleachers are set up along the bay's edge. Almost every home-owner on this side of town throws a party or invites friends over. Many homes are also decorated for the occasion. It's a special night in Ocean City, and if the town ever lets loose, it's during this celebration.

Corson's Inlet State Park

If you drive through Ocean City and remain on Scenic Drive, you'll come upon a short stretch of highway with marshland on both sides. Though there's no visitor center or even a sign to tell you you're on state property, the area is part of Corson's Inlet State Park. Just up ahead is Corson's Inlet, a picturesque, though tricky waterway due to its many shoals. There's a small boat launch here, a bathing area, fishing, bird-watching, hiking and lots of poison ivy. It's also a great place to go sailboarding. During a particularly breezy day in spring, summer or fall, you're apt to see dozens of colorful sails and sleek boards on the water.

A pleasant half-day's outing would be to bicycle down to Corson's Inlet State Park from Ocean City, explore some of the park, perhaps enjoy a picnic and then bike back home. You can do the same if you ride north from Strathmere or Sea Isle City. If you're a fisherman or boater, you'll probably want to spend the day at the park. For more information, write to the Superintendent of Belleplain State Forest, Box 450, Woodbine 08270, or call (609) 861–2404.

Strathmere

Anyone visiting Corson's Inlet State Park who prefers something more to eat than a box lunch or picnic snack should consider the **Deauville Inn** in neighboring Strathmere. Located on Willard's Road, just off Ocean Drive, the Deauville Inn actually sits on Corson's Inlet. The view is as good as the food. The restored country inn serves sit-down dinners, hot and cold sandwiches dockside and breakfast, to boot. During the evening there's live entertainment, and for sailors, the marina has virtually everything you'd need to stock your boat and head out onto the ocean.

Somers Point

When Ocean City gets thirsty, or when the under-30 crowd needs to be revved up with rock 'n' roll, they drive across the bay to Somers Point. But there's more to Somers Point than Ocean City watering holes.

Somers Mansion, built in 1725, is the oldest house in Atlantic County. It overlooks Great Egg Harbor Bay and was the home of John

Somers and family, one of the most important and wealthiest families in colonial South Jersey. Today, Somers Mansion is a New Jersey historical site and open to the public. The mansion, constructed of brick laid in Flemish bond, is three stories high and contains a number of excellent colonial furnishings. When you visit the house, make sure you walk out onto the balcony of the second floor, where you're treated to a view of Great Egg Harbor Bay.

Perhaps the most unusual feature of the house is the roof. Get permission to walk up to the third-floor attic. Notice that the framework supporting the roof, thought to be constructed by a ship wright, resembles the hull of a ship. It is said that if the house were somehow ever flipped over and placed in water, it would simply float away. The Somers Mansion is located on Shore Road at the Somers Point Traffic Circle. Admission is free.

Around the corner from the Somers Mansion is the **Atlantic County Historical Museum and Library.** Located on the lower floor of the building, the museum is stocked with Victorian household items and furniture; a collection of Lenni Lenape Indian tools, weapons and other artifacts; a number of old shipbuilding implements; and a large model of the ship, the *Intrepid.* Upstairs is the library of the Atlantic County Historical Society. Much of the South Jersey historical research that goes on stems from here. On record are deeds, wills, diaries, letters and ships' logs as well as photographs and family trees.

Finally, there's the **South Jersey Regional Theatre** on Bay and Higbee avenues, an area theater group that presents performances of popular plays. Call (609) 653–0553 for further details and this year's schedule of performances.

Did you know that . . .

Richard Somers, a descendant of John Somers, was commander of the *Intrepid,* the ketch that blew up in the Tripoli harbor with all hands on board. This was during the war with the Barbary Pirates and was one of America's first post–revolutionary war naval sorties abroad. From that day on, there has always been a ship named *Intrepid* in the U.S. Navy.

Sea Isle City

Sea Isle City, founded a century ago by Charles Landis, was originally to have been a duplicate of Venice, the Italian city of romance and waterways. Instead, Sea Isle City is somewhat of a scaled-down version of Ocean City. Like Ocean City, Sea Isle City advertises itself as a family resort, even though liquor is sold in town and a lively young crowd plays on the beach each summer. The five-mile stretch of beach is Sea Isle City's biggest attraction. Beach badges are required. They are sold at the Dominic C. Raffa Community Center at 127 John F. Kennedy Boulevard. To cater to the cultural needs of vacationers, the town provides free weekly concerts on the Promenade during July and August. It also sponsors arts and crafts shows, surfing contests and even a baby parade, although it lacks the size and scope of the one held in Ocean City.

Sea Isle City is also known for its fishing. Drive along the Ludlam Bay side of town, and you'll come across a number of party boats that make daily trips offshore. Bluefishing is quite popular here, as is fishing and crabbing in the bay; there are places dockside where one can rent a small skiff and fish the day away on the bay. You'll find commercial fishing boats here as well. Lobster fishing is an important part of the local economy. If you happen to be in the area when a lobster boat is pulling in after a weary couple of days out on the Atlantic, don't hesitate to ask if you might purchase a live lobster or two for dinner that evening. Chances are you'll pay a fair price for a very tasty treat.

Sea Isle City doesn't possess a boardwalk in the traditional sense, that is, wooden planks to walk on—but it does have a paved walkway that parallels the beach. As for an amusement area, **Fun City** is located on Landis Avenue, between 32nd and 33rd streets. It's fine for the kids, but if you're bent on a full night of amusement thrills, best to head south to Wildwood.

Avalon

Avalon and its neighbor, Stone Harbor, share a narrow stretch of barrier-island beach known as Seven Mile Beach. Townsend's Inlet to the north and Hereford Inlet to the south keep these two beautiful beach towns away from the more commercial trappings of Ocean City and Sea Isle City and the Wildwoods. This and the fact that both towns possess a deep interest in preserving the ecological balance of Seven Mile Beach make them two of the most attractive towns on the South Jersey Shore.

Avalon has not succumbed to the lure of developers, at least not yet. True, there are condominiums in town, and Avalon has surely experienced a growth spurt in recent years. But any large-scale development is impossible on Avalon's coveted marshlands because it is the property of the World Wildlife Fund. The organization owns nearly 1,000 acres of wetlands and intends to keep it in its natural state—forever.

Avalon, however, is most noted for its sand dunes and its beach, which rates with the very best found on the Jersey Shore, Its white extra-fine sand, gentle water (thanks to offshore sandbars, which placate much of the ocean's power) and, of course, its beautiful sand dunes make a day at the beach in Avalon a most enjoyable one.

Residents of Avalon are proud of their sand dunes and beach. But they also enjoy a low-key, mild-mannered approach to tourism and the influx of summer visitors. That's not to say that Avalon doesn't have its share of restaurants and nightspots; it does. It also has a boardwalk that runs from 20th to 32nd streets, not to mention the social and recreational programs that originate from the Avalon Community Center at 29th Street and Avalon Avenue. The center offers dances, concerts, roller-skating, and tournaments in tennis, bocce ball, basketball and softball. An Information Center on 30th Street provides the details and dates of such activities as well as information on lodging in Avalon.

But Avalon never seems to forget the individual who comes to town in search of simple peace and relaxation. For the full enjoyment of those two precious elements, few places on the South Jersey shoreline cultivate them as Avalon does.

Stone Harbor

Stone Harbor seems a mere continuation of Avalon as you drive south from the one town to the next. The attitude toward tourism is pretty much the same: Encourage it, but keep it controlled. The commitment to ecology preservation is the same: Stone Harbor's nationally known bird sanctuary and Wetlands Institute (see below) are proof of this. The high quality of beaches is the same, although Stone Harbor does not possess the sand dunes that Avalon does. The lovely lagoons on the bay side of both towns are quite similar. About the only thing that Stone Harbor has that Avalon doesn't is a completely renovated downtown center, filled with interesting shops and eateries.

You can spend the better part of a cloudy morning or afternoon browsing through the Stone Harbor shops. In addition to the usual items found in beach-town stores—beachwear, rafts, umbrellas, mats and boogie boards—you'll also find stores such as the **Irish Pavilion** (9825 Ocean Drive), which carries authentic Irish imports, and the **Sandpiper Galerie** (109th Street and Third Avenue), which sells paintings, duck decoys, antiques and unusual nautical crafts. Most of the shops are on 96th Street or Third Avenue, or at least in the vicinity of them.

For some reason, Stone Harbor has more than its share of top-notch ice-cream parlors. The **Strawberry Patch** (270 96th Street) features imaginative ice-cream concoctions, Belgian waffles and homemade brownies. **Springer's** (9420 Third Avenue) is well known for its deli-

Sand Dunes: The Hows and Whys of Preservation

Question:
Why are sand dunes not only aesthetically pleasing but also critical to the survival of a barrier island?

Answer:
Sand dunes offer the best protection from storms, natural beach erosion and large, pounding waves. Without sand dunes, a barrier island could very well disappear over the course of time.

Question:
Why aren't people allowed to walk on sand dunes?

Answer:
Sand dunes are actually very delicate constructions. People who disregard this fact are sand dunes' worst enemies.

Question:
Why is dune grass so important to the preservation of sand dunes?

Answer:
The dune-grass roots play an important role in keeping the dunes intact. The roots of the dune-grass plant will extend deep into the dune and help control natural dune erosion.

Question:
Aren't stone jetties and seawalls more effective protection for a shoreline than sand dunes?

Answer:
No. Jetties and seawalls actually encourage the loss of beach sand in some cases. When winter-storm waves crash against seawalls and jetties, sand is carried back into the sea as the water retreats. Jetties and seawalls are not effective on barrier islands because a barrier island is in a constantly shifting situation and is made up of nothing but sand. Jetties and seawalls are used in many areas of the Jersey Shore, especially the North Jersey Shore, as a last resort and where sand dunes have already been permanently destroyed by overdevelopment.

Question:
How do environmentalists encourage the growth of sand dunes?

Answer:
With regular dune-grass plantings, regular fertilization and proper placement of snow fences. These three together promote the growth of sand dunes.

Question:
What can I do to help maintain sand dunes on the Jersey Shore?

Answer:
Obey signs that restrict access onto sand dunes. Walk only on established paths. Don't allow your dog to run on or dig in sand dunes. Don't litter. Fully appreciate the value and beauty of sand dunes. Pass this information along to a friend.

ciously rich homemade ice cream. And you'll find wonderfully tempting sundaes at **Le Grand Dipper** (299 97th Street) as well as chocolate-covered strawberries.

Stone Harbor's beaches are wide and clean. Beach badges are mandatory and can be purchased at the Borough Hall (609) 368–5102. There is good surfing, bodysurfing and raft-riding in Stone Harbor as well as boardsailing and wave jumping.

While in Stone Harbor, be sure to spend some time visiting its noted bird sanctuary, located at the southern end of town on Third Avenue between 111th and 117th streets. You don't have to be an experienced bird-watcher to enjoy the egrets, herons and ibises—all long-legged wading birds—flying to and from the 21-acre sanctuary in search of food or a mating partner. You don't even need binoculars. At a small parking lot on Third Avenue, you'll find pay binoculars and information pertaining to the birds.

The best time to visit is just after the break of dawn in late July and early August. It is the busiest time of the year for the birds, as the nesting season is drawing to a close. At this time, environmentalists estimate that are over 10,000 birds in the sanctuary, including seven species of herons.

Did you know that . . .

The Stone Harbor Bird Sanctuary is the only heronry in America sponsored by a municipality. Its only counterpart in the rest of the world is in a small Japanese town outside Tokyo.

No visitor to Stone Harbor should miss a trip to the **Wetlands Institute** on Stone Harbor Boulevard. A nonprofit organization "dedicated to promoting public understanding of, and concern for, the coastal and wetlands ecosystem," the Wetlands Institute is an excellent educational experience for young and old alike.

The Institute is situated on a 6,000-acre tract of coastal marshlands. Inside the cedar-shake building with a balconied, built-in observation deck are laboratories, an auditorium, a gift shop and a small, yet thoroughly delightful, hands-on museum for children. The institute sponsors year-round lectures ("Beach Erosion at Stone Harbor," "Birds of Beach and Bay," and "Do Yourself a Favor: Eat Seafood," among numerous others) conducts guided explorations into salt marshes and sponsors an annual and very popular Wings 'N' Water Festival (decorative bird carving shows, wildlife paintings and seascapes, guided beach and marsh walks) each September. In addition, there are a number of fine programs for children, including educational five-day, summer ecology classes.

When visiting the Wetlands Institute, don't forget to take the self-guided tour along the salt-marsh trail (get a copy of the guide pamphlet from the front desk) and climb the observation tower for an inspiring view of the institute's marshland. Anyone the least bit interested in wetland ecology will find the Wetlands Institute quite fascinating. Open year-round. Admission is free, but a donation is encouraged. One might even want to become a full-time member of the Wetlands Institute. Write to the Wetlands Institute, Stone Harbor Boulevard, Stone Harbor 08247, or call (609) 368-1211.

The Wildwoods

Located just below Seven Mile Beach is Five Mile Beach, another South Jersey barrier island. The three towns on it—North Wildwood, Wildwood and Wildwood Crest—are famous for their beaches. For one thing, they're free; that means no beach badges, a definite rarity on the Jersey Shore. For another, they're incredibly wide and possess extra-fine, seemingly filtered white sand.

If the beaches of the Wildwoods are spectacular, then so is the boardwalk there, with its four amusement piers, all of them stocked with some of the most thrilling, spine-tingling rides in the world. One could spend perhaps an entire week full of exciting nights on the Wildwood boardwalk and still not experience every ride. The Wildwoods also have dozens of restaurants and small-scale eateries featuring a broad range of cuisines, and the best nightlife south of Atlantic City. To ride along Ocean Avenue is to ride through a gamut of neon lights that blaze the names of bars and dance clubs along with the Top 40 bands, trios and solo piano players, which perform in them until early morning.

To fully enjoy what the Wildwoods have to offer, one has to be a day *and* night person. Vacationing here often means spending the day soaking up the sun's rays on the beach and at night, club hopping or boardwalk walking. The next day the routine is repeated. And repeated the day after that. It's a fast, even hectic, pace and a far cry from what's found in Stone Harbor and Avalon, but for those who spend their vacations in Wildwood, anything more staid would be downright disappointing.

The Wildwoods are saturated with hotels and motels and bungalows and guesthouses of every price and fancy. Yet, it is a very good idea to select one before arriving in Wildwood and make the necessary reservations because availability can be a problem during the summer. To do this, write to The Greater Wildwood Hotel and Motel Association for a copy of its Visitor's Guide, a 100 plus-page volume that lists and describes all the accommodations in the Wildwoods. It is a valuable source of making Wildwood vacation plans. Write The Greater Wildwood Hotel

Camping near the South Jersey Shore Resorts

Camping is an excellent alternative means of lodging near the South Jersey Shore because so many campgrounds are close to the beaches and other areas of interest. A campsite is also cheaper than a hotel or motel room. Most of the South Jersey campgrounds are suited for the vacationing family and provide water, electric and sewer hookups, and other basic amenities. Some even have fishing and swimming facilities, children's playgrounds, game rooms and a camp store.

Here's a list of private and state-owned campgrounds that are close to the South Jersey Shore area. For more information on camping here, write to the Cape May County Campgrounds Association, Box 608, Ocean View 08230.

Private Campgrounds

Avalon Campground
492 Shore Road
Clermont 08210
(609) 624–0075

Beachcomber Campground
462 Seashore Road
Cape May 08204
(609) 886–6035

Belleplain State Forest
Box 450
Woodbine 08270
(609) 861–2404

Big Timber Lake Camping Resort
Box 366
Cape May Courthouse 08210
(609) 465–4456

Cape Island Campground
709 Route 9
Cape May 08204
(609) 884–5777

Cold Spring Campground
541 New England Road
Cape May 08204
(609) 884–8717

Delsea Woods Campground
Delsea Drive
Green Creek 08219
(609) 886–3522

Dennisville Lake Campground
Box 36
Dennisville 08214
(609) 861–2461

Driftwood Campground
478 Shore Road (Route 9)
Cape May Courthouse 08210
(609) 624–1899

Fort Apache Campground
Route 47 at Fulling Mill Road
Rio Grande 08242
(609) 886–1076

Frontier Campground
90 Newbridge Road
Ocean View 08230
(609) 390–3649

Green Holly Campground
Box 193
Goshen 08218
(609) 465–9602

Hidden Acres Campground
Box 354C, R.D. #1
Cape May Courthouse 08210
(609) 624–9015

Holly Shores Best Holiday Travel Park
491 Route 9
Cape May 08204
(609) 886–1234

Lake Laurie Campground
669 Route 9
Cape May 08204
(609) 884–3567

North Wildwood Campground
527 Shellbay Avenue
Cape May Courthouse 08210
(609) 465–4440

Outdoor World Lake and Shore Resort
Corson Tavern Road
Ocean View 08230
(609) 624–3369

Pine Haven Campground
(Box 606) 432 Shore Road
Ocean View 08230
(609) 624–3437

Plantation Campground
3065 Shore Road
Seaville 08230
(609) 624–3528

Sea Grove Campground
(P.O. Box 603) 614 Shore Road
Ocean View 08230
(609) 624–3529

Seashore Campsites
720 Seashore Road
Cape May 08204
(609) 884–4010

Shady Oaks Campground
62 State Highway 50
Ocean View 08230
(609) 390–0431

Shellbay Campground
527 North Shellbay Avenue
Cape May Courthouse 08210
(609) 465–4770

Tamerlane Campground
Box 510
Ocean View 08230
(609) 624–0767

Whippoorwill Campground
810 South Shore Road
Marmora 08223
(609) 390–3458

Wildwood Canadian Campground
301 South Shore Road
Rio Grande 08242
(609) 886–2077

State-Owned Campgrounds

Bass River State Forest
Box 118
New Gretna 08224
(609) 296–1114

and Motel Association, P.O. Box 184, Wildwood By-the-Sea 08260. The Greater Wildwood Chamber of Commerce (Box 823, Wildwood, 08260) sends out an Accommodation Directory upon request. It's filled with information on lodging, of course, but it also contains information on restaurants and entertainment. For up-to-the-minute information on Wildwood, call 1–800–WW-BY-SEA.

The Hereford Inlet Lighthouse on First and Central avenues acts as a tourist information outlet and is a good place to pick up brochures and such on the area for those just passing through or spending only the day. Other Wildwood area information centers are Wildwood Information Bureau, Boardwalk and Schellenger Avenue; Wildwood Information Center in Convention Hall at Burk Avenue and Boardwalk; the Wildwood Crest Pier Information Center, Wildwood Crest; and the Wildwood Crest Visitor Center at the end of Rambler Road. Most are seasonal, which means they're open from Memorial Day through Labor Day Weekend and, depending on the weather, on weekends through September.

North Wildwood

North Wildwood is situated at the northern end of Five Mile Beach and is the first of the Wildwoods you'll visit if driving south on Scenic Drive or getting off the Parkway at Exit 6. Lighthouse enthusiasts will want to stop at the Hereford Inlet Lighthouse, located near the entrance to Hereford Inlet before heading to the beach or boardwalk.

It is an interesting lighthouse to tour because, unlike other lighthouses on the Jersey coast, the Hereford Inlet is principally Victorian in design. Built in 1874, the lighthouse was meant to serve as a landmark for those fishermen who fished the waters off Five Mile Beach and returned to shore through the treacherous channel in the inlet. Exceptionally strong tidal currents and everchanging shoals made navigation difficult even in good weather.

Because the original settlement on Five Mile Beach—a village called Anglesea—grew to be a large fishing center, which, at times, rivaled Gloucester, Massachusetts, as the East Coat's fishing capital in the late nineteenth century, the lighthouse and its beacon were especially important to commercial fishermen.

It has been only a few years since the Hereford Inlet Lighthouse was decommissioned (a more modern light-tower now stands on the property and sends its beam out to sea). Thus, restoration continues on the structure; even so, the lighthouse is open to the public during the summer. Admission is free. Future plans call for the creation of a park, museum and cultural center on the lighthouse grounds.

Wildwood

When in Wildwood, think beach and boardwalk: a big beach and a big boardwalk. In the north part of town, near Hunt's Pier, the beach is over 1,000 feet wide. That's a fifth of a mile. Elsewhere in Wildwood the beach isn't quite that wide, but it comes close. Because it's such a long trip from the boardwalk to the water's edge, be sure to wear something on your feet, as the sand can get awfully hot, especially at midday.

The boardwalk owns impressive figures, too. It's more than two miles long, stretching the entire length of Wildwood. To get a good overview of the boardwalk, catch one of Wildwood's Boardwalk Tramcars, which will take you from one end of the boardwalk to the next, if you wish. Those visiting Wildwood for only the day or evening will find the Tramcar a perfect way to see and do as much as time permits. You can flag down a Tramcar at any point on the boardwalk, and you can get off wherever you want.

There are so many amusement rides, concession stands, games of chance, T-shirt outlets, fast-food joints, saltwater taffy and fudge shops, pizza and cheesesteak walk-ins, ice-cream stalls and hot dog/hamburger palaces that for a boardwalk junkie, Wildwood must surely be the closest thing to paradise. Where else can one find a boardwalk chapel, movie theaters and pony rides, of all things, on the beach. Wildwood has got it all—and more.

You'll quickly notice that most of those strolling the boards are young. Wildwood, as already mentioned, lures a young crowd. Still, adults and families come and enjoy Wildwood, too. But the bulk of activities on the boardwalk are most assuredly aimed at teens and those in their twenties.

Some things to do on the boardwalk: Pick a shady spot, put on your sunglasses and treat yourself to an afternoon's worth of people-watching. You'll see all sizes and shapes and some of the skimpiest bathing suits around. Play bingo; it's fun and it's cool in the arcade, and you just might win a prize. For $.99 you can get four hot dogs at the **Wildwood Candy and Ice Cream Company.** For $.50 you get a half quart of Coke. Try a slice of **Angelo's New York Style Pizza** or **Mack's Pizza;** both are delicious. Buy a Belgian waffle at **Snarky's Ice Cream Factory.** Or have **Mrs. Ann** analyze your handwriting.

As for amusement rides, here's a brief rundown on the piers and the best rides. **Midway Pier:** Castle Dracula and the Dungeon Boat Ride (not for those with heart problems), the Matterhorn (a true amusement ride classic). **Hunt's Pier:** Log Flume (wear your bathing suit), the Kamikaze (good but the old Screem Machine was better). **Mariner's Landing:** Sea Serpent (only for the daring and brave and don't eat before you go),

Great Wheel (a huge ferris wheel with a super view at the top). **Morey's Pier:** The Condor (hold onto your hat).

For more cultural entertainment, Convention Hall, also on the boardwalk, frequently hosts big name performers in concert. Melissa Manchester, Laura Branigan, Maynard Ferguson and other pop and jazz greats play there in the summer. Stop by the box office for a calendar of events and ticket information.

Ocean Avenue and those Wildwood streets that run adjacent to it are action-packed until late at night during the summer. Clubs such as **Martinique** (Oak Avenue), the **Rainbow** (Spicer and Pacific avenues), **Sundance** (Oak and New Jersey avenues), **Pier Top Lounge** (Atlantic Avenue at the beach), **Club Cheers** (Cedar and Pacific avenues), **Club Casba** (Spicer and Atlantic avenues), the **Playpen** (Atlantic Avenue at Diamond Beach) and, oh, so many others make the Wildwoods *the* place for club hopping. Some clubs have dress codes; some don't. Most have a cover charge. All have either live entertainment or a fast-spinning disc jockey. To best decide which club or clubs to go to, and also to find out who's playing where, which clubs have all-male revues or go-go girls, or a wet T-shirt contest, or even a quiet table for two where couples go to sip pina coladas and listen to soft rock and pop, consult the free, weekly entertainment newspaper, *Shout.* It's readily available in Wildwood, Wildwood Crest and North Wildwood nightspots.

Wildwood has other things to do besides go to the beach, ride the Sea Serpent and dance the night away. Cloudy days can be spent at the **George Boyer Historical Museum** on the second floor of City Hall (Montgomery and New Jersey avenues). Admission is free. It's a decent museum as far as municipal museums go, and you'll learn quite a bit about Wildwood's past. Open weekdays.

Diamond Beach offers pretty fair surfing when a swell is running. And for fishermen, a number of party and charter boats make daily trips to offshore fishing grounds from the Wildwood area. Most boats depart at 8 A.M. and return at 4 P.M. Check what they're catching at **Otten's Harbor** (Davis and Park Boulevard), the **Wildwood Yacht Basin** (Rio Grande and Susquehanna avenues), and the **Shawcrest Yacht Basin** (Shawcrest Road).

Boaters should know that there are public boat ramps between 4th and 6th avenues on New York Avenue and small boats for rent at **Dad's Place** (North Wildwood Boulevard) in North Wildwood and **Lake View Docks** in Wildwood Crest (Rambler Road and Park Boulevard).

Wildwood Crest

Wildwood Crest is the most quiet—if such a word could be used to describe any of the Wildwoods—and certainly the most family-oriented. It's situated at the southern end of Five Mile Beach. When Wildwood Crest vacationers want the flash and excitement of the boardwalk, Wildwood is mere minutes away. Yet, it's in Wildwood Crest where one can escape all the action when one wants—or needs—to and still enjoy the gorgeous beaches and warm summer sun.

Wildwood Crest boasts more family-owned cottages and summer homes and more higher priced hotels and motels than the other two Wildwoods. It also more resembles a beach community with regular summer residents returning each year than Wildwood, where the average vacation is more apt to be a week rather than a month.

Did you know that . . .

Wildwood's beaches are some of the precious few beaches on the East Coast of the United States that are *growing* instead of diminishing. In some cases, the shoreline has gained an incredible 100 feet in just one year.

Another difference between Wildwood Crest and Wildwood is the former's lakeside, where one can catch splendid sunsets in late August and early September. Sunset Lake and the park nearby often provide a nice alternative to the ocean and beach. Here you'll find sailboarders, waterskiers and jet skiers enjoying the water and picnickers and children enjoying the park.

Other beach alternatives in Wildwood Crest include a possible visit to the **Wildwood Crest Museum** on Seaview Avenue, a concert at the **Gazebo** on Rambler Road or participation in any of a number of athletic programs or social events sponsored by the town.

Where to Eat on the South Jersey Shore

Avanti, Walnut and Old New Jersey avenues, North Wildwood, (609) 729–7277
Price Code: Moderate   Menu: Italian
Homemade pasta dishes to go with veal, steaks and seafood specialties.

Bookers New England Seafood House, 9th and Wesley avenues, Ocean City, (609) 399–4672
Price Code: Moderate   Menu: Seafood
Standard seafood accented with tempting salad bar and tasty appetizers.

Culinary Garden and Inn, 841 Central Avenue, Ocean City,
(609) 399–3713
Price Code: Moderate   Menu: Seafood
Area restaurant critics claim this is the best restaurant in Ocean City. No
disappointing dishes on the menu.

Dragon House, 3616 Pacific Avenue, Wildwood, (609) 522–2320
Price Code: Moderate   Menu: Chinese
The house specialties are Peking duck and any of its soups. Routinely
rated the best Chinese restaurant on the South Jersey Shore.

Johnson's Seafood Restaurant, 4601 Pacific Avenue, Wildwood,
(609) 522–1976
Price Code: Moderate   Menu: Seafood
Johnson's has been a reputable Wildwood restaurant since 1946. It must
be good.

Restaurant Renault Atop the Winery, Renault Winery/Bremen
Avenue, Egg Harbor City, (609) 965–2111
Price Code: Expensive   Menu: Gourmet
Multicourse meals, wine-tasting, superbly prepared dishes and desserts.

Schumann's, 5901 Atlantic Avenue, Wildwood Crest, (609) 522–7050
Price Code: Moderate   Menu: Seafood
Warm, friendly, family restaurant; standard seafood menu, but hearty
servings.

Watson's, 901 Ocean Avenue, Ocean City, (609) 399–1065
Price Code: Moderate   Menu: American
Another fine family restaurant. Those who summer in Ocean City year in
and year out eat at Watson's.

Did you know that . . .

Renault Winery is the oldest continuously operating winery in the
United States. It secured a government permit to make Renault
Wine Tonic throughout the 14 years of prohibition. It had an alco-
hol content of 22 percent and was sold in drugstores.

South Jersey Winery Tours

Most people don't think of New Jersey when the subject of American wines is mentioned. California and New York, yes. But New Jersey? Yet New Jersey is indeed a wine-producing state, and a fairly good one at that. Most of the state's wineries are located in South Jersey and are worth a visit. Those described below are all well within an hour's drive of most South Jersey Shore resort towns. Touring one or more of them is an excellent way to spend a day away from the beach.

Renault Winery. This is the largest and most popular of New Jersey wineries and the one that offers the most for the visitor to see and do. Located on Bremen Avenue in Egg Harbor City (look for the big Renault bottle at the intersection of Route 30 and Bremen Avenue), Renault conducts regular tours of its winery. You'll sample wines and get an up-close glimpse of the wine-making and bottling process. A good time to visit is in early fall, when Renault's Annual Grape Harvest Festival takes place. A big attraction is the grape stomping contest. If you're selected to participate and win the contest, you receive the juice of the grapes you stomped bottled as a souvenir.

Also on the premises is a wine-glass museum, an excellent gourmet restaurant, called the Restaurant Atop the Winery, the Garden Cafe and Ice Cream Parlor, and a wine and champagne shop where you can purchase spirits. Speaking of champagne, Renault is internationally noted for its champagne; 7 of the 28 varieties of wine made at Renault are champagne. Renault is also the only winery in the country that makes blueberry champagne.

For more information on the Harvest Festival, wine tours, and dinner at the Restaurant Renault Atop The Winery, call (609) 965–2111.

Balic Winery. Balic is a small, rather nondescript winery on Route 40 in Mays Landing. Yugoslavian-raised Savo Balic is the proprietor of the family-owned winery, which includes some 30 acres of vineyards and a wine-tasting room. It is the smallest winery in New Jersey and one of the very few wineries that still harvests all grapes by hand.

The public is permitted to tour the vineyards, but arrangements should be made beforehand, as there are no regularly scheduled tours like those at Renault. Call (609) 625–2166 for details. Souvenir wine sets can be purchased in the wine-tasting room. Balic sells 10 different varieties of wine and champagne.

Tomasello Winery. The Tomasello Winery does not conduct regular tours of the winery and vineyards either, but Charles Tomasello will take groups through if arrangements are made in advance. The wine-tasting room, however, is open daily. Those interested in the bottling process of wines should certainly make plans to tour Tomasello, since its setup and Mr. Tomasello's explanation of it is very interesting.

Like Renault, Tomasello is most known for its champagne. There's also a growing demand for its fruity grape wines. Located about halfway between Atlantic City and Camden (farther inland than other area wineries), Tomasello's is on Route 30 in Hammonton, just west of the Route 206 intersection. Tomasello Winery has an outlet and small museum at Smithville for those interested only in purchasing wine. For more information, call (800) 666–WINE.

9

 Cape May

Cape May is not the type of resort you visit just once. There's an irresistible lure, an enchanting touch, to Cape May that pulls you back to it again and again. People come, of course, in the summer. But they also come in the spring, fall and even in the dead of winter. The special warmth and charm of the town, regardless of the season, as well as its live-in museum atmosphere, its tree-lined side streets, its quaint shops and eateries, its history and, ultimately, its firm dedication to the spirit and style of the Victorian Age make Cape May a special place indeed. And over the last few years, more and more people have been finding this out. Today, Cape May ranks with Atlantic City as New Jersey's most popular seaside resort.

Cape May claims that it is America's oldest seaside resort. Long Branch, up on the North Jersey Shore, say historians, has just as much a right to the title as Cape May does (see chapter 2). Yet, it's Cape May that is benefiting most from the claim because it has cultivated a continuous restoration movement and actively seeks to relive its past glories. Long Branch does no such thing; thus, perhaps Cape May wins the decision by default.

Another one of Cape May's claims—that it possesses the largest concentration of authentic Victorian structures in the nation—can also be disputed by another North Jersey Shore town, Ocean Grove (see chapter 2 again). Both are literally filled with beautifully restored Victorian homes, so it really doesn't matter which town has the slight numerical edge. However, it's Cape May that does more, much more, for the sake of tourists, than Ocean Grove does when it comes to marketing its Victorian gems. It centers such popular activities as Victorian Week, Victorian house tours, Victorian candlelight tours, Victorian this and Victorian that around its Victorian heritage. Cape May encourages tourism on the grandest level; Ocean Grove encourages it, too, but not nearly with the enthusiasm that Cape May does.

A visit to Cape May is a visit to an era long gone. The Victorian Age was an age when fancy gingerbread lace adorned verandas with rocking chairs on them; when the rest of the house was painted in bright, bold colors; when flower gardens hugged white picket fences; when the soft, dreamy light of gas lamps lit up the streets each evening; when gracious ladies and gentlemen socialized in rooms filled with ornate furnishings or strolled walkways and paths and talked of Admiral Dewey's Great White Fleet and Teddy Roosevelt and his daring charge up San Juan Hill. The Victorian seemed inundated with niceties and delectable romanticism that's difficult to find these days, except, of course, in Cape May.

Did you know that . . .

Henry Ford and Louis Chevrolet staged automobile races on Cape May's beach in 1905. Later, Ford offered to build the first Ford automotive plant in Cape May, but city officials turned him down.

And that's why people enjoy Cape May so much. The town and its year-round residents live and breathe Victoriana. But unlike other noted historical towns like Williamsburg, Virginia, for instance, Cape May conducts the transformation from present to past without too much spectacle. Although one can easily spend a weekend or week soaking up as much Victorian grandeur as possible, never is what's offered overly contrived or artificial. Cape May holds a strong commitment to authenticity, and the town has just enough restraint not to make it a Victorian circus.

Cape May was named for Cornelius Jacobsen Mey, a Dutch sea captain who explored the Delaware Bay area in 1620. Gradually, the vicinity began to be settled by New England and Long Island whalers and their families who found Cape May's closeness to whaling routes particularly profitable. The first settlement, called Town Bank or Cape May Town, was a whaling village. Unfortunately, the ground where the village was established has been lost to erosion and the sea.

Whaling in Cape May flourished until the early 1700s, and those who mastered the art of killing and beaching whales and the business associated with whaling grew considerably wealthy. However, whale sightings became less and less frequent, due to the indiscriminate slaughter of them. Eventually, this led many settlers to abandon whaling and turn to farming to make a living.

Cape May's economy took still another direction when physicians from Philadelphia began advising their patients to spend a part of the summer in Cape May. It was felt that salt air and water would have a soothing, even curing effect on their ills. Word of Cape May's appeal spread, and soon healthy Philadelphians began visiting Cape May in the mid-1700s to escape the inland summer heat. Thus, the seeds were sown for Cape May's real destiny, namely, that of a resort town.

It wasn't, however, until the 1800s that Cape May really began to take the shape of a summer resort. The first hotel, the Atlantic Hotel, soon had much competition. By the middle of the 1800s, several dozen hotels and inns had been built to accommodate those who came to summer in Cape May. The Mount Vernon, built in 1853, was at the time the largest hotel in the world. Unfortunately, it burned to the ground. Visitors such as Abraham Lincoln, Henry Clay and U. S. Grant signed their names in Cape May guestbooks. Later on, notables such as P. T. Barnum, John Philip Sousa and Henry Ford would also summer in Cape May.

Cape May's progress as a grand resort was stunted by another fire, the Great Fire of 1878. The blaze practically destroyed half the town. Hotels, homes, businesses all fell to the flames. The disaster couldn't have occurred at a worse time. Up north, Long Branch was capturing the attention of the wealthy as well as famous politicians, and its gambling halls were internationally known. But to make matters worse for Cape May, Atlantic City, which was considerably closer, was quickly becoming a major resort, too. That would leave Cape May practically out of the resort picture if it didn't rebuild—and rebuild fast.

Cape May did, in fact, rebuild, and quickly regained most of its reputation as a premier summer resort. This was the Victorian Age, and many of the Victorian structures that grace Cape May's streets today were built in the 1880s and 1890s after the Great Fire. Cape May's resurrection was furthered considerably by President Benjamin Harrison, who spent much of the summer of 1890 and 1891 residing in Cape May Point. He set up the Summer White House in Cape May's Congress Hall.

Cape May enjoyed its rebirth through the early part of the twentieth century. Then came the Great Depression and World War II. People don't spend much money in summer resorts in times of crises, money that Cape May desperately needed to survive. Add to this a major problem with beach erosion coupled with angry Atlantic storms, especially the one that hit the Jersey coast in March 1962 and inflicted over a million dollars worth of damage in Cape May, and Cape May was all but forgotten by summer visitors.

It was, however, Cape May's glorious past that rescued its present and guaranteed its future. As more and more residents began restoring their Victorian homes and the town began witnessing an influx of new blood, Cape May began yet another comeback. The town received National Historic Landmark status, which fostered an aggressive campaign of continued restoration. Soon visitors were coming back to Cape May. As interest in Victoriana spread, Cape May became more and more popular. Today, it is the most popular Victorian town in America.

It is imperative to plan your visit to Cape May in advance for four important reasons. Cape May is a popular resort, and unless you're coming only for the day, you'll need to make lodging reservations in advance of your stay there. In some of the more well-known bed and breakfasts like the Mainstay and Abbey, reservations six or eight months in advance is not a bad idea.

Second, since there is so much to see and do in Cape May, you'll want to make the best of your time there. Sit down and decide beforehand what interests you most and make a point of doing and seeing those things first. The following lists of tours, festivals and activities will help you in your advance planning.

Third, organizations like the Cape May Chamber of Commerce and the Mid-Atlantic Center for the Arts sponsor an amazingly full range of activities, special programs, festivals, shows and concerts for the Cape May visitor. You'll want to make sure you coincide your visit to Cape May with the programs and activities you find most appealing. You can contact the above-mentioned organizations by writing to The Chamber of Commerce of Greater Cap May, P.O. Box 109, Cape May 08204, and The Mid-Atlantic Center for the Arts, P.O. Box 340, Cape May 08204; they will gladly supply you with dates and up-to-the-minute information of current goings-on in Cape May.

And fourth, Cape May is quite a different place in the fall or spring than it is in the summer or winter. Decide what season appeals to you most. Autumn is when Victoriana reaches its zenith. In the summer, Cape May becomes a seaside resort complete with swimming, sunning, surfing and strolling the boardwalk. Then, in the winter Cape May's famous Christmas parade and house tour make it a splendid place to visit during the holiday season. And, finally, in the spring there's the tulip festival when the entire town is brightened by the colorful flowers, and when tours of the city are less crowded.

Those who come only for the day, or on the spur of the moment, can stop at the Welcome Center on Lafayette Street for information on special events and activities. The hostess there will also assist you in finding a room, if you wish, and if none is available, suggest alternative accommodations in the area.

If you approach Cape May from Route 9 or the Garden State Parkway (as opposed to the Cape May-Lewes, Delaware Ferry), the first thing you'll notice as you pass over the Cape May Canal is not the town's wonderful Victorian architecture, but its surprisingly large harbor area and commercial fishing fleet. Cape May is a prime boating area, and many pleasure craft call its marinas home. Its commercial fishing fleet is one of the largest on the East Coast. Numerous party and charter boats are available for full- or half-day fishing excursions. Thus a Cape May vacation need not be exclusively shorebound.

Cape May sponsors a number of antique shows, including the Jersey Cape Antique Auto Show, Victorian Week Antique Show and the Antique Jewelry and Vintage Clothing Show. Call the Cape May Welcome and Information Center for dates, (609) 884–9562.

Cape May Antique Shops

It's only natural that Cape May, a town that celebrates its past every day of the year, should have its share of antique shops. Here is a list of the most popular ones.

Bridgetowne Antiques
523 Broadway
(609) 884–8107

Cape Island Antiques
609 Jefferson Street
(609) 884–6028

Carriage House Antiques
Crystal and Alexander avenues
Cape May Point
(609) 884–7783

Elaine's
513 Lafayette Street
(609) 884–1199

Me Lady's Company
611 Jefferson Street
(609) 884–2421

Midsummer Night's Dream
668 Washington Street
(609) 884–1380

Nostalgia Shop
408 Washington Mall
(609) 884–7071

Past Memories
722 Columbia Street
(609) 884–0415

Rocking Horse Antique Center
405 West Perry Street
(609) 898–0737

Travis Cove Antiques
621 Lafayette Street
(609) 884–5959

Victoria Station
678 Washington Street
(609) 898–0661

After passing Cape May harbor, you'll be on Lafayette Street, which will take you to Cape May's historic district and mall. Parking spaces are hard to come by in Cape May, especially in the summer; you should first try the municipal lots adjacent to **Washington Street Victorian Mall,** Cape May's main shopping area, before venturing into the town's tiny side streets. Once you've found your parking space, you probably won't have to move your car again until you're ready to depart from Cape May. Virtually everything in town is within walking distance, and the very best way to see Cape May is to walk through it at your own pace.

At the beginning of the mall, you'll see an information booth. Here is where nearly all the walking tours, both guided and self-guided, begin (see below). It's also here where you can take a trolley or horse-and-carriage tour of the town.

The Washington Street Victorian Mall contains a collection of boutiques, bookstores, cafes, candy shops, art galleries and other business establishments designed to attract the attention and pocketbook of the Cape May visitor. During Cape May's early 1970s renovation, it was decided to close this section of Washington Street to traffic and make it into a pedestrian mall. Washington Street was Cape May's original downtown shopping district; a number of the buildings there date back to the turn of the century. Most of them got an extensive face-lift, and trees, shrubs and flower beds were planted next to benches, which further spruced up the area.

For those who come to Cape May to shop first and take in the sights later, **McDowell's Gallery** (526 Washington Street Victorian Mall) offers a fine selection of arts and crafts and interesting gifts. **La Patisserie** (524 Washington Street Victorian Mall) is a great place to get a sticky bun and fresh-baked bread. The **Pinebrook** (510 Washington Street Victorian Mall) sells smartly designed Cape May T-shirts and sweatshirts as does **It's a Breeze** (319 Washington Street Victorian Mall). If it's prints or posters you're looking for, try the **Washington Street Gallery** (313 Washington Street Victorian Mall). You can treat your sweet tooth at the **Fudge Kitchen** (513 Washington Street Victorian Mall) and purchase crafted leather items at the **Baileywicke** (656 Washington Street Victorian Mall). The **Old Shire Tavern** (315 Washington Street Victorian Mall) is a good choice for lunch or an afternoon drink. It also has live jazz every night during the summer and on weekends in the winter.

During the summer, the beaches of Cape May are as popular as the Washington Street Victorian Mall and the historical sites around town. Despite their popularity, Cape May's beaches are lacking in size and sand quality. The reason is simple: erosion. In some places, such as in front of the Christian Admiral Hotel, there's no beach left at all. A seawall now holds back the Atlantic Ocean.

As Cape May's beaches shrink, the beaches of the neighboring Wildwoods grow. Currents in the Atlantic are constantly stealing sand from Cape May and depositing it in the Wildwoods. So for those who require fine bathing beaches, Wildwood is much preferred over Cape May.

Cape May's two-mile-long Beach Drive runs the length of the town's waterfront. On one side of the thoroughfare is the beach, boardwalk and seawall; on the other, restaurants, hotels, motels, guesthouses, inns and bed and breakfasts. The east section contains mostly private homes along with the huge, almost overwhelming Christian Admiral Hotel. It is the least crowded part of Beach Drive because there's little or no beach there. The midsection of Beach Drive is where much of the beach and boardwalk activity occur. Convention Hall is located here and is where many beach-related activities sponsored by the Chamber of Commerce are held. Also found here are concession stands, fudge shops, and a few other shops which sell beach items like towels, umbrellas and suntan lotion. Farther along, the beach gets a bit wider than it is in the Convention Hall area and is not usually congested. Near the end of Beach Drive is a view of the Cape May Point Lighthouse and Cape May Point State Park (see below).

In between Beach Drive and Washington Street is the bulk of Cape May's Victorian homes and guesthouses. It's here that you'll see the fairy-talelike gingerbread houses painted in the most cheerful of colors and draped with bargeboard and wood lace. You'll see cupolas and captain's walks, fretwork and featherboarding, magnificent porches and beautiful stained-glass windows that come alive the moment the sun shines on them. Add to this the pretty gardens and meticulously maintained lawns and shrubbery, all on shady, quiet streets. If, somehow, the cars parked there could suddenly disappear, you'd swear the year was 1895.

Walk past the **Mainstay Inn** (635 Columbia Avenue) and the **Abbey** (Columbia and Gurney streets), two of the most exquisite Victorian mansions turned bed and breakfast in America. Both have been photographed and written up in the world's best travel magazines. In the late nineteenth century, the Mainstay was a men's gambling house. Known as Jackson's Clubhouse, it has been painstakingly restored and now is the pride of Cape May's bed and breakfasts (see below for information on tours of the Mainstay and other inns). The Abbey, located across the street from the Mainstay, is a Gothic Revival structure, originally owned by John B. McCreary, a rich businessman who made his money in coal. Built in 1869, it retains much of its original splendor, both inside and out.

Nearby, the **Balt House** (26 Gurney Street) is one of eight identical cottages designed by the noted local architect, Stephen D. Button, in 1871. The **Dr. Henry L. Hunt House** (209 Congress Place) was built in 1881 and possesses a wide range of Victorian designs and architectural styles and is really one of the more unusual homes in Cape May. It has a mansard roof, a beautiful balcony, Gothic gables and an assortment of fancy details that some might think a bit too much. But during the Victorian era there was no such thing as "too much" when it came to architectural decoration.

Finally, one should also walk past **Congress Hall** (Beach and Congress streets). A most prestigious hotel during the Victorian years, American presidents, foreign dignitaries and celebrities of all types stayed in rooms here. And, as already mentioned, President Benjamin Harrison used it as his summer White House. The **Chalfonte Hotel** (307 Howard Street) is also a grand old hotel. Built in 1865, it was one of the few large structures in Cape May to escape the flames of the Great Fire of 1878. It is the oldest hotel in Cape May.

Virtually all the houses on Hughes Street are interesting. Most people who visit Cape May consider it the prettiest street in town. The **Hall House** (645 Hughes Street) and the **Manor House** (612 Hughes Street) are especially attractive. The former was built in 1868, another structure to survive the Great Fire; the latter was built in 1906 and is presently a bed and breakfast inn.

There are many more houses to see in Cape May, some of which are open to the public during specially scheduled tours. It is recommended that you take at least one of these tours. The guides are knowledgeable, and the anecdotes and background history they provide will make your visit to Cape May that much more rewarding.

Tours of Cape May

Virtually all of the tours, activities and special events in Cape May are conducted by one of three groups: the Mid-Atlantic Center for the Arts (MAC), the Cape May Chamber of Commerce or the city of Cape May. Two free publications—*Victorian Cape May,* published by the Chamber of Commerce, and *This Week in Cape May,* published by MAC—list the various activities and goings-on in Cape May. *This Week in Cape May* is particularly useful because it is published weekly during the summer in addition to three fall issues, a winter issue and two spring issues. It lists the time and place for all events in Cape May in the week or season in question and is readily available throughout town.

Trolley Tours. Run by MAC, these half-hour guided tours are intended to give a basic overview of Cape May's history and architectural importance. In the spring and fall, tours begin on Ocean Street, across from the information booth at the Washington Street Victorian Mall, and during the summer at the Trolley Station on Beach Drive and Gurney Street. The tours run many times throughout the day during these three seasons. Choose from three different trolley tours. One takes in the east end of town, the second does the west end and the third deals with Beach Drive and the oceanfront. In the winter, tours combining all three areas are conducted, but on a less frequent basis. They originate from the Emlen Physick Estate (1048 Washington Street). Contact MAC for tour schedule.

Walking Tours. The trolley tours are sufficient for those strapped for time, visiting Cape May only for the day or unable to walk any dis-

Selected Cape May Bed and Breakfasts

Although Cape May boasts many fine hotels and guesthouses, the town is known for its bed and breakfasts. Cape May has far more of these alternative lodgings than anywhere else on the Jersey Shore, and almost all of them will provide the visitor with a memorable stay.

Cape May bed and breakfasts are meticulously restored Victorian mansions that have been decorated with Victorian furniture and graced with Victorian hospitality. They offer all the comforts of home—a cozy fireplace, a library, snacks and small talk in the parlor—with the exception of a private bathroom, although many now offer rooms with private baths at an increased rate.

Breakfasts vary. You're not apt to run into many bacon and egg dishes; the Continental tradition of Danish and beverages is much more common. However, some bed and breakfasts offer gourmet breakfasts. You might be served, for instance, a delicious egg souffle, fruit-filled crepes smothered with cream, homemade waffles and jams, or quiche.

Since the Cape May bed and breakfast experience is so popular, it is highly recommended that you make your reservations well in advance of your visit. Rates are not included because they vary with the season and often change without notice. Expect to pay, however, somewhere in the neighborhood of $85 a night during peak summer and fall months.

The Abbey
Columbia Avenue and Gurney Street
Cape May 08204
(609) 884-4506

Victorian opulence and splendor in a setting that makes this one of Cape May's most popular bed and breakfasts. Three- to four-night minimum stays are required between June 15 and September 30. Rooms with private baths are available. Open April through November.

Abigail Adams
12 Jackson Street
Cape May 08204
(609) 884-1371

Very close to beach; three of the six guest rooms face the ocean. Open April through November. Rates include breakfast, afternoon tea, beach badges and free parking.

Albert G. Stevens Inn
127 Myrtle Avenue
Cape May 08204
(609) 884–4717

Beautiful wraparound veranda complete with white wicker furniture. Three of five guest rooms have private baths. Two-night minimum on weekends. Open year-round.

Barnard-Good House
238 Perry Street
Cape May 08204
(609) 884-5381

Sumptuous breakfast, so good and filling you won't have to eat lunch. Nan Hawkins is a vivacious, charming hostess. Bicycles are available for guests' use. Open mid-March through mid-November.

The Belvidere
26 Gurney Street
Cape May 08204
(609) 884–8713

Built in 1862, house is shown on Historic Walking Tour and is recognized for its exquisite gingerbread architecture. Some rooms with private bath and porch.

Brass Bed
719 Columbia Avenue
Cape May 08204
(609) 884–8075

A classic Victorian Gothic mansion, nicely decorated with antique furnishings. Open all year. Weekly and off-season discounts available.

Captain Mey's Inn
202 Ocean Street
Cape May 08204
(609) 884–7793

Named after Cape May's founder. Located a mere half block from Washington Street Victorian Mall. Open all year. Beautifully decorated. Good, hearty breakfasts.

Duke of Windsor
817 Washington Street
Cape May 08204
(609) 884–1355

Centrally located; large, airy rooms. Bicycles are provided for guests' use. The 45-foot Queen Anne Tower makes the Duke of Windsor an easy landmark. Open year-round.

Gingerbread House
28 Gurney Street
Cape May 08204
(609) 884–0211

Built in 1869, the Gingerbread House survived the Great Fire of 1878. Many impressive Victorian antiques found throughout the house. Continental breakfast.

Humphrey Hughes House
29 Ocean Street
Cape May 08204
(609) 884–4428

One of Cape May's "museumlike" bed and breakfasts filled with antiques. Named after Capt. Humphrey Hughes, who arrived in Cape May in 1692 and became one of the area's first landowners.

John F. Craig House
609 Columbia Avenue
Cape May 08204
(609) 884–0100

Carpenter Gothic in design, the original part of Craig House was built before 1850. Large living room with cozy fireplace and well-stocked library.

Mainstay

635 Columbia Avenue
Cape May 08204
(609) 884-8690

A real gem of a bed and breakfast. Extremely popular, reservations are recommended well in advance. Lavishly restored, museum quality antiques. Innkeepers Tom and Sue Carroll are friendly and are experts in Victoriana. Open April through October.

Manor House

612 Hughes Street
Cape May 08204
(609) 884-4710

Located on the nicest street in all Cape May. Excellent breakfast; impressively decorated. Open year-round.

Manse House

510 Hughes Street
Cape May 08204
(609) 884-0116

Another one that is situated on beautiful Hughes Street. Comfortable, warm atmosphere accented by twin fireplaces. Full breakfast served. Open March through December.

The Mason Cottage

625 Columbia Avenue
Cape May 08204
(609) 884-3358

Continental-plus breakfast; guest rooms with private or shared baths. Open May through October.

The Mooring

801 Stockton Avenue
Cape May 08204
(609) 884-5425

Grand spiral staircase leads to guest rooms, which feature period antiques. All rooms have private baths. Open year-round.

The Prince Edward

38 Jackson Street
Cape May 08204
(609) 884-2131

One- and two-bedroom Victorian suites and guest apartments, each with a parlor, kitchen and private bath; furnished with period antiques.

Queen Victoria

102 Ocean Street
Cape May 08204
(609) 884-8702

Queen Victoria rates with Abbey and Mainstay as top-notch. A good time to visit is during Christmas season. There's tree decoration, caroling, Dickens read by the fireplace. Full country breakfast. Minimum stay of two nights required on weekdays; three or four on holidays, during the summer and for rooms with private bath. Open year-round.

Windward House

24 Jackson Street
Cape May 08204
(609) 884-3368

Edwardian inn with spacious rooms, a wraparound front porch, second-floor porch and third-floor sundeck. All rooms have private baths and air conditioners. Open all year.

tance. Far more comprehensive are the walking tours, also sponsored by MAC, which usually last for 90 minutes. They also begin in front of the information booth and take in sections of both east and west ends of town. Much more of an emphasis is put on architectural detail as well as spicy gossip concerning the people who once lived in the houses. Offered daily during the summer and on weekends the rest of the year.

Horse-and-Carriage Tours. Privately run by the Cape May Carriage Company, this tour combines parts of all three trolley tours. You ride in a horse-drawn carriage, which is much more romantic and personal than a trolley. It, too, is a half-hour long and begins across the street opposite the information booth at the Washington Street Victorian Mall.

Mansions by Gaslight Tour. Beginning at the **Emlen Physick Estate,** home of the Mid-Atlantic Arts Center, this once-a-week tour (Wednesday evenings in the summer and holiday weekends year-round) includes interior tours of the Emlen Physick House, Cape May's most noted Victorian gem; the **Mainstay** and **Abbey;** and the **Humphrey Hughes House,** which contains some of the finest Victorian furnishings in Cape May. Visitors are shuttled by bus from one mansion to the next. Since this is a popular tour, one should get tickets at the Emlen Physick Estate as early as possible. Call MAC at (609) 884–5404 for more information.

Victorian Sampler Tour. View the restored interiors of five of Cape May's top bed and breakfasts. Some of the bed and breakfasts visited include **Captain Mey's Inn,** the **Brass Bed, Windward House, Albert G. Stevens Inn** and **Wilbraham Mansion.** Tour transportation is provided by MAC's trolley-bus. Check with the Welcome and Information Center for the current listing of bed and breakfasts included on the tour and ticket information.

Christmas Candlelight Tour. The Christmas Candlelight Tour is a popular holiday tour of a dozen Cape May houses and two or three churches, all of which have been handsomely decorated for Christmas. It is a rather long tour; it often runs four hours. A trolley is used to shuttle people from house to house. Order your tickets well in advance from MAC. The tour is usually conducted the Saturday after Christmas.

Christmas Lights Trolley Tour. Many of the same houses are covered on this tour as on the Candlelight Tour except here visitors get to see only the exterior of the houses. Sponsored by MAC.

Physick Estate Tours. Built by the renowned architect, Frank Furness, for Dr. Emlen Physick, the 16-room mansion is the main focus of the tour. The estate is located at 1048 Washington Street, six blocks from the mall. You'll marvel at the elegant natural wood paneling, Furness-designed mantelpieces, luxurious furnishings and much more. Behind the mansion is the estate's **Carriage House.** Open year-round, it is the home of the Cape May County Art League and contains an art gallery and museum. The work of Cape May County artists is exhibited, and during monthly wine and cheese receptions, the public can meet the artists whose work is on exhibit. The Art League also sponsors a county-wide house tour of its own the last weekend in June, plus a boardwalk art show, lectures, art classes and other special programs. For further information, write to the Cape May County Art League, P.O. Box 596, 1050 Washington Street, Cape May 08204, or call (609) 884–8628.

Children's Tours of the Physick Estate and Trolley Tours. During the summer, tours of the Physick Estate are held for children between the ages of 6 and 12. The guides are usually retired schoolteachers. Trolley tours of Cape May are also conducted for children; contact the MAC for time and departure information.

Romantic Moonlight Trolley Ride. This is more of a drive than a tour. Couples take the trolley ride and absorb the evening's ambiance as the trolley winds its way slowly through Cape May's gas-lighted streets. Sponsored by MAC; contact its office for details.

Cape May Festivals

The **Cape May Tulip Festival** occurs each spring on the last weekend in April; it's a carnival of color as more than 50,000 tulip bulbs are planted to celebrate Cape May's Dutch heritage. The two-day fest includes special MAC-sponsored Tulip Garden Trolley Tours, Dutch folk dancing and food, garden walks and a juried crafts show held in historic Congress Hall that attracts some 70 master craftsmen.

In July, MAC sponsors two notable events: the annual **Quilt and Decoy Show and Sale,** held in Cape May's Convention Hall, and a **Historic House Tour.** During this tour, 10 Victorian homes are open to the public. Victoriana buffs should consider this tour a must.

The **Victorian Fair** is usually held on the third Saturday in June on the Emlen Physick Estate. Everything from antique handicraft items to doll's clothing and glassware is sold at the fair. To keep the children occupied while mom and dad shop, Victorian games and contests are held throughout the day and include a dunking booth, beanbag toss and hoop rollings.

During the summer MAC sponsors a **Vintage Film Festival.** The films shown are Hollywood classics such as *The Jolson Story, State Fair, A Star Is Born* and *Cheaper by the Dozen.* Movies are shown once a week in the Henry Sawyer Room of the Chalfonte Hotel (301 Howard Street). Contact MAC for this year's selection of films and the dates when they'll be shown.

One can also take in a professionally produced play. Produced indoors at the Chalfonte Hotel, at the Cape May Institute (1511 New York Avenue) and at the Cape May County Art League stage (1050 Washington Street), the theater company stages three productions in revolving repertory (usually musicals, murder mysteries and Victorian period pieces). Contact MAC for this year's schedule and information on purchasing tickets.

Cape May's annual **Seafood Festival** and **Founder's Day** celebration are September highlights. Concerts, a five-mile road race and an arts-and-crafts show help celebrate the discovery of Cape May by Captain Mey and its eventual settlement by New England whalers.

The biggest festival, **Victorian Week,** occurs in October. Here's a sampling of what one can expect: guided tours of private homes, square-dancing contests, antique and crafts shows, Victorian vaudeville, stained-glass tours, walking and trolley tours, and a restoration workshop in which Victorian house restoration experts lead seminars and discussion groups on such themes as "A Victorian Parlor," "Victorian Furnishings" and "Victorian Lighting Devices and Wallcoverings."

In December, there's **Christmas in Cape May.** It's impossible not to get in the holiday spirit as Cape May is decorated with lavish Christmas displays. Carolers stroll through the street, Old Saint Nick visits with the kids; candlelight walks and tours are conducted nightly; merchants and innkeepers have open houses. There's even an annual Christmas Ball and a Charles Dickens Christmas Extravaganza. For more information, call (609) 697–2564.

Did you know that . . .

Cape May is known as a "lost colony" of *Mayflower* descendants. Some genealogists believe there are as many *Mayflower* descendants residing in and around Cape May today as there are in Plymouth, Massachusetts, the place where the *Mayflower* settlers started their first colony in America.

Things to Do in Cape May and Cape May Area

Go Deep-sea Fishing. Several charter and party boats make daily trips out onto the ocean and Delaware Bay for bluefish, tuna and flounder. Cape May waters are also a good place to fish for weakfish and drumfish. Also, there are good opportunities for white marlin. The **Miss Chriss Fishing Center** is the home port of the *Lady Chris.* The *Sea Mist* sails out from the South Jersey Marina and is a favorite with shark fishermen. The *Sea Star II* offers six-hour fishing trips and free fishing instruction, while the *Fiesta* specializes in bluefishing. Finally, the tall ship

Yankee, an 80-foot schooner, takes Cape May visitors on three-hour cruises along the scenic Intracoastal Waterway. For sailing reservations, call (609) 884–1919.

Go Whale Watching. Whale watchers can sign up for cruises at the Cape May Whale Watching and Sightseeing Center, 1286 Wilson Drive. More and more fin humpback and minke whales as well as bottle-nose dolphins are being sighted off Cape May and other Shore towns.

Take a Bicycle Tour of Cape May. Bicycling through the streets of Cape May at your own pace is a wonderful way to spend an afternoon. You can cover more ground then you can walking, and you're not confined to a trolley; you can also stop when and for how long you please. Once you've ridden through the town's Victorian district, bike down to **Cape May Point State Park.** Simply take Lafayette Street to Sunset Boulevard and watch for signs to the lighthouse. The distance is not more than six miles round-trip. The grade is flat and the scenery is that of the **Cape May Bird Sanctuary.** Bicycle riders with more ambition should then ride to **Higbee Beach** through picturesque farmland and Cape May countryside. Get back on Sunset Boulevard, make a left onto Bayshore Road, and then a left onto New England Road and follow it to the end.

You can rent bikes from **Buckingham Bikes** (1111 Beach Drive), **La Mer Bicycle Rentals** (Beach Drive and Pittsburgh Avenue), and **Village Bicycle Shop** (Victorian Village Plaza). All three shops are seasonal, however. All open early in the morning, so you can get a full day's worth of bicycle touring in if you want to. Serious bicyclists should consider riding their own bikes.

Visit the U.S. Coast Guard Training Center. If you ride to the north end of Beach Drive, turn left onto Pittsburgh Avenue, where you'll find the entrance to the U.S. Coast Guard Training Center. It is here where fresh recruits come to complete an eight-week training session. After graduation, sailors are then assigned to various Coast Guard units around the globe. The public is invited to attend recruit graduation parades every Friday morning on Parade Field. Advance permission, however, is necessary to visit the base. Call (609) 884–8451 for more information.

Go Horseback Riding. Saddle horses for hire are available at the **Hidden Valley Ranch** (4070 Bayshore Road, 609–884–8205). The ranch specializes in family trial rides. A series of horse shows and special equestrian events are held at Hidden Valley on Saturdays. The riding center is also a wildlife refuge that offers excellent bird-watching opportunities to experienced and novice birders alike.

Take a Ferry Ride. The Cape May-Lewes, Delaware Ferry cuts across the entrance to the Delaware Bay. There's not much to see en route except whitecaps and blue water; nor is there anything of significance in Lewes. Why go? To relax, soak up the sun and simply enjoy the boat ride.

The trip is approximately 70 minutes long and is usually a smooth voyage. There are four ferries in the fleet. They leave from the Cape May Terminal at the end of Ferry Road. The service is seven days a week, but the times and the number of runs differ from season to season. Call (609) 886-2718 for details.

Visit the Cape May County Museum. You'll find no better museum in the Cape May area than the Cape May County Museum on Route 9 in Cape May Courthouse. Run by the Cape May County Historical and Genealogical Society, the **John Holmes House** was built prior to the revolutionary war and is the museum complex's main attraction. Guides take you through the rooms of the house, where there are collections of fine china, furniture and excellent examples of eighteenth- and nineteenth-century household items. The eighteen-century antiques are especially interesting as is the display in the basement of the Holmes House, which includes guns, swords and uniforms, plus the flag of the Civil War ironclad, the *Merrimac.*

Outside in the barn, you'll find maritime artifacts, whaling implements and shipbuilding tools from Cape May's golden era of shipbuilding, as well as Indian weapons and arrowheads and a lens from the Cape May Point Lighthouse. The museum also sponsors a lecture series and special theme open-houses. If you live in Cape May County, you might even want to spend time in the museum's library, where you can trace your family tree. Many in the county have done so and have found out that their ancestors were related to Hannah Willdin, whose grandfather, John Howland, came to this country aboard the *Mayflower.* The museum is open April to December 10. Small admission fee.

Take the Kids to the Cape May County Park and Zoo. Up the road on Route 9, north of the Cape May County Museum, is the Cape May County Park and Zoo. The park is a good size—150 acres—and contains a variety of things to do. Hiking, biking, picnicking and jogging are popular activities. So are shuffleboard, badminton, horseshoes and softball, and the facilities for these are well maintained. Wedding ceremonies are often held at the Gazebo, and kids are permitted to fish in the pond there. But the biggest attraction is the zoo. It's one of Cape May's best-kept secrets. More than 100 species of animals, including tigers, a lion, cougars, bears, monkeys, a giraffe and bobcats, live at the zoo. Many of the animals can be seen up close. Great for children and free. Open year-round. For more information call (609) 465–5271.

Spend an Afternoon at Leaming's Run Botanical Gardens. Those seeking respite from the bustling activity of Cape May, with its many tours, busy streets and rich Victoriana, will find Leaming's Run Botanical Gardens a sheer delight. Carved out of a lower reach of the Pine Barrens, the Gardens consists of 25 separate gardens, each immaculately kept and cared for by the Aprill family.

All the gardens have themes. The Bridal Garden, for instance, has white flowers against a backdrop of green. The Yellow Garden consists of some 50 varieties of domestic and wild yellow flowers. The Blue Garden is noted for its morning glories. The Houseplant Garden is filled with only houseplants. There are also lawns, ferneries and lily ponds at Leaming's Run.

Those familiar with botanical gardens and standard English gardens will find Leaming's Run quite different simply because it's not manicured "prim and proper." Aprill calls Leaming's Run an "American garden," meaning "it's a place to be in and enjoy and feel a part of, rather than to merely walk through and look." Unlike most botanical gardens, which bloom in the spring, Leaming's Run is a summer garden. That means if you visit at the height of summer, you'll be sure to see a dizzying display of colorful flowers.

Leaming's Run is also considered an important hummingbird center on the East Coast. When you come to the garden's Gazebo, sit quietly and look around you. In five minutes or so, you're quite certain to see your share of these remarkably tiny birds feeding on the flowers nearby.

In the middle of the gardens is a re-creation of an old South Jersey farm from the time when Thomas Leaming first settled the area in the late 1600s. The main cabin was constructed from logs cut from the pasture area. There's also an herb and kitchen garden to see. At the end of the main path in the gardens is the Cooperage, a barn built in 1730 that has been transformed into a gift shop. Inside, you'll find all sorts of dried flowers hanging from the rafters as well as baskets and candles for sale. The barn was used by Christopher Leaming, a prominent South Jersey whaler in the 1700s, to make barrels for whale oil. The white house next door is where the Aprill family resides. It was Christopher Leaming's house and is the oldest whaler's house in Cape May County.

The 30 acres that constitute Leaming's Run are open daily from May through October, weather permitting. The best time to visit the Gardens is in the first week of October, says Jack Aprill. Admission is charged, but once you're in the gardens, you can stay as long as you like. Leaming's Run is located on the west side of Route 9 in Swainton. For more information, call (609) 465–5871.

Visit Cold Spring Village. Cold Spring Village is a re-creation of a nineteenth-century South Jersey farm village made up of old buildings from Cape May County that were originally earmarked for destruction. Instead, they were moved to Cold Spring Village and have been turned into minimuseums, shops and places where craftspeople perform traditional trades (candlemaking, spinning, weaving).

Presently, there are about 20 buildings to visit with more slated to be moved to Cold Spring Village and restored in the near future. You can visit the Spicer-Leaming House, for example, a structure thought to be the second oldest house in Cape May County, and which is now an antique shop; two old railroad stations, one from the nearby town of Rio Grande, and the other from Woodbine; the old Cape May Point jailhouse; and the Heislerville schoolhouse, among others. In all of these are crafts, food and souvenirs for sale, the profits of which help in restoration and upkeep.

Cold Spring Village sponsors a full slate of activities throughout the summer. Antique shows, craft festivals, square dancing competition, antique auto shows and banjo and fiddle concerts highlight the Cold Spring Village calendar. Call (609) 898–2300 for this year's schedule of events. Cold Spring Village is located just outside the town of Cape May on Seashore Road.

Spend the Day at Cape May Point State Park. Cape May Point State Park is well known for its outstanding bird-watching and its picturesque lighthouse. It's located about two miles southwest of Cape May proper and is adjacent to the Cape May Migratory Bird Refuge. Before the area became a state park, it was part of the U.S. Coastal Defense network, and during World War II, a huge concrete bunker and gun stood guarding the entrance to Delaware Bay. Today, if you walk along the beach, preferably at low tide, you can view and even climb on the remains of the bunker and gun emplacement. Built in 1942, the bunker was 900 feet from the water's edge. Today, it's in the water, a victim of Cape May's erosion problem.

Did you know that . . .

Bottle-nosed dolphins calve in lower Delaware Bay during June each year and can be seen from the shores of Cape May Point State Park.

While visiting Cape May Point State Park, be sure to climb the 199 steps that lead to the top of the lighthouse, where the view of the South Jersey Shore on a clear day is excellent. The present lighthouse was built in 1859 and was recently restored by Cape May's Mid-Atlantic Center for the Arts (MAC).

If you're an avid bird-watcher, be sure to bring your binoculars when you visit Cape May Point State Park. The area is one of the more popular bird-watching sites in South Jersey because it, like so many other Shore sites, is located on the Atlantic Flyway. Both spring and fall are good times to view birds, although veteran bird-watchers say the best time to view birds of prey, such as hawks, is September and October. Regular hawk sightings occur at the Cape May Point Hawkwatch Observation

Deck in the park. You'll also see shorebirds and songbirds, peregrine and other falcons, bald and golden eagles, and you'll meet members of the New Jersey Audubon Society who come to the park to conduct their annual hawk count.

Before you begin your day of bird-watching, stop first at the Visitor Center, where you can pick up pamphlets pertaining to the birds you might see and the general ecology of the area. Also, you can pick up trail guides so that you can spend part of your day hiking over the more than three miles of trails and boardwalks through the Natural Area. Here you'll find photography blinds and more bird-watching platforms. Do stay on the trails, though. The area is well stocked with poison ivy. A half-mile-long nature trail has been built exclusively for use by the handicapped.

Cape May Point State Park doesn't have lifeguarded beaches, but visitors are permitted to swim at their own risk. Fast-moving currents can, however, make swimming somewhat dangerous, so be careful, use common sense and don't venture out too far if you decide to go into the water. If you want a beach-oriented activity, try fishing. Surf fishing is permitted in the park, and weakfish, blues and flounder are common catches.

Visit Cape May Point. The quiet, cozy town of Cape May Point is often ignored by visitors to Cape May, even though they must pass through it to get to Cape May Point State Park. It is a small town; in the winter its population barely rises above 200, and in the summer it goes to 2,000. There are no hotels or tourist facilities, just summer bungalows and cottages that are rented out by the month or season. But that shouldn't prevent a visitor to Cape May from spending a couple of hours in the town and taking in some of its charm and history.

Along with Avalon and Stone Harbor, Cape May Point's beaches rank with the prettiest of the South Jersey Shore, due mainly to the preservation of the sand dunes there, and their clean, scrubbed sand. But like its neighbor, Cape May, Cape May Point is suffering badly from erosion as any local will sadly point out. If you walk along Cape May Point's beaches and head northeast, you'll cross into Cape May Point State Park. You'll also pass a large hotellike structure just behind the dunes. That's St. Peter's-by-the-Sea, an old religious retreat. If you walk in the opposite direction, you'll come to Higbee Beach Wildlife Management Area. But before you do, at the end of Sunset Boulevard you'll see what looks like a concrete bunker lying some 200 yards offshore. Actually, it's the hull of a concrete ship called the *Atlantus*. In World War I, the United States government commissioned the experimental construction of concrete ships due to a serious shortage of steel. The *Atlantus* was a 3,000-ton freighter built in 1918 and, for a year, was used as a coal steamer. But it was obvious that concrete ships were not the ships of the future. The incredible bulkiness and excessive weight made for very difficult handling in both harbors and the open sea. Decommissioned after the war, the *Atlantus* and two other concrete vessels were purchased by a private company, which planned to use them as ferry docking facilities for a Delaware Bay ferry service. However, during a storm in 1926, the *Atlantus* broke free and went aground off Sunset Boulevard, where you see it today. Due to the weight of the ship and the shallow water where it came to rest, salvage efforts were discouraged. Today the ship is a state historic site.

Sunset Boulevard is important for yet another reason. It is the only place left where one can find "Cape May Diamonds," clear, nearly pure quartz crystals that resemble expensive diamonds. The main source of the quartz is the upper part of the Delaware River, where the water breaks up the quartz into pebbles. The swift current then takes them down the river to its mouth—the Delaware Bay—a journey that, say some scientists, takes thousands of years. Because of the strong tides in the bay and the position of the *Atlantus* offshore, the quartz crystals come ashore today only at Sunset Beach. Before the *Atlantus* went aground, however, they could be found all along Higbee Beach. In fact, Higbee Beach was once known as Diamond Beach.

Did you know that . . .

The largest Cape May Diamond ever found at Cape May was nearly the size of a hen's egg and weighed almost eight ounces.

When the quartz crystals are polished, they assume a regal appearance. Gift shops at the edge of Sunset Boulevard sell polished Cape May Diamonds. You can find your own diamonds, though, in the sand in front of the *Atlantus*. Of course, you'll have to polish them for them to resemble diamonds. The best time to search for the quartz crystals is just after a storm. Beachcombers also find, on occasion, Indian arrowheads and fossils.

Visit the Higbee Beach Wildlife Management Area. Higbee Beach is a rich, mostly secluded 600-acre expanse of holly and scrub oak forest, sand dunes blanketed with beachgrass, beach, meadows and ponds. Although it may seem to be facing the ocean, Higbee Beach actually borders Delaware Bay. Higbee Beach is a limited resource area because it's an important stopover for migrating birds, including many endangered species of raptors such as the bald eagle and peregrine falcon.

Nonetheless, Higbee Beach offers a number of things to do to make a visit worthwhile. The sand dunes offer protection from the wind, and the area gets a terrific afternoon sun. Thus, Higbee Beach is one of the best places to begin work on an early summer tan. If you walk along the beach in early summer, you'll find hundreds of horseshoe crabs on the beach, where they deposit their eggs. There's also good fishing at Higbee Beach. Four-wheel drive permits are available to fishermen who wish to bring their vehicles on the beach.

As one might expect, Higbee Beach in a good place to bird-watch, especially in the fall. Two of Higbee Beach's southwestern fields have observation blinds. Some bird-watchers actually prefer Higbee Beach over Cape May Point State Park since the former is usually much less crowded.

Higbee Beach also allows hunting; actually, it's one of the best places on the East Coast to hunt woodcock. The Higbee hunting season, however, begins in November due to the area's importance as a rest stop for migrating birds. Hunting licenses are mandatory and can be obtained, after passing a hunter's safety course, at most New Jersey sporting goods shops. You're also allowed to go horseback riding in the Higbee Beach preserve, but you'll need a permit for this activity. You can get an annual permit at the Higbee Beach Field House on the main road as you approach the access to the beach. Expect to pay about $15 for it.

Beach plum preserves spread on a piece of homemade bread is a true Shore treat. The preserves are easy to make, and Higbee Beach is *the* place on the South Jersey Shore to pick beach plums. Bring baskets to put the plums in—and bring helpers. Beach plums are tiny, and you need many of them to make a worthwhile batch of preserves.

Two things you can't do at Higbee Beach are swimming and nude sunbathing. The water is shallow, rocky and dangerous, and there are no lifeguards. As for nudity on Higbee Beach, people do sunbathe in the buff, but if they're spotted by a ranger, they're given a summons and can be arrested.

Where to Eat in Cape May

A & J Blue Claw, Ocean Drive, (609) 884–5878
Price Code: Moderate   Menu: Seafood
A & J has a retail fish store next to the restaurant. That means you can count on very fresh fish.

Alexander's, 653 Washington Street, (609) 884–2555
Price Code: Expensive   Menu: Continental
Great Cape May atmosphere. Alexander's is a restored Victorian mansion where the Sunday brunches are nearly legendary.

Bayberry Inn, Perry Street and Congress Place, (609) 884–8406
Price Code: Moderate   Menu: International
The spicy Hot Thai Chicken Wings in honey sauce ought not to be missed.

Chalfonte Hotel, 307 Howard Street, (609) 884–8409
Price Code: Moderate   Menu: Southern
The Southern fried chicken is great, but you should try something more adventurous and zesty. A great choice for breakfast, too.

Fresco's Ristorante Italiano, 412 Bank Street, (609) 884–0366
Price Code: Expensive   Menu: Italian
Fresh seafood, homemade pasta, garden vegetables and the best veal dishes in Cape May.

Louisa's Cafe, 104 Jackson Street, (609) 884–5882
Price Code: Inexpensive/moderate   Menu: Original
Small, crowded cafe, but excellent food. One of Cape May's best eateries. Arrive early so you can find a table.

Mad Batter, 19 Jackson Street,(609) 884–5970
Price Code: Moderate   Menu: Original
Acclaimed by restaurant critics everywhere, you can't visit Cape May without dining at the Mad Batter. This excellent restaurant dares to be different.

Maureen, Beach and Decatur streets, (609) 884–3774
Price Code: Moderate   Menu: Mostly seafood
This nationally recognized restaurant specializes in the finest sea-food dishes, but Medallions of Veal au Bec Rouge and Tournedos Royale are true dining treats.

Peaches Cafe, Perry and Jackson streets, (609) 884–0202
Price Code: Moderate   Menu: Mostly seafood
New England clam chowder is unbeatable. Great choice for casual lunch or supper.

Washington Inn, 801 Washington Street, (609) 884–5697
Price Code: Moderate   Menu: International
The inn is an 1856 plantation house. Good atmosphere, good food. Quite popular, as indeed it should be.

Index

Other Books of Interest from The Globe Pequot Press

◆

Off the Beaten Path Series
New Jersey ◆ New York ◆ Pennsylvania

◆

Short Bike Rides Series
New Jersey ◆ Eastern Pennsylvania ◆ Long Island

◆

Short Nature Walks on Long Island, Third Edition

◆

A Museum Guide to Washington, D.C., Second Edition

◆

Guide to Washington, D.C. and Beyond

◆

Daytrips, Getaway Weekends, and Vacations
in the Mid-Atlantic States, Second Edition

◆

Recommended Country Inns Mid-Atlantic
and Chesapeake Region, Third Edition

◆

Treasury of Bed & Breakfast

◆

Factory Outlet Guide to the Mid-Atlantic States, Second Edition

◆

Northern Lighthouses

◆

The above listed books may be obtained in major bookstores
or by writing the publisher, The Globe Pequot Press, P.O. Box Q,
Chester, CT 06412, or call 1–800–234–0495.
In Connecticut call 1–800–962–0973.